Hippocrene
CHILDREN'S
ILLUSTRATED
SPANISH
DICTIONARY

ENGLISH - SPANISH
SPANISH - ENGLISH

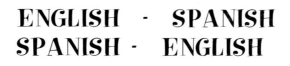

Compiled and translated by the Editors of Hippocrene Books

Interior illustrations by S. Grant (24, 81, 88); J. Gress (page 10, 21, 24, 37, 46, 54, 59, 65, 72, 75, 77);
K. Migliorelli (page 13, 14, 18, 19, 20, 21, 22, 25, 31, 32, 37, 39, 40, 46, 47, 66, 71, 75, 76, 82, 86, 87);
B. Swidzinska (page 9, 11, 12, 13, 14, 16, 23, 27, 28, 30, 32, 33, 35, 37, 38, 41, 42, 45, 46, 47, 48, 49, 50,
52, 53, 56, 57, 58, 59, 60, 61, 62, 63, 66, 68, 69, 70, 71, 72, 73, 75, 77, 78, 79, 83), N. Zhukov (page 8, 13,
14, 17, 18, 23, 27, 29, 33, 34, 39, 40, 41, 52, 64, 65, 71, 72, 73, 78, 84, 86, 88).

Design, prepress, and production: Graafiset International Inc.

Cataloging-in-Publication Data available from the Library of Congress.

ISBN 0-7818-0889-8

Printed in Hong Kong.

For information, address:
Hippocrene Books, Inc.
171 Madison Avenue
New York, NY 10016

INTRODUCTION

With their absorbent minds, infinite curiosities and excellent memories, children have enormous capacities to master many languages. All they need is exposure and encouragement.

The easiest way to learn a foreign language is to simulate the same natural method by which a child learns English. The natural technique is built on the concept that language is representational of concrete objects and ideas. The use of pictures and words are the natural way for children to begin to acquire a new language.

The concept of this Illustrated Dictionary is to allow children to build vocabulary and initial competency naturally. Looking at the pictorial content of the Dictionary and saying and matching the words in connection to the drawings gives children the opportunity to discover the foreign language and thus, a new way to communicate.

The drawings in the Dictionary are designed to capture children's imaginations and make the learning process interesting and entertaining, as children return to a word and picture repeatedly until they begin to recognize it.

The beautiful images and clear presentation make this dictionary a wonderful tool for unlocking your child's multilingual potential.

Deborah Dumont, M.A., M.Ed.,
Child Psychologist and Educational Consultant

Spanish Pronunciation

Letter(s)	Pronunciation system used
a	**ah** as in English 'art'
ai/ay	**igh** as in English 'high'
b	**b** as in English 'bent'
c	**k** as in English 'kitten'
ci	**see** as in English 'see'
ch	**ch** as in English 'cheese'
cua	**qu** as in English 'quarrel'
cue	**que** as in English 'quench"
d	**d** as in English 'dog'
e	**eh** as in English 'leg'
er	**air** as in English 'hair'
f	**f** as in English 'father'
g	**g** as in English 'goat'
	j as in English 'jewel'
	h as in English 'ham'
h	most often silent, sometimes a *h*-sound
i	**ee** as in English 'meet'
j	**j** as in English 'jewel'
ju	**hoo** as in English 'hoof'
k	**k** as in English 'kitten'
l	**l** as in English 'lemon'
ll	**y** as in English 'yes'
m	**m** as in English 'man'
n	**n** as in English 'new'
ña	**nya** as in the name 'Tonya'
ño	**nyo** as in 'El Niño'

Letter(s)	Pronunciation system used
o	**o** as in English 'row'
p	**p** as in English 'pan'
qu	**k** as in English 'kitten'
r	**r** as in English 'rabbit'
rr	longer, sustained *r* (rolled *r*)
s	**s** as in English 'sing'
t	**t** as in English 'tall'
u	**oo** as in English 'broom'
ue	**weh** like the *wh* in English 'when'
v	**v** as in English 'violet'
w	**w** as in English 'water'
y	**ee** as in English 'free'
z	**s** as in English 'sand'

Note: Adjectives are listed in their masculine form.
The feminine is formed by changing the −o ending into −a.
This is also valid for nouns that can be both masculine and feminine.

airplane   **(el) avión**
(ehl) ah-vee-yohn

alligator   **(el) caimán**
(ehl) kigh-mahn

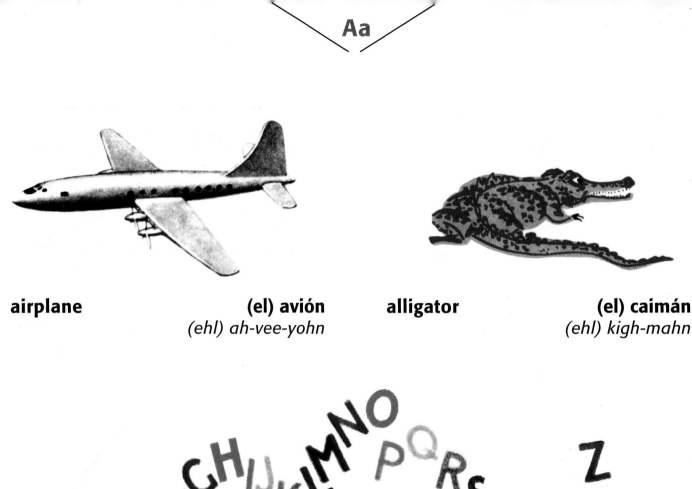

alphabet   **(el) alfabeto**
(ehl) al-fah-beh-to

antelope   **(el) antílope**
(ehl) an-tee-loh-peh

antlers   **(las) cuernas**
(lahs) quehr-nas

apple   **(la) manzana**
(lah) man-sah-na

aquarium   **(el) acuario**
(ehl) ah-qua-ree-o

arch   **(el) arco**
(ehl) ar-ko

arrow   **(la) flecha**
(lah) fleh-cha

autumn   **(el) otoño**
(ehl) oh-ton-yo

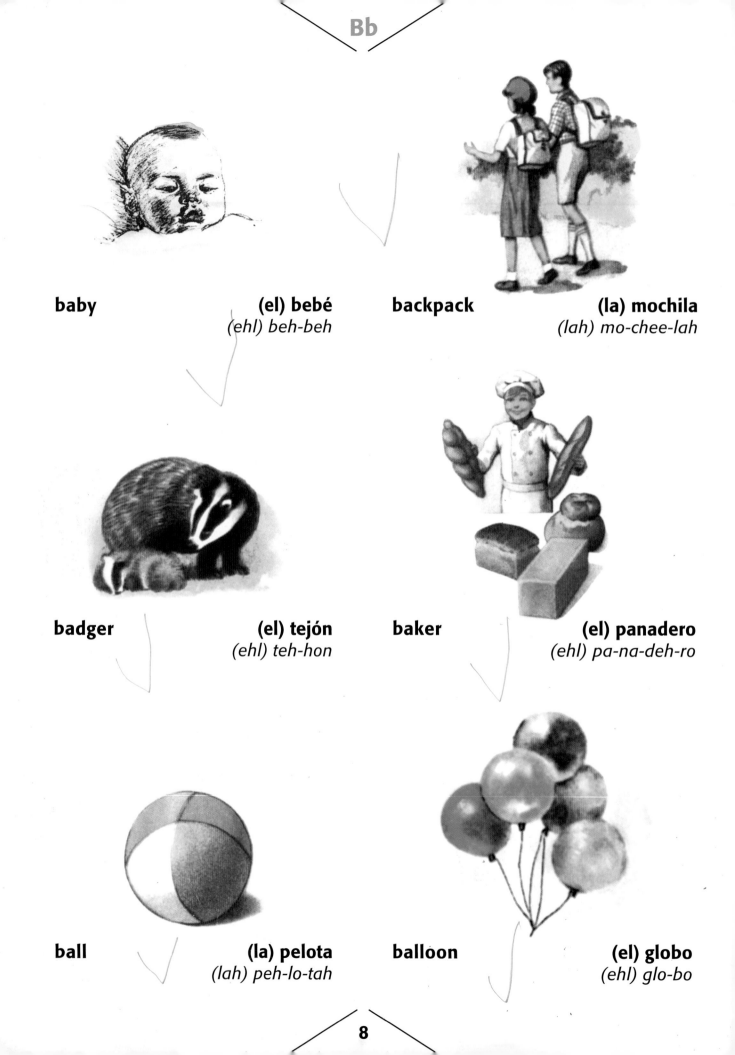

baby   **(el) bebé**
(ehl) beh-beh

backpack   **(la) mochila**
(lah) mo-chee-lah

badger   **(el) tejón**
(ehl) teh-hon

baker   **(el) panadero**
(ehl) pa-na-deh-ro

ball   **(la) pelota**
(lah) peh-lo-tah

balloon   **(el) globo**
(ehl) glo-bo

banana   **(la) banana**
(lah) bah-nah-na

barley   **(la) cebada**
(lah) seh-ba-da

barrel   **(el) barril**
(ehl) bahr-reel

basket   **(el) cesto**
(ehl) seh-sto

bat   **(el) murciélago**
(ehl) moor-see-eh-lah-go

beach   **(la) playa**
(lah) pligh-ya

bear   **(el) oso**
(ehl) oh-so

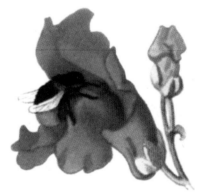

beaver   **(el) castor**
(ehl) kah-stor

bed   **(la) cama**
(lah) kah-ma

bee   **(la) abeja**
(lah) ah-beh-hah

beetle   **(el) escarabajo**
(ehl) ehs-kar-a-bah-ho

bell   **(la) campana**
(lah) kam-pah-na

belt   **(el) cinturón**
(ehl) seen-too-rohn

bench   **(el) banco**
(ehl) ban-ko

bicycle   **(la) bicicleta**
(lah) bee-see-kleh-ta

binoculars   **(los) gemelos**
(lohs) hem-eh-los

bird   **(el) pájaro**
(ehl) pah-ha-ro

birdcage   **(la) jaula**
(lah) howl-a

black   **negro**
neh-gro

blocks   **(los) bloques**
(los) blo-kehs

blossom   **(la) flor**
(lah) flohr

blue   **azul**
ah-sool

boat   **(el) barco**
(ehl) bar-ko

bone   **(el) hueso**
(ehl) weh-so

book   **(el) libro**
(ehl) lee-bro

boot   **(la) bota**
(lah) boh-ta

bottle   **(la) botella**
(lah) bo-teh-ya

bowl   **(la) escudilla**
(lah) eh-skoo-dee-ya

boy   **(el) niño**
(ehl) neen-yo

bracelet   **(el) brazalete**
(ehl) bra-sa-leh-teh

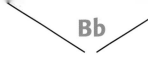

branch   **(la) rama**
(lah) rah-ma

bread   **(el) pan**
(ehl) pahn

breakfast   **(el) desayuno**
(ehl) deh-sigh-oo-no

bridge   **(el) puente**
(ehl) pwehn-teh

broom   **(la) escoba**
(lah) ehs-ko-ba

brother   **(el) hermano**
(ehl) air-mah-no

brown   **pardo**
pahr-do

brush   **(el) cepillo**
(ehl) seh-pee-yo

bucket   **(el) cubo**
(ehl) koo-bo

bulletin board

(la) tablilla
(lah) tah-blee-ya

bumblebee   **(el) abejorro**
(ehl) ah-beh-hor-ro

butterfly   **(la) mariposa**
(lah) mah-ree-po-sa

cab **(el) taxi**
(ehl) tak-see

cabbage **(la) col**
(lah) kol

cactus **(el) cacto**
(ehl) kak-to

café **(el) café**
(ehl) kah-feh

cake **(el) pastel**
(ehl) pah-stel

camel **(el) camello**
(ehl) kah-meh-yo

camera   **(la) cámara**
(lah) ka-ma-ra

candle   **(la) vela**
(lah) veh-la

candy   **(el) caramelo**
(ehl) ka-ra-me-lo

canoe   **(la) canoa**
(lah) kah-no-a

cap   **(la) gorra**
(lah) gor-ra

captain   **(el) capitán**
(ehl) kah-pee-tan

car   **(el) carro**
(ehl) kar-ro

card   **(la) carta**
(lah) kar-ta

carpet   **(la) alfombra**
(lah) ahl-fom-bra

carrot   **(la) zanahoria**
(lah) zah-na-ho-ree-a

(to) carry   **llevar**
yeh-vahr

castle   **(el) castillo**
(ehl) ka-stee-yo

cat **(el) gato**
(ehl) gah-to

cave **(la) cueva**
(lah) queh-va

chair **(la) silla**
(lah) see-ya

cheese **(el) queso**
(ehl) keh-so

cherry **(la) cereza**
(lah) seh-reh-sa

chimney **(la) chimenea**
(lah) chee-men-eh-ya

chocolate   **(el) chocolate**
(ehl) cho-ko-lah-teh

Christmas tree   **(el) árbol de Navidad**
(ehl) ahr-bol deh nah-vee-dad

circus   **(el) circo**
(ehl) seer-ko

(to) climb   **subir**
soo-beer

cloud   **(la) nube**
(lah) nu-beh

clown   **(el) payaso**
(ehl) pigh-ah-so

coach   **(el) coche**
(ehl) ko-cheh

coat   **(el) abrigo**
(ehl) ah-bree-go

coconut   **(el) coco**
(ehl) ko-ko

comb   **(el) peine**
(ehl) peh-ee-neh

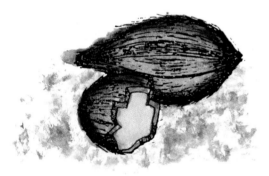

comforter   **(el) edredón**
(ehl) eh-dreh-don

compass   **(la) brújula**
(lah) broo-hoo-la

(to) cook   **cocinar**
ko-see-nahr

cork   **(el) corcho**
(ehl) kor-cho

corn   **(el) maíz**
(ehl) ma-ees

cow   **(la) vaca**
(lah) vah-ka

cracker   **(la) galleta**
(lah) ga-yeh-ta

cradle   **(la) cuna**
(lah) koo-na

(to) crawl   **gatear**
gah-teh-ahr

(to) cross   **cruzar**
kroo-sahr

crown   **(la) corona**
(lah) ko-roh-na

(to) cry   **llorar**
yo-rahr

cucumber   **(el) pepino**
(ehl) peh-pee-no

curtain   **(la) cortina**
(lah) kor-tee-na

(to) dance — **bailar**
bigh-lahr

dandelion — **(el) diente de león**
(ehl) dee-en-teh deh leh-ohn

date — **(la) fecha**
(lah) feh-cha

deer — **(el) ciervo**
(ehl) see-air-vo

desert — **(el) desierto**
(ehl) deh-see-air-to

desk — **(el) escritorio**
(ehl) eh-skree-to-ree-oh

dirty — **sucio**
soo-see-oh

dog

(el) perro
(ehl) pehr-ro

doghouse

(la) perrera
(lah) pehr-re-ra

doll

(la) muñeca
(lah) moon-yeh-ka

dollhouse

(la) casa de muñecas
(lah) kah-sa deh moon-yeh-kas

dolphin

(el) delfín
(ehl) dehl-feen

donkey

(el) burro
(ehl) boor-ro

dragon

(el) dragón
(ehl) dra-gohn

dragonfly   **(la) libélula**
(lah) lee-beh-loo-la

(to) draw   **dibujar**
dee-boo-hahr

dress   **(el) vestido**
(ehl) veh-stee-do

(to) drink   **beber**
beh-bair

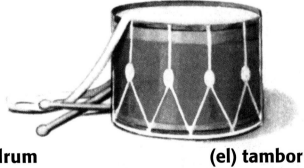

drum   **(el) tambor**
(ehl) tam-bor

duck   **(el) pato**
(ehl) pah-to

eagle **(el) águila**
(ehl) ah-gwee-la

(to) eat **comer**
ko-mair

egg **(el) huevo**
(ehl) weh-vo

eggplant **(la) berenjena**
(lah) beh-ren-heh-na

eight **ocho**
oh-cho

elbow **(el) codo**
(ehl) ko-do

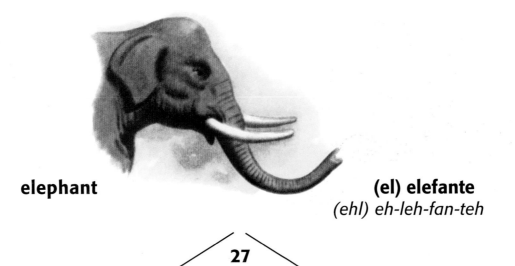

elephant **(el) elefante**
(ehl) eh-leh-fan-teh

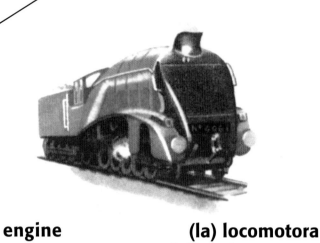

empty **vacio**
vah-see-o

engine **(la) locomotora**
(lah) lo-ko-mo-to-ra

envelope **(el) sobre**
(ehl) so-breh

escalator **(la) escalera mecánica**
(lah) eh-ska-leh-ra meh-ka-nee-ka

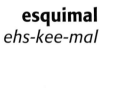

Eskimo **esquimal**
ehs-kee-mal

(to) explore **explorar**
ehk-splor-ahr

eye **(el) ojo**
(ehl) oh-jo

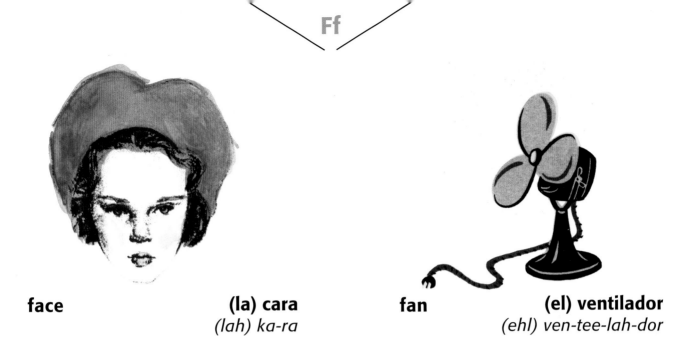

face   **(la) cara**
(lah) ka-ra

fan   **(el) ventilador**
(ehl) ven-tee-lah-dor

father   **(el) padre**
(ehl) pah-dreh

fear   **(el) miedo**
(ehl) mee-eh-do

feather   **(la) pluma**
(lah) ploo-ma

(to) feed   **alimentar**
ah-lee-men-tahr

fence   **(la) cerca**
(lah) sair-ka

fern   **(el) helecho**
(ehl) eh-leh-cho

field   **(el) campo**
(ehl) kam-po

field mouse   **(el) ratón de campo**
(ehl) rah-ton deh kahm-po

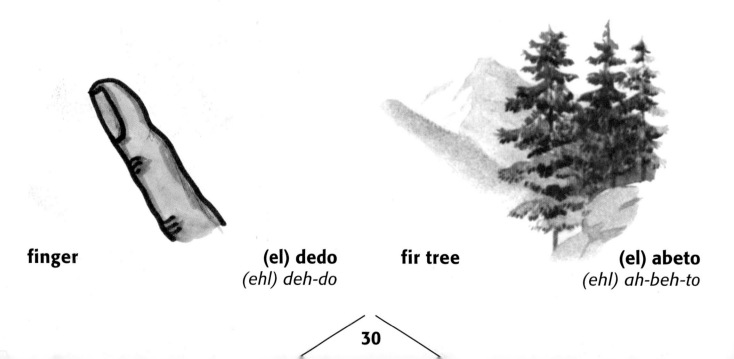

finger   **(el) dedo**
(ehl) deh-do

fir tree   **(el) abeto**
(ehl) ah-beh-to

fire   **(el) fuego**
(ehl) fweh-go

fish   **(el) pez**
(ehl) pehz

(to) fish   **pescar**
pe-skahr

fist   **(el) puño**
(ehl) poo-nyo

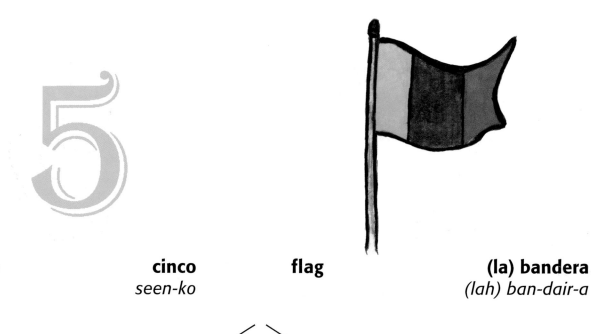

five   **cinco**
seen-ko

flag   **(la) bandera**
(lah) ban-dair-a

flashlight **(la) linterna eléctrica**
(lah) leen-tair-na eh-lek-tree-ka

(to) float **flotar**
flo-tahr

flower **(la) flor**
(lah) flor

(to) fly **volar**
vo-lahr

foot **(el) pie**
(ehl) pee-eh

fork **(el) tenedor**
(ehl) teh-ne-dor

fountain **(la) fuente**
(lah) fwehn-teh

four   **cuatro**
quah-tro

fox   **(el) zorro**
(ehl) zor-ro

frame   **(el) marco**
(ehl) mar-ko

friend   **(el) amigo**
(ehl) ah-mee-go

frog   **(la) rana**
(lah) rah-na

fruit   **(la) fruta**
(lah) froo-ta

furniture   **(los) muebles**
(lohs) mweh-blehs

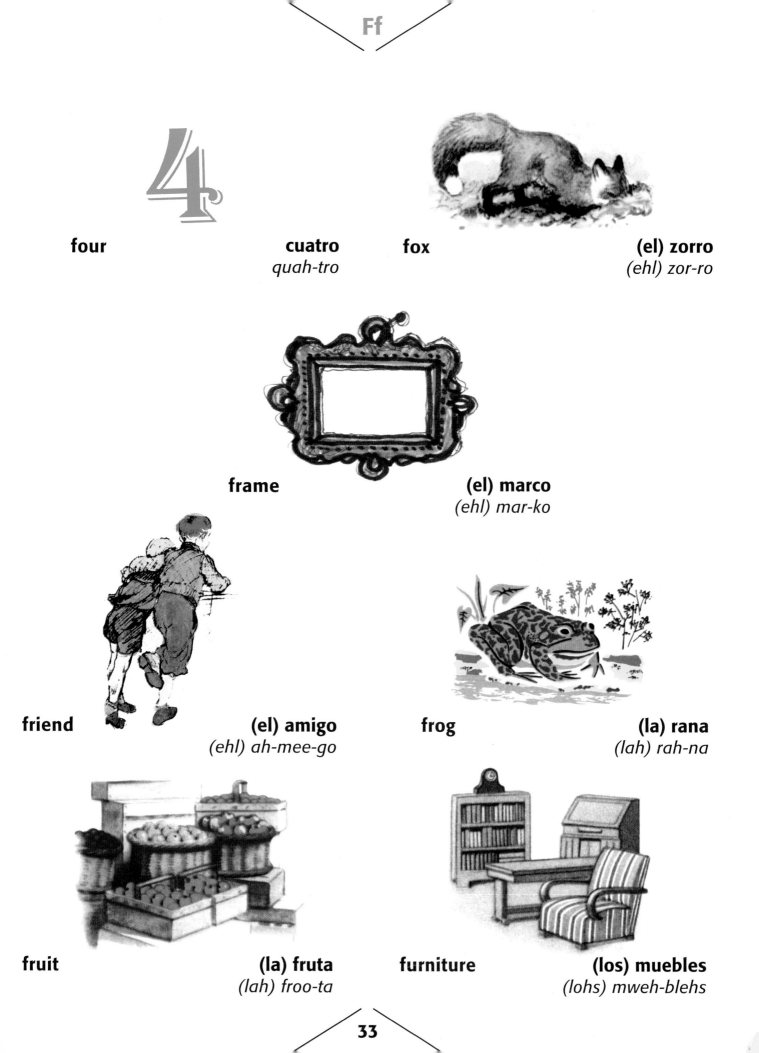

garden   **(el) jardín**
(ehl) har-deen

gate   **(la) puerta**
(lah) pwehr-ta

(to) gather   **coger**
ko-hair

geranium   **(el) geranio**
(ehl) he-rah-nee-o

giraffe   **(la) jirafa**
(lah) hee-ra-fa

girl   **(la) niña**
(lah) neen-ya

(to) give   **dar**
dahr

glass   **(el) vaso**
(ehl) vah-so

glasses   **(las) gafas**
(lahs) gah-fas

globe   **(la) esfera**
(lah) es-feh-ra

glove   **(el) guante**
(ehl) gwan-teh

goat   **(la) cabra**
(lah) kah-bra

goldfish   **(el) pez de colores**
(ehl) pays deh ko-lo-rehs

"Good Night"   **"Buenas noches"**
bweh-nahs no-chehs

"Good-bye"   **"Adiós"**
ah-dee-os

goose   **(el) ganso**
(ehl) gahn-so

grandfather   **(el) abuelo**
(ehl) ah-bweh-lo

grandmother   **(la) abuela**
(lah) ah-bweh-la

grapes   **(las) uvas**
(lahs) oo-vas

grasshopper   **(el) saltamontes**
(ehl) sal-ta-mon-tehs

green   **verde**
vair-deh

greenhouse   **(el) invernadero**
(ehl) een-vair-na-de-ro

guitar   **(la) guitarra**
(lah) gee-tahr-ra

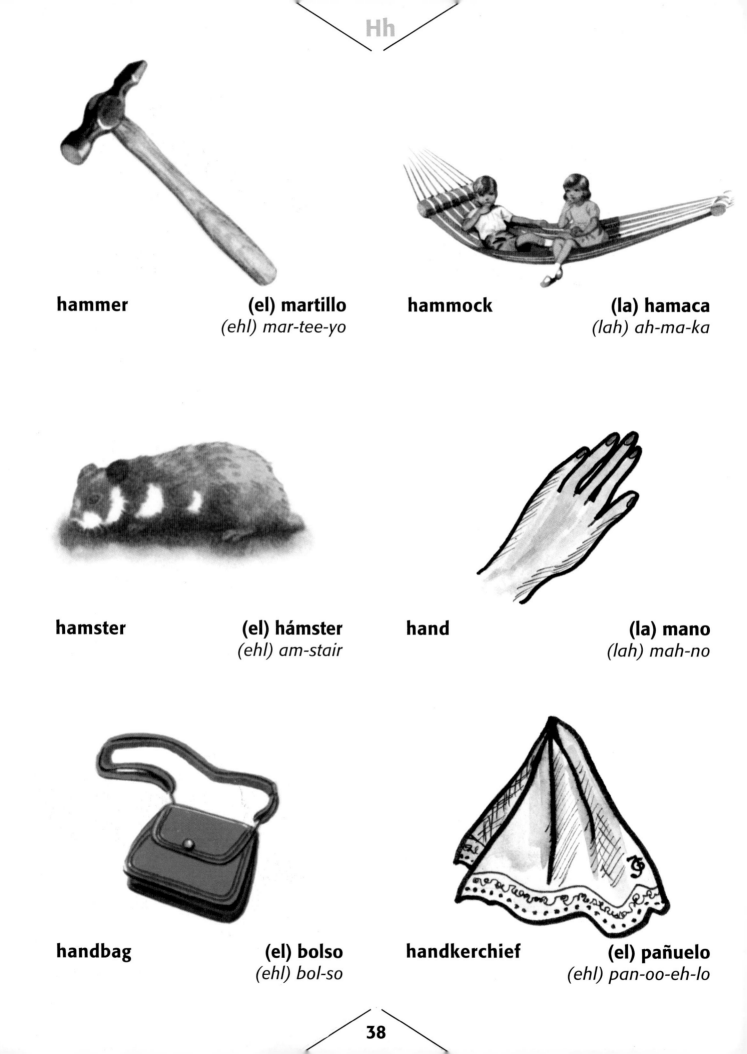

hammer   **(el) martillo**
(ehl) mar-tee-yo

hammock   **(la) hamaca**
(lah) ah-ma-ka

hamster   **(el) hámster**
(ehl) am-stair

hand   **(la) mano**
(lah) mah-no

handbag   **(el) bolso**
(ehl) bol-so

handkerchief   **(el) pañuelo**
(ehl) pan-oo-eh-lo

harvest   **(la) cosecha**
(lah) ko-seh-cha

hat   **(el) sombrero**
(ehl) som-breh-ro

hay   **(el) heno**
(ehl) eh-no

headdress   **(el) tocado de plumas**
(ehl) to-kah-do deh plu-mas

heart   **(el) corazón**
(ehl) kor-ah-sohn

hedgehog   **(el) erizo**
(ehl) air-ee-so

hen   **(la) gallina**
(lah) ga-yee-na

(to) hide   **esconder**
ehs-kon-dair

highway   **(la) carretera**
(lah) car-reh-teh-ra

honey   **(la) miel**
(lah) mee-el

horns   **(los) cuernos**
(lohs) quehr-nos

horse   **(el) caballo**
(ehl) ka-bah-yo

horseshoe   **(la) herradura**
(lah) air-ra-doo-ra

hourglass   **(el) reloj de arena**
(ehl) reh-loh deh ah-rain-a

house   **(la) casa**
(lah) kah-sa

(to) hug   **abrazar**
ah-bra-sahr

hydrant   **(la) boca de riego**
(lah) bo-ka deh ree-eh-go

ice cream   **(el) helado**
(ehl) eh-lah-do

ice cubes   **(los) cubitos de hielo**
(los) koo-bee-tos deh ee-yeh-lo

ice-skating   **patinar**
pah-tee-nar

instrument   **(el) instrumento**
(ehl) een-stroo-men-to

iris   **(el) iris**
(ehl) eer-ees

iron   **(la) plancha**
(lah) plan-cha

island   **(la) isla**
(lah) ees-la

jacket **(la) chaqueta**
(lah) cha-keh-ta

jam **(la) mermelada**
(lah) mer-meh-la-da

jigsaw puzzle **(el) rompecabezas**
(ehl) rom-peh-ka-beh-sas

jockey **(el) jockey**
(ehl) jaw-kee

juggler **(el) malabarista**
(ehl) ma-la-ba-ree-sta

(to) jump **saltar**
sal-tahr

kangaroo   **(el) canguro**
(ehl) kan-goo-ro

key   **(la) llave**
(lah) yah-veh

kitten   **(el) gatito**
(ehl) gah-tee-to

knife   **(el) cuchillo**
(ehl) koo-chee-yo

knight   **(el) caballero**
(ehl) kah-ba-yeh-ro

(to) knit   **tejer**
teh-hair

knot   **(el) nudo**
(ehl) noo-do

koala bear   **(el) koala**
(ehl) ko-ah-la

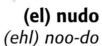
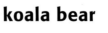

ladder **(la) escala**
(lah) eh-skah-la

ladybug **(la) mariquita**
(lah) ma-ree-kee-ta

lamb **(el) cordero**
(ehl) kor-dair-o

lamp **(la) lámpara**
(lah) lahm-pa-ra

(to) lap **lamer**
lah-mair

laughter **(la) risa**
(lah) ree-sa

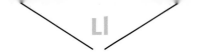

lavender   **(la) lavanda**
(lah) la-vahn-da

lawn mower   **(el) cortacésped**
(ehl) kor-ta-ses-ped

leaf   **(la) hoja**
(lah) oh-ha

leg   **(la) pierna**
(lah) pee-air-na

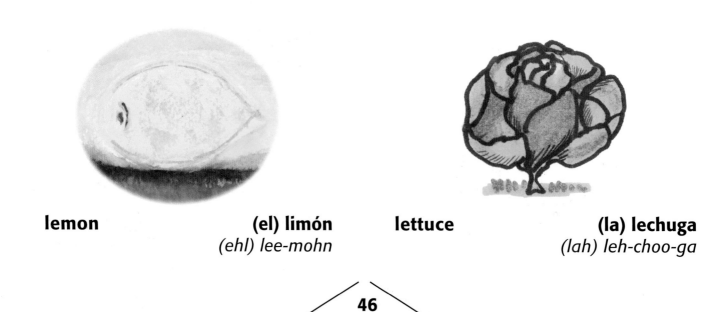

lemon   **(el) limón**
(ehl) lee-mohn

lettuce   **(la) lechuga**
(lah) leh-choo-ga

lightbulb   **(la) bombilla**
(lah) bom-bee-ya

lighthouse   **(el) faro**
(ehl) fah-ro

lilac   **(la) lila**
(lah) lee-la

lion   **(el) león**
(ehl) leh-ohn

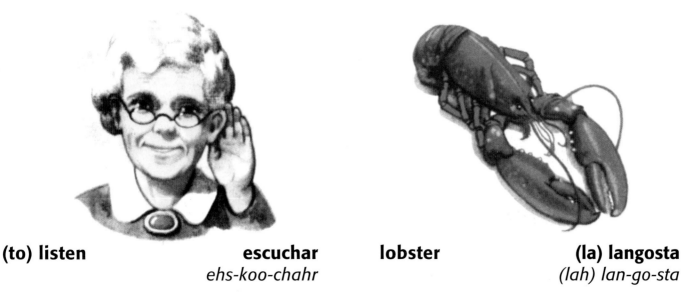

(to) listen   **escuchar**
ehs-koo-chahr

lobster   **(la) langosta**
(lah) lan-go-sta

lock   **(la) cerradura**
(lah) sehr-rah-doo-ra

lovebirds   **(los) periquitos**
(lohs) peh-ri-kee-tos

luggage   **(las) maletas**
(lahs) ma-leh-tas

lumberjack   **(el) leñador**
(ehl) len-ya-dor

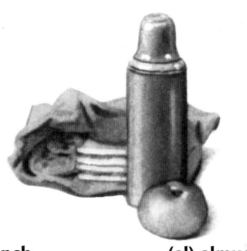

lunch   **(el) almuerzo**
(ehl) ahl-mwehr-so

lynx   **(el) lince**
(ehl) leen-seh

magazine **(la) revista**
(lah) reh-vee-sta

magician **(el) mago**
(ehl) mah-go

magnet **(el) imán**
(ehl) ee-man

map **(el) mapa**
(ehl) mah-pa

maple leaf **(la) hoja del arce**
(lah) oh-ha dehl ahr-seh

marketplace **(la) plaza del mercado**
(lah) plah-sa dehl mer-ka-do

mask **(la) máscara**
(lah) mah-sca-ra

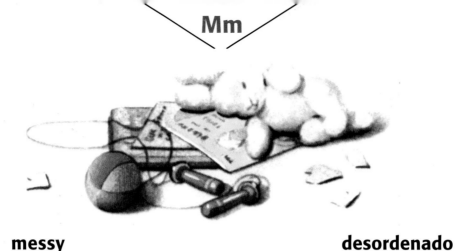

messy

desordenado
dehs-or-deh-nah-do

milkman **(el) lechero**
(ehl) leh-cheh-ro

mirror **(el) espejo**
(ehl) ehs-peh-ho

mitten **(el) mitón**
(ehl) mee-tohn

money **(el) dinero**
(ehl) dee-nair-o

monkey **(el) mono**
(ehl) mo-no

moon **(la) luna**
(lah) loo-na

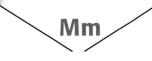

Mm

mother   **(la) madre**
(lah) mah-dreh

mountain   **(la) montaña**
(lah) mon-tahn-ya

mouse   **(el) ratón**
(ehl) rah-ton

mouth   **(la) boca**
(lah) boh-ka

mushroom   **(el) hongo**
(ehl) on-go

music   **(la) música**
(lah) moo-see-ka

naked   **desnudo**
dehs-noo-do

necklace   **(el) collar**
(ehl) koh-yar

needle   **(la) aguja**
(lah) ah-goo-ha

nest   **(el) nido**
(ehl) nee-do

newspaper   **(el) periódico**
(ehl) pair-ee-o-dee-ko

9

nightingale   **(el) ruiseñor**   **nine**   **nueve**
(ehl) roo-ee-sen-yor   *nweh-veh*

12 3 4 5 6 7 8 9 10

notebook   **(el) cuaderno**   **number**   **(el) número**
(ehl) quah-dehr-no   *(ehl) noo-meh-ro*

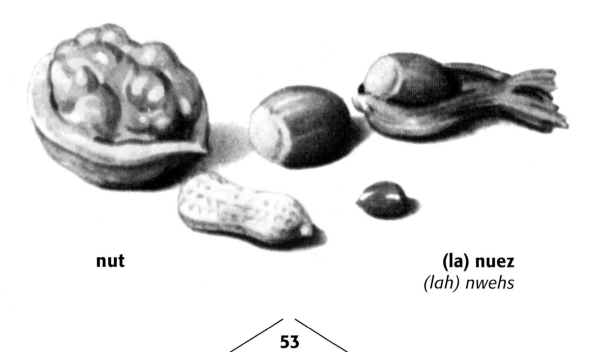

nut   **(la) nuez**
(lah) nwehs

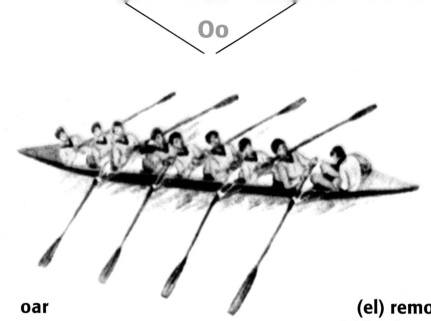

oar   **(el) remo**
(ehl) reh-mo

ocean liner   (el) buque transoceánico
(ehl) boo-keh trans-o-see-ahn-ee-ko

old   **viejo**
vee-eh-ho

one   **uno**
oo-no

onion   **(la) cebolla**
(lah) seh-boh-ya

open   **abierto**
ah-bee-air-to

orange   **(la) naranja**
(lah) na-ran-ha

ostrich   **(el) avestruz**
(ehl) ah-veh-stroos

owl   **(la) lechuza**
(lah) leh-chu-za

ox   **(el) buey**
(ehl) boo-ay

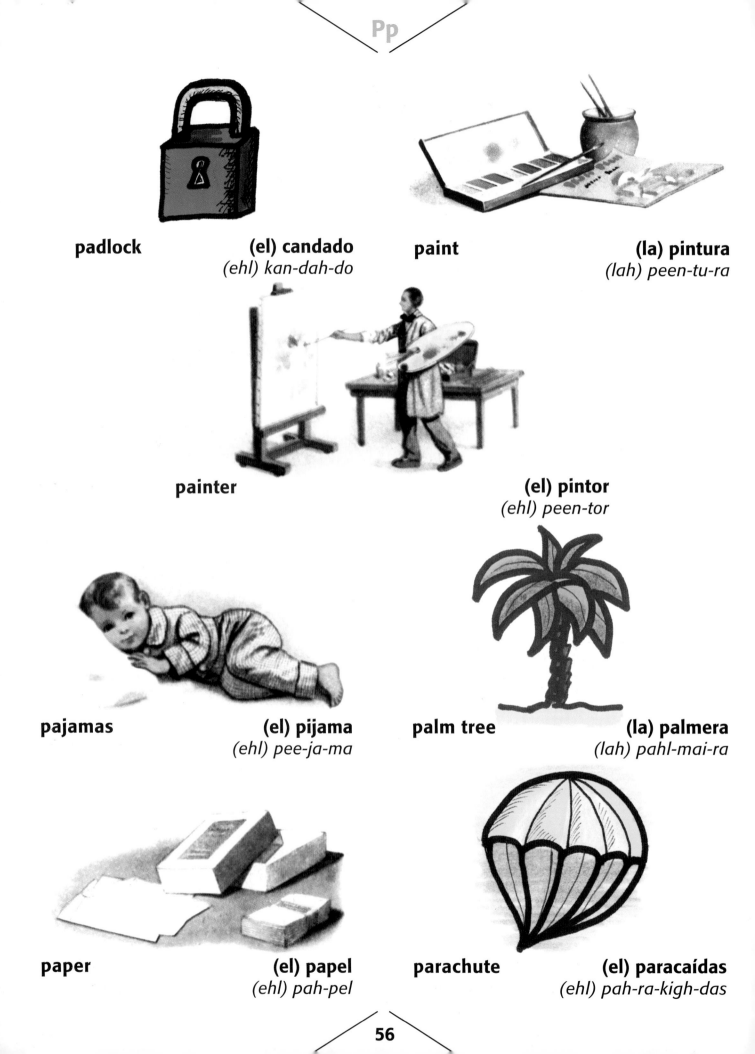

padlock   **(el) candado**
(ehl) kan-dah-do

paint   **(la) pintura**
(lah) peen-tu-ra

painter   **(el) pintor**
(ehl) peen-tor

pajamas   **(el) pijama**
(ehl) pee-ja-ma

palm tree   **(la) palmera**
(lah) pahl-mai-ra

paper   **(el) papel**
(ehl) pah-pel

parachute   **(el) paracaídas**
(ehl) pah-ra-kigh-das

park   **(el) parque**
(ehl) par-keh

parrot   **(el) loro**
(ehl) loh-ro

passport   **(el) pasaporte**
(ehl) pas-a-por-teh

patch   **(el) remiendo**
(ehl) reh-mee-en-do

path   **(la) senda**
(lah) sehn-da

peach   **(el) melocotón**
(ehl) mel-o-ko-ton

pear   **(la) pera**
(lah) peh-ra

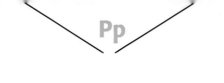

pebble

(la) guija
(lah) gee-ha

(to) peck

picotear
pee-ko-teh-ahr

(to) peel

pelar
peh-lahr

pelican

(el) pelícano
(ehl) pel-ee-ka-no

pencil

(el) lápiz
(ehl) lah-pees

penguin

(el) pingüino
(ehl) peen-gwee-no

people

(la) gente
(lah) hen-teh

piano   **(el) piano**
(ehl) pee-ah-no

pickle   **(el) pepinillo**
(ehl) peh-pee-nee-yo

pie   **(el) pastel**
(ehl) pas-tel

pig   **(el) puerco**
(ehl) pwehr-ko

pigeon   **(la) paloma**
(lah) pah-lo-ma

pillow   **(la) almohada**
(lah) al-mo-ha-da

pin   **(el) alfiler**
(ehl) ahl-fee-lehr

pine   **(el) pino**
(ehl) pee-no

pineapple   **(la) piña**
(lah) peen-ya

pit   **(el) hoyo**
(ehl) oy-yo

pitcher   **(el) jarro**
(ehl) jahr-ro

plate   **(el) plato**
(ehl) plah-to

platypus   **(el) platypus**
(ehl) plah-tee-poos

(to) play **jugar**
hoo-gahr

plum **(la) ciruela**
(lah) see-rweh-la

polar bear **(el) oso polar**
(ehl) oh-so po-lar

pony **(el) caballito**
(ehl) kah-bai-yee-to

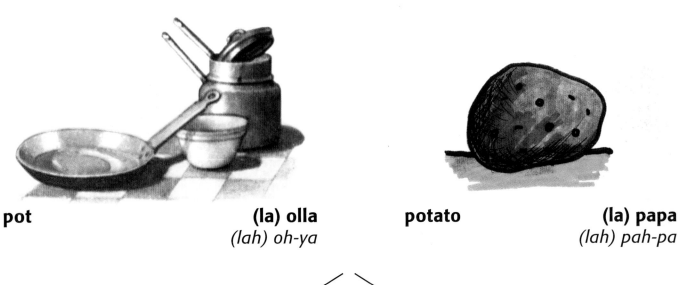

pot **(la) olla**
(lah) oh-ya

potato **(la) papa**
(lah) pah-pa

(to) pour   **vaciar**
vah-see-ahr

present   **(el) regalo**
(ehl) reh-ga-lo

(to) pull   **halar**
ah-lahr

pumpkin   **(la) calabaza**
(lah) kal-a-bah-sa

Qq

puppy   **(el) perrito**
(ehl) pehr-ree-to

queen   **(la) reina**
(lah) reh-ee-na

rabbit　　　　　　　　　**(el) conejo**
(ehl) ko-neh-ho

raccoon　　　**(el) mapache**　　　**racket**　　　**(la) raqueta**
(ehl) ma-pah-cheh　　　　　　　　*(lah) rah-keh-ta*

radio　　　**(la) radio**　　　**radish**　　　**(el) rábano**
(lah) rah-dee-o　　　　　　　　*(ehl) rah-ba-no*

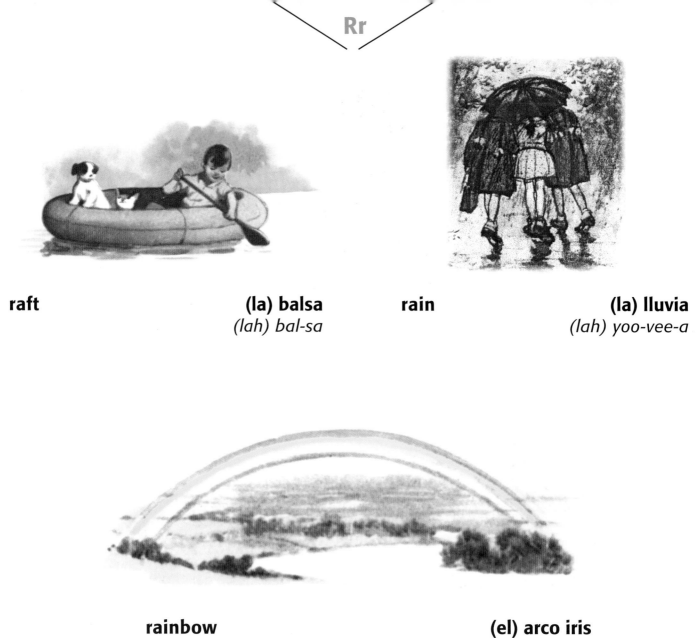

raft   **(la) balsa**
(lah) bal-sa

rain   **(la) lluvia**
(lah) yoo-vee-a

rainbow   **(el) arco iris**
(ehl) ar-ko eer-ees

raincoat   **(el) impermeable**
(ehl) een-pair-mee-ah-bleh

raspberry   **(la) frambuesa**
(lah) fram-bweh-sa

(to) read

leer
leh-air

red

rojo
ro-ho

refrigerator

(el) refrigerador
(ehl) reh-freh-her-ah-dor

rhinoceros

(el) rinoceronte
(ehl) ree-no-sair-an-teh

ring

(el) anillo
(ehl) ah-nee-yo

(to) ring　　**sonar**
so-nahr

river　　**(el) río**
(ehl) ree-o

road　　**(la) calle**
(lah) ka-yeh

rocket　　**(el) cohete**
(ehl) ko-eh-teh

roof　　**(el) techo**
(ehl) teh-cho

rooster　　**(el) gallo**
(ehl) gah-yo

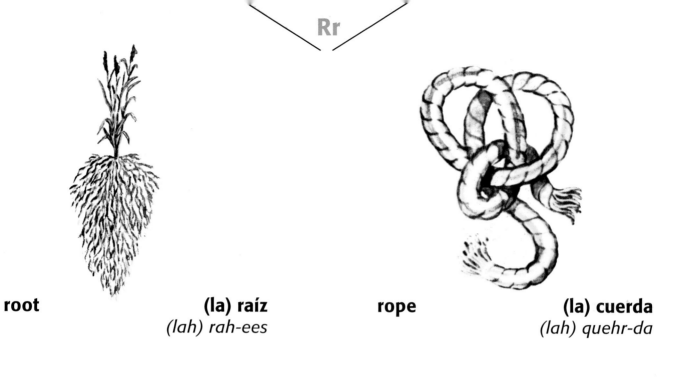

root   **(la) raíz**
(lah) rah-ees

rope   **(la) cuerda**
(lah) quehr-da

rose   **(la) rosa**
(lah) ro-sa

(to) row   **remar**
reh-mahr

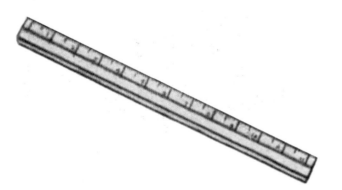

ruler   **(la) regla**
(lah) reh-gla

(to) run   **correr**
kor-rair

safety pin　　**(el) imperdible**
(ehl) eem-pehr-dee-ble

(to) sail　　**navegar**
nah-veh-gahr

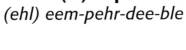

sailor　　**(el) marinero**
(ehl) mar-ee-neh-ro

salt　　**(la) sal**
(lah) sal

scarf　　**(la) bufanda**
(lah) boo-fahn-da

school　　**(la) escuela**
(lah) ehs-que-la

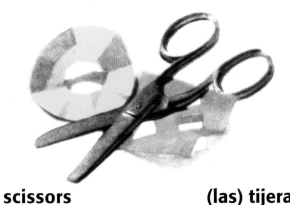

scissors   **(las) tijeras**
(lahs) tee-ehr-as

screwdriver   **(el) destornillador**
(ehl) dehs-tor-nee-ya-dor

seagull   **(la) gaviota**
(lah) gah-vee-o-ta

seesaw   **(el) balancín**
(ehl) bal-an-seen

seven   **siete**
see-eh-teh

(to) sew   **coser**
ko-sair

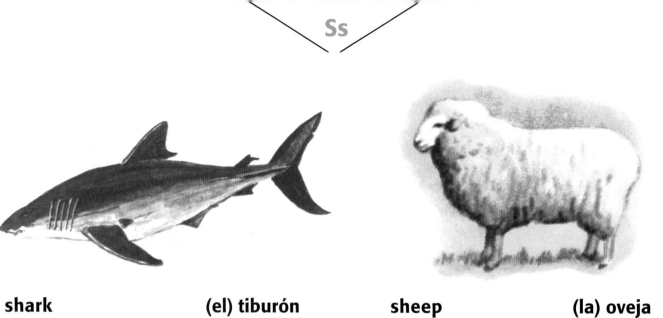

shark   **(el) tiburón**
(ehl) tee-boo-ron

sheep   **(la) oveja**
(lah) oh-veh-hah

shell   **(la) concha**
(lah) kohn-chah

shepherd   **(el) pastor**
(ehl) pahs-tohr

ship   **(el) barco**
(ehl) bahr-koh

shirt   **(la) camisa**
(lah) kah-mee-sah

shoe   **(el) zapato**
(ehl) sah-pah-toh

shovel   **(la) pala**
(lah) pah-lah

(to) show   **mostrar**
moh-strahr

shower   **(la) ducha**
(lah) doo-cha

shutter   **(la) contraventana**
(lah) kohn-trah-vehn-ta-nah

sick   **enfermo**
ehn-fair-moh

sieve   **(el) tamiz**
(ehl) tah-meez

(to) sing   **cantar**
kahn-tahr

(to) sit   **sentar(se)**
sehn-tahr-(seh)

six   **seis**
sai-s

sled   **(el) trineo**
(ehl) tree-neh-oh

(to) sleep   **dormir**
dohr-meer

small **pequeño**
peh-keh-nyoh

smile **(la) sonrisa**
(lah) sohn-ree-sah

snail **(el) caracol**
(ehl) kah-rah-kohl

snake **(la) serpiente**
(lah) sehr-pee-ehn-teh

snow **(la) nieve**
(lah) nee-eh-veh

sock **(el) calcetín**
(ehl) kahl-seh-teen

sofa   **(el) sofá**
(ehl) soh-fah

sparrow   **(el) gorrión**
(ehl) gohr-ree-ohn

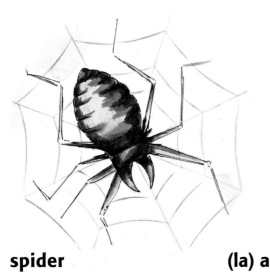

spider   **(la) araña**
(lah) ah-rahn-yah

spiderweb   **(la) telaraña**
(lah) teh-lah-rahn-yah

spoon   **(la) cuchara**
(lah) koo-chah-rah

squirrel   **(la) ardilla**
(lah) ahr-dee-yah

stairs   **(la) escalera**
(lah) eh-ska-le-ra

stamp   **(la) estampilla**
(lah) eh-stam-pee-ya

starfish   **(la) estrella de mar**
(lah) eh-streh-ya deh mahr

stork   **(la) cigüeña**
(lah) see-gwehn-yah

stove   **(la) estufa**
(lah) eh-stoo-fah

strawberry   **(la) fresa**
(lah) freh-sah

subway

(el) metro
(ehl) meh-troh

sugar cube   **(el) cubito de azúcar**
(ehl) koo-bee-toh deh ah-soo-kahr

sun

(el) sol
(ehl) sol

sunflower   **(el) girasol**
(ehl) gee-rah-sol

sweater

(el) suéter
(ehl) sweh-tehr

(to) sweep   **barrer**
bahr-rair

swing

(el) columpio
(ehl) ko-loom-pi-o

table   **(la) mesa**
(lah) meh-sa

teapot   **(la) tetera**
(lah) teh-te-rah

teddy bear   **(el) oso de juguete**
(ehl) oh-soh deh hoo-geh-teh

television   **(el) televisor**
(ehl) tehl-eh-vee-sor

ten   **diez**
dee-ehs

tent   **(la) tienda de campaña**
(lah) tee-yen-dah deh cam-pahn-yah

theater   **(el) teatro**
(ehl) teh-ah-tro

thimble   **(el) dedal**
(ehl) deh-dahl

(to) think   **pensar**
pehn-sahr

three   **tres**
trehss

tie   **(la) corbata**
(lah) kor-bah-ta

(to) tie   **atar**
ah-tahr

tiger **(el) tigre**
(ehl) tee-greh

toaster **(la) tostadora**
(lah) tos-tah-do-ra

tomato **(el) tomate**
(ehl) toh-mah-teh

toucan **(el) tucán**
(ehl) too-kan

towel **(la) toalla**
(lah) to-ah-yah

tower **(la) torre**
(lah) tohr-reh

toy box | **(la) caja de juguetes**
(lah) ka-ja de hoo-geh-tes

tracks | **(la) vía**
(lah) vee-yah

train station | **(la) estación del tren**
(lah) eh-sta-see-on dehl train

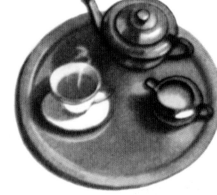

tray | **(la) bandeja**
(lah) bahn-deh-hah

tree | **(el) árbol**
(ehl) ahr-bol

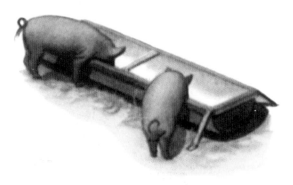

trough | **(el) abrevadero**
(ehl) ah-breh-vah-deh-roh

truck   **(el) camión**
                            (ehl) kah-mee-yohn

trumpet   **(la) trompeta**
              (lah) trom-peh-tah

tulip   **(el) tulipán**
                        (ehl) too-leh-pahn

tunnel   **(el) túnel**
                  (ehl) toon-ehl

turtle   **(la) tortuga**
                        (lah) tohr-too-ga

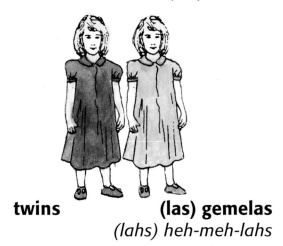

twins   **(las) gemelas**
            (lahs) heh-meh-lahs

two   **dos**
                    dohs

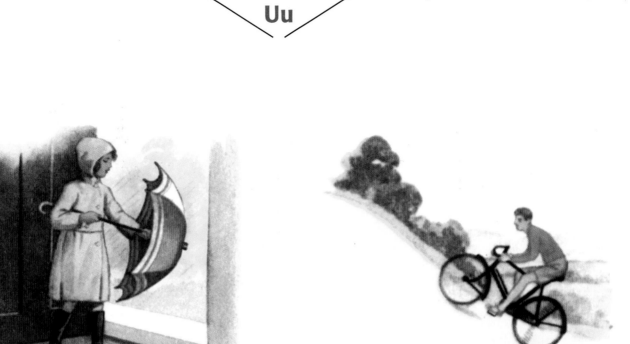

umbrella   **(el) paraguas**
(ehl) par-ah-gwahs

uphill   **cuesta arriba**
koo-es-tah ah-ree-ba

Vv

 vase   **(el) jarrón**
(ehl) hah-rohn

veil   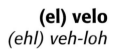 **(el) velo**
(ehl) veh-loh

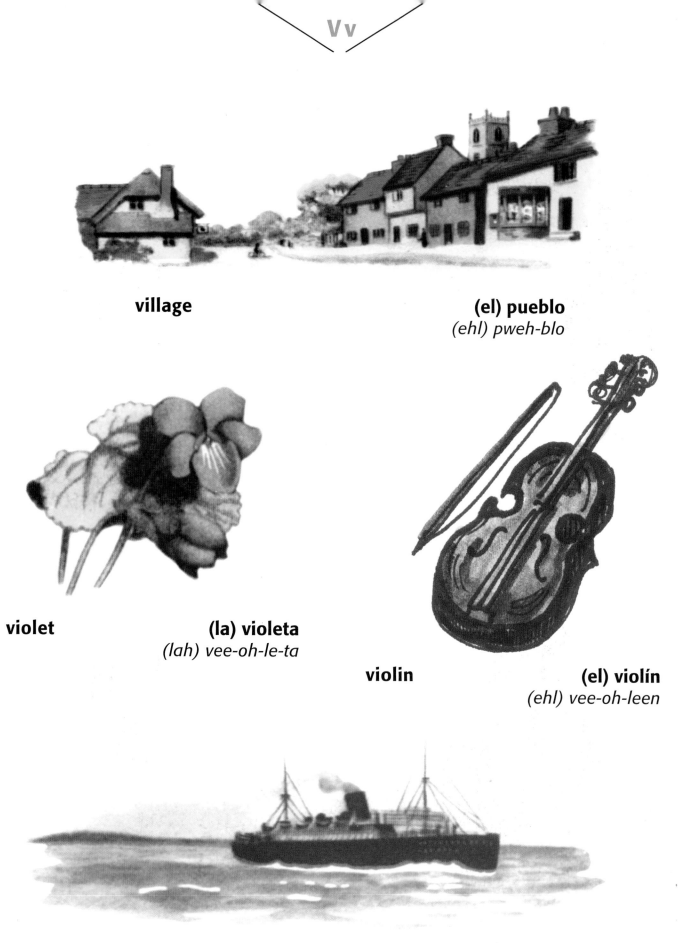

village

(el) pueblo
(ehl) pweh-blo

violet

(la) violeta
(lah) vee-oh-le-ta

violin

(el) violín
(ehl) vee-oh-leen

voyage

(el) viaje
(ehl) vee-ah-heh

waiter   **(el) camarero**
(ehl) kah-ma-reh-ro

(to) wake up   **despertar(se)**
dehs-per-tahr-(seh)

walrus   **(la) morsa**
(lah) mor-sa

(to) wash   **lavar**
lah-vahr

watch   **(el) reloj**
(ehl) reh-lo

(to) watch   **mirar**
mee-rahr

(to) water   **regar**
reh-gahr

waterfall   **(la) cascada**
(lah) kahs-kah-dah

watering can   **(la) regadera**
(lah) reh-ga-deh-ra

watermelon   **(la) sandía**
(lah) sahn-dee-yah

weather vane   **(la) veleta**
(lah) veh-leh-tah

(to) weigh   **pesar**
peh-sahr

whale   **(la) ballena**
(lah) ba-yeh-na

wheel   **(la) rueda**
(lah) roo-eh-dah

wheelbarrow   **(la) carretilla**
(lah) kahr-reh-tee-yah

whiskers   **(el) bigote**
(ehl) bee-go-teh

(to) whisper   **susurrar**
suh-sur-rahr

whistle   **(la) chifla**
(lah) chee-flah

white   **blanco**
blahn-ko

wig   **(la) peluca**
(lah) peh-loo-kah

wind   **(el) viento**
(ehl) vee-ehn-toh

window   **(la) ventana**
(lah) vehn-tah-na

wings   **(las) alas**
(lahs) ah-lahs

winter   **(el) invierno**
(ehl) een-vee-air-no

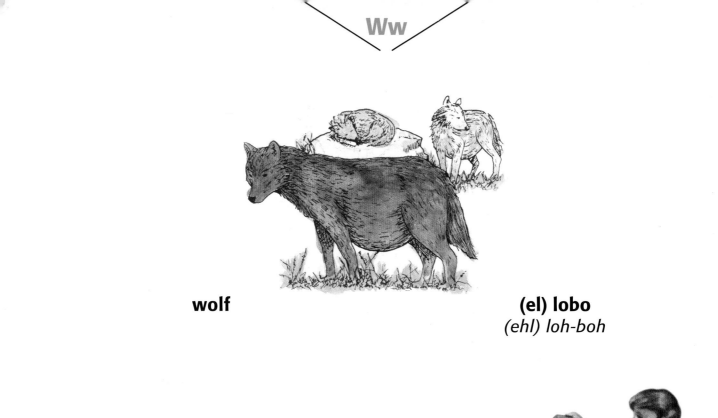

wolf

(el) lobo
(ehl) loh-boh

wood

(la) madera
(lah) ma-deh-ra

word

(la) palabra
(lah) pah-lah-bra

(to) write

escribir
eh-skree-beer

yellow   **amarillo**
ah-ma-ree-yoh

Zz

zebra   **(la) cebra**
(lah) seh-bra

A

abeja (la) bee
abejorro (el) bumblebee
abeto (el) fir tree
abierto open
abrazar (to) hug
abrevadero (el) trough
abrigo (el) coat
abuela (la) grandmother
abuelo (el) grandfather
acuario (el) aquarium
"Adiós" "Good-bye"
águila (el) eagle
aguja (la) needle
alas (las) wings
alfabeto (el) alphabet
alfiler (el) pin
alfombra (la) carpet
alimentar (to) feed
almohada (la) pillow
almuerzo (el) lunch
amarillo yellow
amigo (el) friend
anillo (el) ring
antílope (el) antelope
araña (la) spider
árbol (el) tree
árbol de Navidad (el)
    Christmas tree
arco (el) arch
arco iris (el) rainbow
ardilla (la) squirrel
atar (to) tie
avestruz (el) ostrich
avión (el) airplane
azul blue

B

bailar (to) dance
ballena (la) whale
balsa (la) raft
banco (el) bench
bandeja (la) tray

bandera (la) flag
banana (la) banana
barco (el) boat; ship
barrer (to) sweep
barril (el) barrel
bebé (el) baby
beber (to) drink
berenjena (la) eggplant
bicicleta (la) bicycle
bigote (el) whiskers
blanco white
bloques (los) blocks
boca (la) mouth
boca de riego (la) hydrant
bolso (el) handbag
bombilla (la) lightbulb
bota (la) boot
botella (la) bottle
brazalete (el) bracelet
brújula (la) compass
"Buenas noches" "Good Night"
buey (el) ox
bufanda (la) scarf
buque transoceánico (el)
    ocean liner
burro (el) donkey

C

caballero (el) knight
caballito (el) pony
caballo (el) horse
cabra (la) goat
cacto (el) cactus
café (el) café
caimán (el) alligator
caja de juguetes (la) toy box
calabaza (la) pumpkin
calcetín (el) sock
calle (la) road
cama (la) bed
cámara (la) camera
camarero (el) waiter
camello (el) camel
camión (el) truck
camisa (la) shirt
campana (la) bell

campo (el) field
candado (el) padlock
canguro (el) kangaroo
canoa (la) canoe
cantar (to) sing
capitán (el) captain
cara (la) face
caracol (el) snail
caramelo (el) candy
carretera (la) highway
carretilla (la) wheelbarrow
carro (el) car
carta (la) card
casa (la) house
casa de muñecas (la) dollhouse
cascada (la) waterfall
castillo (el) castle
castor (el) beaver
cebada (la) barley
cebolla (la) onion
cebra (la) zebra
cepillo (el) brush
cerca (la) fence
cereza (la) cherry
cerradura (la) lock
cesto (el) basket
chaqueta (la) jacket
chifla (la) whistle
chimenea (la) chimney
chocolate (el) chocolate
ciervo (el) deer
cigüeña (la) stork
cinco five
cinturón (el) belt
circo (el) circus
ciruela (la) plum
coche (el) coach
cocinar (to) cook
coco (el) coconut
codo (el) elbow
coger (to) gather
cohete (el) rocket
col (la) cabbage

Index

columpio (el) swing
comer (to) eat
concha (la) shell
conejo (el) rabbit
contraventana (la) shutter
corazón (el) heart
corbata (la) tie
corcho (el) cork
cordero (el) lamb
corona (la) crown
correr (to) run
cortacésped (el) lawn mower
cortina (la) curtain
cosecha (la) harvest
cruzar (to) cross
cuadero (el) notebook
cuatro four
cubito de azúcar (el) sugar cube
cubitos de hielo (los) ice cubes
cubo (el) bucket
cuchara (la) spoon
cuchillo (el) knife
cuerda (la) rope
cuernas (las) antlers
cuernos (los) horns
cuesta arriba uphill
cueva (la) cave
cuna (la) cradle

D

dar (to) give
dedal (el) thimble
dedo (el) finger
delfín (el) dolphin
desayuno (el) breakfast
desierto (el) desert
desordenado messy
despertar(se) (to) wake up
destornillador (el) screwdriver
dibujar (to) draw
diente de león (el) dandelion
diez ten

dinero (el) money
dormir (to) sleep
dos two
dragón (el) dragon
ducha (la) shower

E

edredón (el) comforter
elefante (el) elephant
enfermo sick
erizo (el) hedgehog
escala (la) ladder
escalera (la) stairs
escalera mecánica (la) escalator
escarabajo (el) beetle
escoba (la) broom
esconder (to) hide
escribir (to) write
escritorio (el) desk
escuchar (to) listen
escudilla (la) bowl
escuela (la) school
esfera (la) globe
espejo (el) mirror
esquimal Eskimo
estación del tren (la) train station
estampilla (la) stamp
estrella de mar (la) starfish
estufa (la) stove
explorar (to) explore

F

faro (el) lighthouse
fecha (la) date
flecha (la) arrow
flor (la) blossom; flower
flotar (to) float
frambuesa (la) raspberry
fresa (la) strawberry
fruta (la) fruit
fuego (el) fire
fuente (la) fountain

G

gafas (las) glasses
galleta (la) cracker
gallina (la) hen
gallo (el) rooster
ganso (el) goose
gatear (to) crawl
gatito (el) kitten
gato (el) cat
gaviota (la) seagull
gemelas (las) twins
gemelos (los) binoculars
gente (la) people
geranio (el) geranium
girasol (el) sunflower
globo (el) balloon
gorra (la) cap
gorrión (el) sparrow
guante (el) glove
guija (la) pebble
guitarra (la) guitar

H

halar (to) pull
hamaca (la) hammock
hámster (el) hamster
helado (el) ice cream
helecho (el) fern
heno (el) hay
hermano (el) brother
herradura (la) horseshoe
hoja (la) leaf
hoja del arce (la) maple leaf
hongo (el) mushroom
hoyo (el) pit
hueso (el) bone
huevo (el) egg

I

imán (el) magnet

luna (la) moon

imperdible (el) safety pin
impermeable (el) raincoat
instrumento (el) instrument
invernadero (el) greenhouse
invierno (el) winter
iris (el) iris
isla (la) island

J

jardín (el) garden
jarro (el) pitcher
jarrón (el) vase
jaula (la) birdcage
jirafa (la) giraffe
jockey (el) jockey
jugar (to) play

K

koala (el) koala bear

L

lamer (to) lap
lámpara (la) lamp
langosta (la) lobster
lápiz (el) pencil
lavanda (la) lavender
lavar (to) wash
lechero (el) milkman
lechuga (la) lettuce
lechuza (la) bowl
leer (to) read
leñador (el) lumberjack
león (el) lion
libélula (la) dragonfly
libro (el) book
lila (la) lilac
limón (el) lemon
lince (el) lynx
linterna eléctrica (la) flashlight
llave (la) key
llevar (to) carry
llorar (to) cry
lluvia (la) rain
lobo (el) wolf
locomotora (la) engine
loro (el) parrot

M

madera (la) wood
madre (la) mother
mago (el) magician
maíz (el) corn
malabarista (el) juggler
maletas (las) luggage
mano (la) hand
manzana (la) apple
mapa (el) map
mapache (el) raccoon
marco (el) frame
marinero (el) sailor
mariposa (la) butterfly
mariquita (la) ladybug
martillo (el) hammer
máscara (la) mask
melocotón (el) peach
mermelada (la) jam
mesa (la) table
metro (el) subway
miedo (el) fear
miel (la) honey
mirar (to) watch
mitón (el) mitten
mochila (la) backpack
mono (el) monkey
montaña (la) mountain
morsa (la) walrus
mostrar (to) show
muebles (los) furniture
muñeca (la) doll
murciélago (el) bat

N

naranja (la) orange
navegar (to) sail
negro black
nido (el) nest
nieve (la) snow
niña (la) girl
niño (el) boy
nube (la) cloud
nudo (el) knot

nueve nine
nuez (la) nut
número (el) number

O

ocho eight
ojo (el) eye
olla (la) pot
oso (el) bear
oso de juguete (el) teddy bear
oso polar (el) polar bear
otoño (el) autumn
oveja (la) sheep

P

padre (el) father
pájaro (el) bird
pala (la) shovel
palabra (la) word
palmera (la) palm tree
paloma (la) pigeon
pan (el) bread
panadero (el) baker
pañuelo (el) handkerchief
papa (la) potato
papel (el) paper
paraguas (el) umbrella
pardo brown
parque (el) park
pasaporte (el) passport
pastel (el) cake; pie
pastor (el) shepherd
patinar ice-skating
pato (el) duck
payaso (el) clown

peine (el) comb
pelar (to) peel
pelícano (el) pelican
pelota (la) ball
peluca (la) wig
pensar (to) think
pepinillo (el) pickle
pepino (el) cucumber
pequeño small
pera (la) pear
periódico (el) newspaper
periquitos (los) lovebirds
perrera (la) doghouse
perrito (el) puppy
perro (el) dog
pesar (to) weigh
pescar (to) fish
pez (el) fish
pez de colores (el) goldfish
piano (el) piano
picotear (to) peck
pie (el) foot
pierna (la) leg
pijama (el) pajamas
piña (la) pineapple
pingüino (el) penguin
pino (el) pine
pintor (el) painter
pintura (la) paint
plancha (la) iron
plato (el) plate
platypus (el) platypus
playa (la) beach
plaza del mercado (la) marketplace
pluma (la) feather
pueblo (el) village
puente (el) bridge
puerco (el) pig
puerta (la) gate
puño (el) fist

Q

queso (el) cheese

R

rábano (el) radish

radio (la) radio
raíz (la) root
rama (la) branch
rana (la) frog
raqueta (la) racket
ratón (el) mouse
ratón de campo (el) field mouse
refrigerador (el) refrigerator
regadera (la) watering can
regalo (el) present
regar (to) water
regla (la) ruler
reina (la) queen
reloj (el) watch
reloj de arena (el) hourglass
remar (to) row
remiendo (el) patch
remo (el) oar
revista (la) magazine
rinoceronte (el) rhinoceros
río (el) river
risa (la) laughter
rojo red
rompecabezas (el) jigsaw puzzle
rosa (la) rose
rueda (la) wheel
ruiseñor (el) nightingale

S

sal (la) salt
saltamontes (el) grasshopper
saltar (to) jump

sandía (la) watermelon
seis six
senda (la) path
sentar(se) (to) sit
serpiente (la) snake
silla (la) chair
sobre (el) envelope
sofá (el) sofa
sol (el) sun
sombrero (el) hat
sonar (to) ring
sonrisa (la) smile
subir (to) climb
sucio dirty
suéter (el) sweater
susurrar (to) whisper

T

tablilla (la) bulletin board
tambor (el) drum
tamiz (el) sieve
taxi (el) cab
teatro (el) theater
techo (el) roof
tejer (to) knit
tejón (el) badger
telaraña (la) spiderweb
televisor (el) television
tenedor (el) fork
tetera (la) teapot
tiburón (el) seesaw
tienda de campaña (la) tent
tigre (el) tiger
tijeras (las) scissors
toalla (la) towel
tocado de plumas (el) headdress
tomate (el) tomato
torre (la) tower
tortuga (la) turtle
tostadora (lah) toaster
tres three
trineo (el) sled
trompeta (la) trumpet

tucán (el) toucan
tulipán (el) tulip
túnel (el) tunnel

U

uno one
uvas (las) grapes

V

vaca (la) cow
vaciar (to) pour
vacio empty
vaso (el) glass
vela (la) candle
veleta (la) weather vane
velo (el) veil
ventana (la) window
ventilador (el) fan
verde green
vestido (el) dress
vía (la) tracks
viaje (el) voyage
viejo old
viento (el) wind
violeta (la) violet
violín (el) violin
volar (to) fly

Z

zanahoria (la) carrot
zapato (el) shoe
zorro (el) fox

Folk Tales from Bohemia
Adolf Wenig
This folk tale collection is one of a kind, focusing uniquely on humankind's struggle with evil in the world. Delicately ornate red and black text and illustrations set the mood.
Ages 9 and up
90 pages • red and black illustrations • 5 1/2 x 8 1/4 • 0-7818-0718-2 • W • $14.95hc • (786)

Czech, Moravian and Slovak Fairy Tales
Parker Fillmore
Fifteen different classic, regional folk tales and 23 charming illustrations whisk the reader to places of romance, deception, royalty, and magic.
Ages 12 and up
243 pages • 23 b/w illustrations • 5 1/2 x 8 1/4 • 0-7818-0714-X • W • $14.95 hc • (792)

Glass Mountain: Twenty-Eight Ancient Polish Folk Tales and Fables
W.S. Kuniczak
Illustrated by Pat Bargielski
As a child in a far-away misty corner of Volhynia, W.S. Kuniczak was carried away to an extraordinary world of magic and illusion by the folk tales of his Polish nurse.
171 pages • 6 x 9 • 8 illustrations • 0-7818-0552-X • W • $16.95hc • (645)

Old Polish Legends
Retold by F.C. Anstruther
Wood engravings by J. Sekalski
This fine collection of eleven fairy tales, with an introduction by Zymunt Nowakowski, was first published in Scotland during World War II.
66 pages • 7 1/4 x 9 • 11 woodcut engravings • 0-7818-0521-X • W • $11.95hc • (653)

Folk Tales from Russia
by Donald A. Mackenzie
With nearly 200 pages and 8 full-page black-and-white illustrations, the reader will be charmed by these legendary folk tales that symbolically weave magical fantasy with the historic events of Russia's past.
Ages 12 and up
192 pages • 8 b/w illustrations • 5 1/2 x 8 1/4 • 0-7818-0696-8 • W • $12.50hc • (788)

Fairy Gold: A Book of Classic English Fairy Tales
Chosen by Ernest Rhys
Illustrated by Herbert Cole
Forty-nine imaginative black and white illustrations accompany thirty classic tales, including such beloved stories as "Jack and the Bean Stalk" and "The Three Bears."
Ages 12 and up
236 pages • 5 1/2 x 8 1/4 • 49 b/w illustrations • 0-7818-0700-X • W • $14.95hc • (790)

Tales of Languedoc: From the South of France

Samuel Jacques Brun

For readers of all ages, here is a masterful collection of folk tales from the south of France.

Ages 12 and up

248 pages • 33 b/w sketches • 5 1/2 x 8 1/4 • 0-7818-0715-8 • W • $14.95hc • (793)

Twenty Scottish Tales and Legends

Edited by Cyril Swinson

Illustrated by Allan Stewart

Twenty enchanting stories take the reader to an extraordinary world of magic harps, angry giants, mysterious spells and gallant Knights.

Ages 9 and up

215 pages • 5 1/2 x 8 1/4 • 8 b/w illustrations • 0-7818-0701-8 • W • $14.95 hc • (789)

Swedish Fairy Tales

Translated by H. L. Braekstad

A unique blending of enchantment, adventure, comedy, and romance make this collection of Swedish fairy tales a must-have for any library.

Ages 9 and up

190 pages • 21 b/w illustrations • 51/2 x 81/4 • 0-7818-0717-4 • W • $12.50hc • (787)

The Little Mermaid and Other Tales

Hans Christian Andersen

Here is a near replica of the first American edition of 27 classic fairy tales from the masterful Hans Christian Andersen.

Ages 9 and up

508 pages • b/w illustrations • 6 x 9 • 0-7818-0720-4 • W • $19.95hc • (791)

Pakistani Folk Tales: Toontoony Pie and Other Stories

Ashraf Siddiqui and Marilyn Lerch

Illustrated by Jan Fairservis

In these 22 folk tales are found not only the familiar figures of folklore—kings and beautiful princesses—but the magic of the Far East, cunning jackals, and wise holy men.

Ages 7 and up

158 pages • 6 1/2 x 8 1/2 • 38 illustrations • 0-7818-0703-4 • W • $12.50hc • (784)

Folk Tales from Chile

Brenda Hughes

This selection of 15 tales gives a taste of the variety of Chile's rich folklore. Fifteen charming illustrations accompany the text.

Ages 7 and up

121 pages • 5 1/2 x 8 1/4 • 15 illustrations • 0-7818-0712-3 • W • $12.50hc • (785)

All prices subject to change. **To purchase Hippocrene Books** contact your local bookstore, call (718) 454-2366, or write to: HIPPOCRENE BOOKS, 171 Madison Avenue, New York, NY 10016. Please enclose check or money order, adding $5.00 shipping (UPS) for the first book and $.50 for each additional book.

Technical Recruiting

Jorge Ocampo
Senior Account Manager

Suite 290
Three Centerpointe Drive
Lake Oswego, OR 97035
(503) 620-1838 (800) 936-2342
Fax (503) 620-0798
Mobile (503) 789-8305
jocampo@ajilon.com
www.ajilon.com

Technical Recruiting

For information, address:

SemCo Enterprises, Inc.
PO Box 147
Winter Park, FL 32790
phone: 407.830.5400
fax: 407.830.0016
email: semco@semcoenterprises.com
http://www.semcoenterprises.com

ISBN # 0-9668422-3-5
© Copyright 1999 by M. Susan Hodges

Contents

Part One
Technical Recruiting

1. Introduction

Recruiting is the process of finding the right person to fill a job opening. This is not necessarily an easy thing to do, especially when there are more job openings than there are potential candidates. Even if there are plenty of candidates, it still takes a lot of work and talent to find the right person for the job.

Technical recruiting is a specialty with its own unique requirements. A technical recruiter fills jobs for Information Technology (IT); programmers, analysts, software engineers, etc. Because technical recruiters are dealing with a group of people that seem to speak a different language, communication is not easy. The job requirement originates from a technical person and the job applicants are technical, but everyone else involved in the recruiting process is nontechnical.

There are different kinds of technical recruiters. Some recruiters work with permanent placement, and others deal with contract, or consulting, jobs. Permanent placement is hiring an employee whose income is usually expressed in terms of annual salary and a benefit package. A contract worker is one who is hired for a specific (and temporary) assignment. Their salary is most often defined on an hourly basis and benefits are limited or even nonexistent. This hourly salary is also referred to as hourly rate, billing rate, or daily rate. Corporate recruiters recruit only for one company, most often the one they work for. They do permanent placement and are rarely involved with contract hires. Employment agency recruiters (also called headhunters) also do permanent placement, but of course they are recruiting for client companies. Recruiters in consulting firms do either permanent or temporary placement and, in fact, often do both.

Recruiters are filling jobs for a manager who has a job opening, but they might not be working directly with that manager. Corporate recruiters usually deal directly with the hiring manager, but recruiters in employment agencies and consulting firms must often work with an intermediary. In consulting firms the job requestor is usually an account manager who works for the consulting firm. Employment agents usually work with the client companies HR department. The person the recruiter works with is called the job requestor, whether he or she is the actual hiring manager or is an intermediary. The job requestor is the person responsible for defining the job that needs to be filled. This job

RECURITING PROCESS

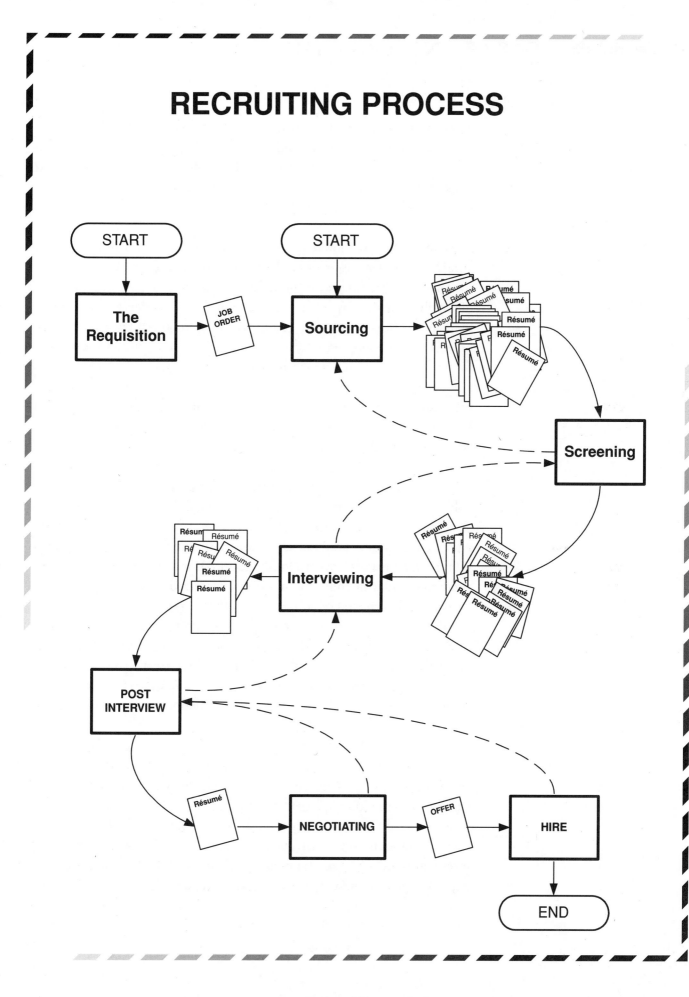

description must contain information about specific skill requirements, personal characteristics desired, and pertinent logistical information such as date needed and salary range. This job description can be called many things including job order, job requisition, job specs (specifications), and job requirement.

Most of the time the job requisition is the start of the recruiting process. The recruiter uses the job order defining what kind of person is needed for the job to "source" for the job. Sourcing the candidate is gathering résumés of possible hires, and quantity is important. The recruiter wants to find as many résumés as possible that fit the basic job requirements. Recruiters, however, often source without a specific job description in hand, especially for temporary or contract jobs. Recruiters know what skills are in demand and will collect résumés for these skill sets, because they know they will eventually receive a pertinent job requirement. Sourcing often results in hundreds of résumés, so the next phase, screening, is necessary to sift through and find the best possible applicants.

Once possible candidates have been found, the next step is to find probable candidates from the collection of possible ones. This is called screening. A screen determines whether the person is worth interviewing for the job, and the screen itself often includes a limited phone interview. Screening covers a lot of ground. It is used to determine if the candidate's résumé reflects the appropriate skills, if the candidate's availability fits the job opening, and if the necessary soft skills are there. While there are no hard percentages, screening should eliminate most of the résumés from consideration. Some of the time screening eliminates all of the résumés, so the recruiter is back to the sourcing phase. Most of the time, the screening identifies candidates to be interviewed. These applicants are often ranked or classified so the strongest can be interviewed first.

Interviewing for most jobs includes multiple interviews. At minimum the recruiter conducts an interview to determine whether to present the candidate to the job requestor, and the job requestor conducts an interview to decide whether they would like to hire the candidate. Often there are more than the two interviews, and there are different types of interviews and different types of questions to ask. The quantity and depth of the interviewing required varies depending upon the seniority and importance of the job. Interviewing again reduces the number of potential candidates, and the candidates who interview well move into the post-interview phase. Again, the interviews might eliminate all candidates, so the second-ranked candidates can be interviewed, or the recruiter can go back to sourcing.

The post-interview phase in many ways is a time of reflection. First, the job requestor and the recruiter review the job requirements and the candidates that are being seriously considered. Candidates can now be evaluated and compared with each other. Reference checking is also done at this point, as is drug testing if required. This is the decision point—should an offer be made? When the answer is yes, it's time to start negotiating.

Negotiating is actually a sales job. The recruiter now has to sell the job and the company to the candidate, and has to do so by countering unknown potential offers from other companies. Negotiating actually starts with the initial contact with a candidate, as it's the recruiter's job to determine what is important to the candidate—what will make the candidate choose his or her offer above others. The recruiter needs this information to successfully negotiate the hire. With some applicants it's salary, with others location, and with some something as small as being provided with business cards can be the most important part of the job offer. The end of the negotiating phase is either a successful hire or a return to the recruiting process if the candidate turns down the offer.

The recruiting process is a cycle of sequential phases, but not necessarily sequential steps. While ideally the process cycles through in order, at any phase the recruiter might have to go back even to the beginning as candidates are eliminated. Recruiters also work on different phases in the cycle for each job and each candidate. Recruiters maintain a pipeline, or queue, of candidates and must keep track of where in the pipeline each candidate is. Each phase has its own requirements for follow-up (both to the candidate and to the job requestor), and recruiters are asked how many candidates they have in the pipeline, how many interviews they have scheduled, and so on. It might appear confusing, as a typical work-day could consist of:

ACTIVITY	PHASE
Interviewing two or three candidates for a Web Programmer job	Interviewing
Checking the Internet to source job requirement that just came in	Sourcing
Calling a company to do a reference check	Post Interview
Meeting with a hiring manager to discuss new openings	The Requisition
Sending thank you, offer, and/or reject letters	Negotiating
Writing a job ad to be posted to the company's Web page	Sourcing
Analyzing résumés that came in over the weekend	Screening

Obviously a recruiter has to be well-organized to keep track of everything that's happening on any given day. A good recruiter keeps track of an infinite number of details, but has to have the big picture in mind at all times.

2. The Requisition

JOB REQUISITION

CORE DESCRIPTION

Logistics (location, hours, start date, contact information, etc.)

Job requirements (logistical, personal, technical)

Job description (job type, technical environment, seniority level)

TECHNICAL SKILL SET

Platforms (computer, operating system)

Development (languages, methodologies, tools)

Data management (files, databases, warehouses)

Communications (networks, client/server, Internet)

A requisition, or job order, sounds fairly simple, but actually there's a lot of activity going on during this phase. The requisition is, of course, the description of the job opening and originates from the manager who has the opening. Original job orders are inevitably incomplete. It's not unusual for a manager to say "I need a C++ programmer" and sit back and wait for candidates to interview. The recruiter knows this is impossible. There are literally thousands of C++ programmers out there, and no one is going to interview them all. The recruiter must fill out job orders and get the rest of the requirements in order to start the process. Corporate recruiters usually work directly with the job requestor, who is also the hiring manager, and can establish communications so they can do this, but other recruiters don't have it quite as easy. Often they never talk directly to the manager, but must work with intermediaries. Recruiters from employment agencies are usually talking to HR people—the job requestor is often a corporate recruiter! Recruiters in consulting firms usually get job orders from account managers in their own firms. The job requestor is now an account manager who has the actual contact with the hiring managers in the client companies. This makes the recruiting effort more difficult, as only the hiring manager really knows what kind of person he or she needs, and having to work through a third party raises the possibility of misunderstanding the job requirements. The recruiter needs to have a correct picture of the job to be filled, and the difficulty of doing so increases with the number of people between the recruiter and the hiring manager, therefore the recruiter should do whatever is possible to get to talk directly to this manager. Hopefully this will happen, but if it doesn't the recruiter must get the appropriate information from the job requestor. This information includes job logistics, the job description and job requirements.

See: *Requisition for Technical Position* on page 143.

Job Logistics

Logistical information can include many things, but at minimum the recruiter must know the job location, the job requestor identity and contact information, the desired start date, and the salary:

Location can mean different things. It has to start with city and state, because of the number of people that relocate for technical jobs. For corporate recruiters, location could include a branch location, but usually states a department within the company. For agency and consulting firm recruiters, location starts with the identity of the client company, then proceeds to add branch and department. Remote assignments (or even interviews) require extra logistical information. Candidates will need to know about airports, public transportation, restaurants, etc. A standard form can be used to collect this information and pass it on to the candidate.

See: *Site Information* on page 147.

The name, and probably title, of the job requestor is obviously important, along with phone number, fax, and e-mail information. The recruiter will be getting in touch with the requestor many times throughout the process—to get more information about the job, to schedule interviews, to get feedback on a candidate, etc.

Most technical jobs have a desired start date of yesterday, but this is important to pin down. For contract jobs, this information should include the proposed length of the assignment. The recruiter also needs to know how long the job requestor can wait to fill the job. Some jobs are more critical and the recruiter can concentrate on the most important.

Finally, salary must be known and should be expressed as a range, but the recruiter should check to see if there is an absolute maximum that will be paid. Salary discussions can also cover whether there is a sign-on bonus and whether relocation expenses will be paid.

Additional logistical information can be included in the job requisition. This varies from company to company. Perhaps the most common additional information is the signature and identity of the authorizing manager. Other things could include special benefits, or even restrictions. For example, an assignment might include gym privileges. On the other hand, perhaps there is no handicapped access at a certain location. Every job has its own unique logistics, and the more the recruiter knows, the easier it is to find the right candidates.

Job Description

There are literally hundreds of different jobs being performed by Information Technology professionals, and every job can be defined by a core description and an associated skill set. The core description includes three things: the job type, the computer environment, and the seniority required. Job types fall into three categories: application development, technical development, and systems support. Applications developers are responsible for creating and maintaining the business software a company needs. Technical developers work with the system software— the operating systems, the database management systems, and the network systems. Systems support personnel are responsible for the daily operation of all the computer systems, both hardware and software. The computer environment refers to a mainframe, midrange or desktop system. Seniority is defined as senior, mid, or junior. These levels can be equated to years—a senior has over five years of experience, mid-level developers have from two to five years, and a junior has under two years of experience. Each job also has an associated skill set, which can now be added to the description, to have a complete understanding of the job. Skills come from four areas: the platform, development issues, data management, and communications skills. A detailed explanation of what needs to be included in a technical job description is covered in Section 3, Technical Job Descriptions.

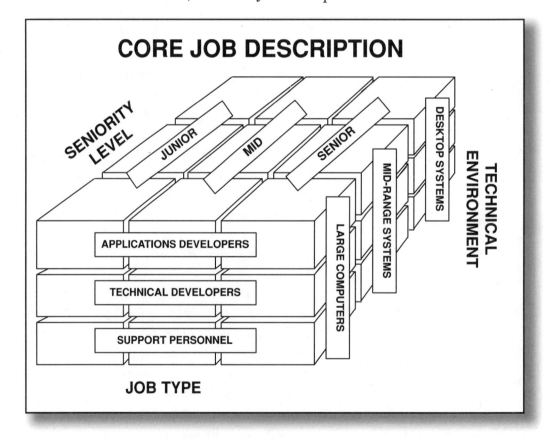

Job Requirements

Job requirements are things that are absolute musts; there can be no negotiation on these issues. Companies insist that candidates satisfy these needs and are even willing to pay higher salaries when the requirement is hard to fill. Requirements are usually not technical, but reflect personal, nontechnical, or logistical needs. They come from many sources and can even be government issued, eg.working on defense systems might require a security clearance. On a personal level many companies now require candidates to pass drug tests. An example of a nontechnical skill requirement could be that a global company needs applicants to be fluent in a second language. Logistically, many jobs in consulting firms require that the candidate be willing to travel regularly. The most common requirement is a college degree. Some jobs not only require a degree, they require a specific major such as Computer Science.

There is one common technical requirement, and it's for certification. Certification, especially for networking professionals, is provided by vendors who provide training in specific skills, then test to confirm that the person has learned what the courses cover. These vendors will certify the participant if he or she passes the test(s). Networking certification, especially that for Microsoft and Novell networking, is a good example of requirements for which companies pay extra.

The logistics, job description, and job requirements complete a job order, and this is the information the recruiter needs in order to look for good candidates. Sometimes a company uses an actual form to collect this information, but even if no form exists the information needed is the same and the recruiter should build his or her own form to consistently collect complete information for each job.

See: *Requisition for Technical Position* on page 143.

Requisition Processing

Even in the best-case situation where the recruiter has a detailed requisition form that is filled out by the hiring manager, the recruiter inevitably has to go back to the job requestor with questions. Obviously, some of the questions could be to fill in missing information, but after that is done there are still issues that should be resolved with the hiring manager. For example, both the job requestor and the recruiter bring certain assumptions to the process, and it's worth taking the time to uncover what these are.

Most job requestors have an assumption, or expectation, about how many interviews they will conduct and how soon they should start interviewing. The recruiter should be prepared to set expectations based on experience with similar job requisitions. With some hard-to-find skills, there will be very few résumés coming in, with even fewer interviews, and the recruiter should be sure the job requestor understands filling this job will take time. Other assumptions are made about the timing and kind of feedback the job requestor expects. Does he or she expect weekly phone calls detailing how many résumés have been received, how many candidates have been screened, etc.? Or, are they willing to wait until actual interviews need to be scheduled? The recruiter needs to get feedback, too. If résumés are sent to a manager, how long should the recruiter wait before hearing back? And, what kind of feedback? Simply being told that "none of the résumés you sent me are any good" doesn't help the recruiter at all. The recruiter needs to know why these résumés were unacceptable. This means that a regular method of communications must be established.

The requisition phase is the first chance the recruiter has to discover benefits about the job or about the company offering the job. Each company and each job has its own unique benefits and attractive points, and it's important for the recruiter to know what they are. A company's benefit package is only the starting point. Be sure to find out about flex hours, relocation expenses and, perhaps, availability of a corporate credit card. These are only a few things that could convince a candidate to accept an offer. Corporate recruiters working with only one company can define corporate benefits once, and usually do so within the HR Department (which undoubtedly knows more about benefits than any hiring manager). Standard forms make it easier to collect this information. Recruiters in employment agencies and consulting firms have a bigger job, as they must determine the corporate benefits for many companies. In addition, the recruiter should check on benefits for each specific job. For example, a certain job might include the opportunity for technical training, another might offer a completion bonus. All recruiters have to check with the job requestor to see if a particular job has specific benefits.

> See: *Company/Client Analysis* on page 125.

Process control also starts with the requisition phase. Recruiters manage two queues, or pipelines, as they do their work. One is a queue of applicants, the other is a queue of open jobs. At any given time the recruiter must know how many applicants he or she is working with, and how many job orders have not yet been filled. These queues are commonly called pipelines. Each job order must be entered (by date) in the pipeline when it is received. Standard forms are used to quickly summarize the recruiting activity.

> See: *Pipeline Report/Open Jobs* on page 141.

3. Technical Job Descriptions

A job description for a technical job requires both a core description and a technical skill set. The core description has three elements, each of which has three possibilities. The background of the job must be defined as being either applications development, technical development, or support. Every job also requires a certain experience level, which is stated as junior, mid, or senior. Finally, the technical environment of the job completes the core description. A technical job can be any combination of the options in the three categories. One job could be for a junior applications developer working with desktop systems, another may need a senior technical developer working with large computers, a third might require a senior applications developer working with large computers. The second part of the job description describes the technical skill set the job needs. Technical skills fall into four categories; platforms, development tools, data management, and communications, or networking, skills.

Background and Experience

Applications Developers   Most IT jobs fall into this category. These are the people who create and maintain the business, or application, software. This includes, but is not limited to, human resources, payroll, accounting, administration, and industry specific software such as MRP (Manufacturing Resource Planning), financial software for banks, insurance companies and brokerages, education packages for schools, and statistical programs for the pharmaceutical industry. Any software that helps a company run its business is produced by these people. Applications developers work with the logical functioning of software systems, are concerned with business solutions, and know relatively little about hardware.

Junior (up-to-two-years experience) applications developers write and modify programs. They work on several programs at once, but are not responsible for program interaction. They work under the supervision of mid- or senior-level developers and stay within the confines of the programming department. They have many technical skills, and their jobs are defined exclusively by these skills. Job titles usually include the word "programmer" or perhaps "engineer."

Mid-level (two-to-five-years experience) applications developers continue to create and maintain software, but do much more. They must work with the interactions and interfaces in the system, so system analysis and design start to be important. The job also requires interpersonal skills as mids have direct contact with the users, or the business men and women within the company. At this point in a development career, programmers often start to specialize. The two specialities in this area are applications and data.

TECHNICAL JOB DESCRIPTIONS

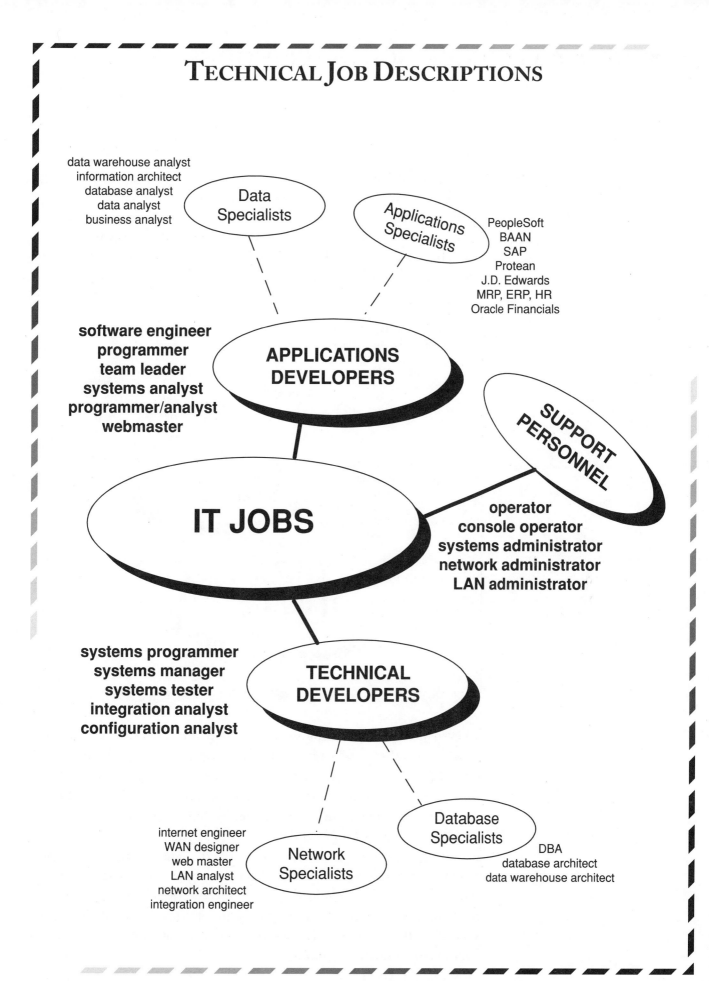

data warehouse analyst
information architect
database analyst
data analyst
business analyst

Data Specialists

Applications Specialists

PeopleSoft
BAAN
SAP
Protean
J.D. Edwards
MRP, ERP, HR
Oracle Financials

software engineer
programmer
team leader
systems analyst
programmer/analyst
webmaster

APPLICATIONS DEVELOPERS

IT JOBS

SUPPORT PERSONNEL

operator
console operator
systems administrator
network administrator
LAN administrator

systems programmer
systems manager
systems tester
integration analyst
configuration analyst

TECHNICAL DEVELOPERS

internet engineer
WAN designer
web master
LAN analyst
network architect
integration engineer

Network Specialists

Database Specialists

DBA
database architect
data warehouse architect

Applications specialists have developed a body of knowledge about an industry, such as banking, a business process, such as benefits processing, or a software product, such as SAP. Often the requirements for mid-level applications developers list the application skill first. In fact, SAP knowledge is often listed as the only skill. There has been such a shortage of developers who know this product that companies don't care about any other skills. Titles for these developers can reflect the specific application, such as EDI Analyst and SAP Programmer.

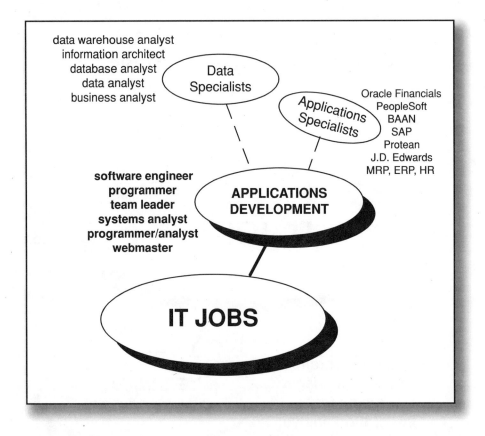

The data specialty requires knowledge of DBMSs (DataBase Management Systems) and data design and analysis tools. These people build the logical data structures that can be specific to a single application or can be enterprise-wide. This logical design requires knowledge of the business environment, as it defines what fields of information will be grouped together, and the data specialists work closely with the user departments. Data specialists can be titled Data Analyst, Database Analyst, or even Information Architect although the noun "architect" is more often used for technical developers. Data Modeler is a title that is used for anyone doing data design on an enterprise-wide basis. Data specialists also work with data warehousing, so Warehouse Architect or Warehouse Analyst are common.

Mid-level applications developers work under the supervision of seniors, but are much more independent than juniors. Job titles still use the word "programmer" and "engineer" is even more popular. New titles include "analyst," "designer," "modeler," and "architect."

Seniors are the most important people in the Information Technology Department. They do everything the mid-level developers do, but are responsible for both the supervision of the mid- and junior-level staff and the correctness of the systems being produced. Those two words— "supervise" and "responsible"—are the key to identifying a job or person as senior-level. Titles often simply add the word "senior" to the noun, so we have Senior Programmer, Senior Software Engineer, etc. Seniors also can specialize in applications or data, but there are two jobs that are senior only—project leader and systems analyst.

A system analyst is someone skilled and experienced in the analysis phase of the system development cycle. It requires strong interpersonal skills, as analysts spend much of their time with the users determining needs and processing functions. Analysts usually have programming backgrounds, although some companies have moved people from user departments into this position. Analysts have thorough knowledge of the applications systems and often know as much about the company's work, eg. banking, as anyone in the company. Analysts usually do much of the system design in addition to the analysis work. A minimum of five-years programming experience is usually required. This is not a managerial job, and in many companies is on the same level as project leader.

A project leader, or team leader, must have managerial skills as well as technical skills. A project leader is responsible for scheduling and planning the systems development. He or she establishes time frames for completion of the project and sets priorities for the work to be done. Occasionally project leaders do some of the analysis, design, and programming work, but usually their work is to provide technical assistance and leadership during these phases. This job is also responsible for evaluating, training, and monitoring the career paths of the programmers. A minimum of five years of programming experience is required.

Technical Developers   Technical developers create, maintain, and develop system software: operating systems, database management systems, and communications systems. The software has nothing to do with the company's business, but rather manages the computer environment. Technical developers know a great deal about the hardware and are responsible for the physical design of data and systems. They are concerned with making sure software runs effectively in the computer environment and often mention tuning, or performance tuning. They are responsible for integrating the different systems within the company. Interpersonal skills are not as important, as there is no contact with the company's business men and women. In fact, many technical developers work alone or in very loose teams. As with applications developers, titles often include the nouns "programmers" and "engineers." In addition, technical developers are likely to have the title "architect."

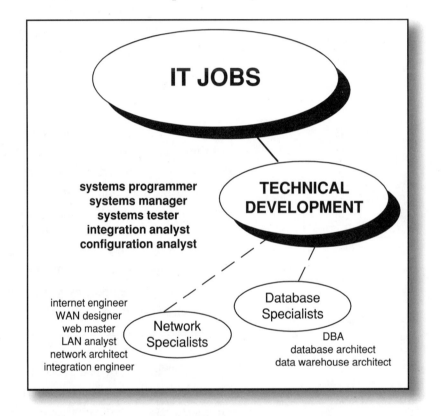

Junior, mid-level, and senior technical developers can be associated with the same time periods as the applications developers (under two years, two to five years, and over five years), but with technical jobs the specialization is what is important. The technical staff specializes in either operating systems, data, or communications.

Operating systems specialist titles often include the word "systems" as in Systems Programmer or Systems Architect, and the job is to make sure the operating system effectively manages the resources of the company. Each developer is usually responsible for the performance of certain operating system programs. For example, one systems programmer might monitor device handlers, while another would work with the job schedulers. In more senior jobs, technical developers are responsible for such things as capacity planning (making sure the computer environment has hardware and management systems that are large enough and fast enough to effectively run the application systems) and configuration management (keeping track of all the hardware and/or software). Titles can reflect the job duties, such as Configuration Manager, or can be generic, such as Systems Programmer, Integration Analyst, and System Architect.

Data specialists have thorough knowledge of physical database design and implementation. The physical design of a database takes the logical design (the field groupings) and stores the various groups on disk accounting for hardware facts such as: data stored in the center of a disk will be retrieved faster than data stored on the outside. Once the database is built, the technical developers are now responsible for tuning the database to make sure it continues to provide good response time, even as situations change. More specific titles for data specialists include data architect, data warehouse designer, or DBA.

The DBA, or DataBase Administrator, is usually a technical developer, although some large installations have both technical and applications DBAs. This job administers and controls the organizations' database resources and is responsible for the performance and tuning of the database. Companies have a DBA for each DBMS (eg. an Oracle DBA). DBAs are responsible for the accuracy, security, and backups of the data.

Communications, or network specialists, are the highest paid people in Information Technology, and should be, as these jobs require knowledge of two industries—the computer industry and the communications industry. These are the people who create, maintain, and develop the networking necessary for all the online services a company provides. An online program is one where a person on a terminal is interacting with a program on a separate computer. This basic definition indicates the level of hardware knowledge required; something is online because of the hardware usage. This specialty includes client/server systems and the Internet access. Because of the growth of both of those areas, communications specialists are much in demand.

Technical developers use the words "network" or "communications" rather than the word "online." They, in fact, have a lot of words they use to describe their work. Topology defines how a LAN (Local Area Network) is set up. A protocol is a set of rules; communications protocols are rules that govern the data transmission. Middleware is software that connects programs following different protocols. A firewall is software that protects a company's internal systems from Internet browsers. Reference to any of these terms identifies the person or the job as a technical developer, specifically a networking specialist. Most of the titles have the word "network" in the title, as in Network Analyst, Network Designer, and Network Manager. Many new titles have appeared that use the word "Internet." There are Internet Programmers, Web Analysts, and, of course, Webmaster.

Support Personnel   The support staff in a company is part of the technical staff, but support personnel have a very different job. Support people do not create, maintain, or develop software. They are responsible for running and supporting the software that the developers create. They do not know programming logic, languages, or development tools and do no analysis or design. They are responsible for installing hardware and software, running system backups, monitoring the hardware, distributing reports, mounting tapes and toner cartridges, and trouble-shooting problems. Support personnel know how to run both hardware and software. It is the job of the support staff to ensure that the daily production schedule is completed correctly.

Support jobs differ with the computer environment. The support staff in a mainframe installation is called operations, and variations on the title "operator" are the norm. In addition to Operators, Senior Operators, Tape Operators, and Console Operators, titles include Tape Handlers, Distribution Managers and Shift Supervisors. The computer runs 24-hours a day, so the operators work in shifts. Juniors perform most of the manual labor—mounting tapes and distributing reports— and seniors do the troubleshooting and supervision. It would be the senior, or console, operator who would notice that a certain job was taking longer than usual. He or she would then query the operating system to determine the status of the job. Based on the status, the shift supervisor would call the programmer (at perhaps 2:00 a.m.) to come in and fix the problem. Operators sometimes move into technical development as they have necessary hardware knowledge.

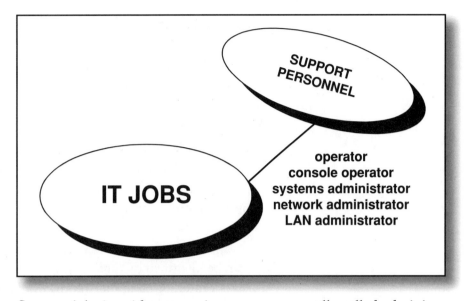

Support jobs in midrange environments are usually called administrators—System Administrator and Network Administrator. System Administrator is, in fact, an official title in a Unix environment, although it is used in any midrange installation. This job is responsible for such things as installing new software, adapting software to the system, performing system backups, recovering lost data, and maintaining security. Systems administrators have some of the same duties as mainframe system operators, but have more responsibility. In a mainframe system, the operators run backups. In a midrange system, the systems administrator plans and runs the backups. Network administrators will actually install and maintain the networks. They do the actual cabling, respond to problem calls, add and remove devices from the network, and run monitor programs to check hardware and software. These support people often move into technical development. Because they have more responsibility they learn more about the software and many decide the move to development would be a good one.

Another job that is often considered to be part of the support staff is that of Help Desk personnel. The Help Desk is the department within a company that users go to when they encounter a problem or need assistance. Help Desks were originally set up to provide support for desktop environments, and, in general, support included purchasing desktop equipment, training users in desktop software such as Access and Word, establishing networks for desktops, and acting as consultants when problems are encountered. Help Desks do have access to technical developers to assist with problems, but most of the personnel are nonprogrammers who provide training, basic consulting, and purchasing functions. These individuals are skilled in using desktops and prewritten software packages, but are not programmers. There is no accepted title for Help Desk personnel, and length of experience and specific skills vary greatly. Help Desks have been expanded beyond just servicing desktop systems, but this is still their dominant use.

Environment

Every IT job requires skills and experience in a specific technical environment; large computers, midsize, also called midrange, or desktop systems. All computers and all software systems fall into one of these three areas, and job requestors want to see applicants who have worked in the appropriate area.

Large computer systems include mainframes and supercomputers and can be identified by three characteristics. First, the computer resides in a data center, or computer room, which is generally locked and access is controlled through keys and/or passwords. The second and third characteristics are the people who normally have access to the computer room: the support personnel and technical developers. A large computer system has support personnel, or operators, who are responsible for the daily running of the computer and associated equipment. Operators mount tapes, change toner cartridges in printers, perform equipment maintenance functions, and troubleshoot problems that occur. They are concerned mostly with the hardware and its operation, but do get to know something of the software. Technical developers, called "systems programmers," are the people who work with the support software—the operating systems, database management systems, and communications systems. Systems programmers ensure that all software in the installation works with the hardware and interfaces properly with other software systems. Mainframe systems are, of course, the largest. These are machines that can run systems that handle billions (even trillions) of pieces of information. They have the fastest speeds and the most storage, so are naturally used by large companies. This classification means the job requestor wants someone used to working with large systems and vast amounts of data.

Midsize, or midrange systems, consists of two types of computers; the midsize computers (which could really be called small mainframes) and the RISC machines, or workstations. A midsize computer is an intermediate-size computer that can perform the same kinds of applications as a mainframe, but lacks the speed and storage capacity. One typical function is to serve as the main computer in a medium-size business, and, as such, they are similar to mainframes. They can handle a hundred or more terminals and can have dozens of data storage devices. A second function is to act as the server system in a client/server environment. A client/server environment is one in which one computer acts as the server and provides data distribution and security functions to other computers that are independently running various applications. Although a RISC (Reduced Instruction Set Computer) is really a large desktop computer, its speed and storage capacity equal that of midsize computers, so RISC machines can be categorized as midrange systems. These machines are fast, have high-resolution graphics capabilities, and usually use Unix as the standard operating system. Midsize systems have applications and technical developers, and support personnel are called operators or administrators. The computers are housed in computer rooms, but these rooms are rarely locked, and all IT personnel have access.

A desktop computer requires no special environmental controls, nor does it always require support personnel. Desktop systems vary from a completely contained, single-user microcomputer sitting on someone's desk, to a network of computers linked together sharing printers and data files, to a sophisticated workstation, usually a RISC machine, that is housed in a computer room and supported by a staff of administrators and programmers. Unlike the large systems the computer room is rarely locked. Support personnel are usually called "administrator" instead of "operator" because they not only run the hardware but also provide some software support in terms of running backups for data collections, and maintaining passwords for logons. Desktop environments rarely have technical developers. The applications programmers and support personnel do what technical work is necessary and these applications programmers tend to know more about hardware than do applications people in other environments, and the support people know more about software than other administrators or operators.

Technical Skill Set

There is a skill set associated with each job. There are literally tens of thousands of products used by IT professionals. In addition, there are sets of rules, methodologies, and knowledge sets that appear in job descriptions. The skills can be categorized in four areas: platforms, development, data management, and communications. Some jobs require knowledge of skills in all four areas, while others will ask for a single skill.

Skills that are part of the platform reflect the computer systems and the operating systems. Both can be explicitly stated, as in Sun SPARC/ Solaris, but they need not be. Often the platform will be referred to simply as Unix. This kind of platform reference means any computer

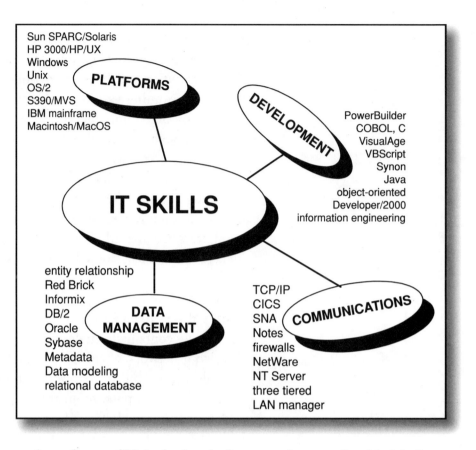

and any flavor of Unix fit the platform requirement for this job. In another situation, both machine and operating system might be required.

Development skills include programming languages (such as COBOL, C and Java), development tools, and techniques. Techniques are the rules and standards defined by developmental methodologies or architectures. Included with techniques are object-oriented and component-based development. Protocols and specifications also fit this category. Development tools are programs that automate some function of the development cycle and include CASE, RAD and ADE tools. Development skills are not required of support personnel.

The data management category includes data files, databases, and data warehousing. Data files are usually handled by the operating system, so are considered part of the platform but there are exceptions like IBM's VSAM. Databases should really be referred to as DBMSs and DB/2 and Oracle are examples. Data warehousing is a new use of data and uses DBMS skills and complex query skills. In addition to the product skills, data management requires design skills such as data modeling and designing metadata.

Technical Job Descriptions

The knowledge and skills necessary to develop online applications fall into the communications category. Skills include OLTP monitors such as CICS, LANs, NOS (Network Operating Systems), and communications protocols. In addition, client/server, component-based architecture, the Internet, and data warehousing all require communications knowledge and skills. This is the most technical area in Information Technology.

All technical recruiters must learn enough about computer technology in order to communicate with both the job requestors and the applicants. Much learning is done on-the-job, but there is some training available.

See: *Training for Technical Recruiters* on page 197.

4. Sourcing

Internet
Colleges
Cold Calls
Career Fairs
Open Houses
Internal Sources
Advertising
Networking

Sourcing

Sourcing is finding possible candidates. That's a simple statement, but the activities involved in this phase can be very complex. Recruiters find people who are actively job hunting (active candidates) but also source for passive candidates—people who aren't looking for a new job, but can be enticed with the right offer. Sourcing can follow the receipt of a requisition, or it can be the start of the recruiting process. Most of the time recruiters look for applicants for a specific job, but sometimes recruiters collect résumés first and then try to find the jobs. This is rare in a corporate setting, happens sometimes in a consulting firm, but might be the norm in an employment agency. Because both consulting firms and employment agencies work with job openings from many companies, they can call clients to see if there is an opening for a good applicant. Even without openings, some recruiters regularly source and screen qualified applicants to build a database of good candidates for future openings.

There are many different ways to find candidates, and recruiters must not limit themselves to a single source. Each has its pros and cons, and a combination of sources does best. Sources to be considered are:

The Internet	Open Houses
Internal sources	College Recruiting
Advertising	Cold Calling
Career Fairs	Networking

The Internet

The Internet is quickly becoming the major source recruiters use to find applicants for technical jobs. It's natural for people working in the computer field to use the Internet to search for jobs, so recruiters have access to tens of thousands of potential candidates, if they know how to find them. There are tools and techniques for recruiters to find both active and passive candidates. Internet sourcing is covered separately in Section 5.

Internal Sources

Corporate recruiters have many internal sources to use when searching for candidates, and job posting can often find good candidates from existing employees. Companies often approve internal transfers when a job opens, and many times existing employees are the first candidates for promotions, but these situations usually occur on a departmental basis. People within the department know of the opening and ask about it, or a manager knows someone they think would do a good job. This, however, ignores the entire rest of the company. Job posting makes information about current openings available to the entire company. This information can be posted on online networks, available from HR,

INTERNAL SOURCES

Current Employees

Transfers and promotions within the same department fill many jobs, and company-wide job postings attract even more people. PRO: dealing with known quantities. CON: small candidate pool.

Employee Referrals

Current employees are rewarded when friends they recommend are hired. PRO: cost effective, morale booster. CON: could cause problems with current employees, if referral is not hired, or worse, is hired and fired.

Former Staff

If someone left on good terms, rehiring can be a good move. PRO: known quantity. CON: potential conflicts with existing staff, especially if the person is rehired in a senior position.

Internal Databases

Internal databases that are kept of prior applicants. Many good applicants might fit a present opening. PRO: already have the résumé on file. CON: the best have probably accepted other jobs.

or even put on bulletin boards throughout the company. The important thing is that all employees have access to the information. Every company has employees that are under-employed and could, with training, move into a more challenging and interesting job. Information Technology has a persistent shortage of skilled workers, and it can be very cost-effective to train current staff for positions as programmers and/or support jobs. The best thing about filling a job with an existing employee is that a known quantity is hired—a good worker who knows the company. The major weakness of this source is that it accesses a very small pool of potential candidates and creates another opening.

Another internal source is employee referrals. This form of recruitment is cost-effective and has a positive impact on employee morale. With this method employees are advised every time there is a job opening and are given the job description with all its responsibilities. If someone an employee refers is hired, the current employee is given a bonus. Typically the bonuses are less than agency fees or advertising, but are significant—even several thousand dollars for high-paying technical jobs. One problem with this technique is that it, too, accesses a small pool of candidates. Problems can also occur if the referral is not hired or worse, fired shortly after hiring. Employee referrals are used most often by corporate recruiters, but are also used by recruiters in consulting firms. Consulting firms and employment agencies also use a simple referral plan where anyone from any company who refers a successful candidate gets a bonus. These bonuses are typically smaller than employee referral bonuses, but because they're open to anyone, they reach a broader pool of candidates.

Other internal sources are former staff (if they left favorably) and internal applicant databases. In a corporate environment, former staff means people who left the company to take another position. For consulting firms, former staff could mean the same as many consulting firms do have permanent employees, but it also could mean someone who was previously hired on a contract basis. When former staff is hired, both the company and the new hire have realistic expectations of each other. Very often a former employee has learned new skills since leaving and now has even more to offer. A main drawback is potential problems with former colleagues, especially if the person is re-hired into a higher-level or higher-paying position than employees who were peers when the person left. This is not too big a problem in consulting firms, because the consultants work for many different companies, but can be a significant problem with an internal hire who returns to the same department to work with many of the same people he or she worked with before. In addition to using former staff as a source, companies build internal databases of applicants, especially those who have actually been interviewed. Even though a prior interaction might not have resulted in a hire, conditions change and the job opening you have now might be more attractive to the candidate, or the skills the candidate has might fit an opening that didn't exist when the candidate applied before. This is a critical sourcing technique for consulting firms and employment agencies because of the diversity of the job requirements.

Advertising

One of the most common recruiting sources for all recruiters is advertising, and recruiters can advertise in many media including print, radio, television, billboards, banners, and even movie ads. Some things are important in all advertising:

1. All ads must clearly state how an applicant can respond. A recruiter's name, phone number, fax number, e-mail address, regular address, (or any combination) can be included. The "recruiter's name" doesn't have to be real; many companies use dummy names so they can see what ads get a good response.
2. If the ad is running in a national magazine or newspaper, or ads for a job that is not local, state the job location. Often companies have several locations, or will advertise eg. in the Boston area for jobs in the Sunbelt.
3. All ads should have a focus. Advertising is used to sell things. Decide what's being sold—is it the job, the company, or the opportunity? Concentrate on one of the three.
4. Identify the potential respondent. Make sure the ad clearly identifies the person who could fill the job, or jobs, currently open. Most ads use a job "title" that really isn't a title at all, but is rather a short description of the job.
5. Indicate the type of job, whether it's permanent, contract, part-time, intern, etc.

Print advertising is the most common and usually means newspaper advertising in the classified section of Sunday's local newspaper, but also refers to magazines and trade papers. This can be especially effective when the paper runs a special technical section, which most metropolitan papers do regularly. Advertising works if the ads are well designed,

ADVERTISING
Internet postings
Print—Newspapers,
Magazines
Radio & Television
Billboards
Banners
Movie Ads

and it simply wastes money if they aren't. Good ads have a distinctive logo or corporate name that appears in the same place in every ad. In fact, one of the benefits of advertising is name recognition. People like working for familiar companies and are likely to respond to an ad if they've heard of the company. Make sure the ad has enough white space to let the logo, and the most important selling points about the job stand out. Ads should either emphasize a single job and headline the job description and required skills, or should emphasize opportunities and highlight corporate benefits—including, of course, technical areas of opportunities. Decide how many résumés are desired—broad "great opportunity" ads usually draw many résumés, while a very specific ad might not get a single response. Blind ads that don't identify the company can be run, but should be job specific. When blind ads are run, the company should decide ahead of time what should be done when current employees respond! Ads are not effective if they generate either too few or too many responses, and good ads are hard to develop. There are advertising agencies that specialize in technical advertising, and some companies have had success with them.

While print advertising requires the applicant actively look for the ad, radio and television advertising can also be effective and have the extra benefit of reaching passive applicants. Radio advertising during commuting hours can generate a lot of interest and is usually not too expensive. Network television can be expensive, but cable channels are usually much cheaper and can reach a specific audience. Television has the extra benefit of showing potential applicants the actual job environment. No matter the length of the radio or TV spot, make sure the ad repeats the contact information at least twice.

Billboards can be effective locally. Banners attractively displayed on the company's building can describe job openings, and movie ads are a possibility. All of these sources require ads that quickly grab the viewer's attention and entice a response. All these sources reach passive applicants, and all are fairly inexpensive, but none generate many responses.

Career Fairs

Career, or job, fairs are organized by a host who then runs the fair and are attended by corporations and consulting firms. Employment agencies rarely attend job fairs. Most fair participants are looking for any technical professional, but some fairs are held for specialties such as networking professionals. At minimum the host determines the date and the location, and advertises the fair so potential job seekers will come. Sometimes a company will host a job fair and invite other local companies to participate, but more often the host is a company who specializes in conducting job fairs. These companies usually provide other services such as providing refreshments, printing a program for attendees that includes information about the participating companies, and collecting résumés from attendees to distribute to the participating companies. The résumé distribution can be invaluable because at well-attended fairs it's impossible to speak with all the candidates, and at least companies will get résumés of the attendees they didn't have a chance to meet. Some fairs also include social functions in the evening, and some even provide speakers before or after the applicants arrive. This gives recruiters a chance to network with their peers.

When participating in a job fair, be prepared. Have plenty of information about your company available and consider creating information specifically for fairs. Many companies make videos that play continually, giving a picture of the work atmosphere and opportunities. An information flier, clearly stating how to contact the company and briefly describing opportunities, should be available to hand to applicants. It's also important to have enough people working at the fair to talk with all interested applicants. Most of the people working at the fair are recruiters, but, if possible, make sure there's at least one technical person available to answer questions from technical applicants. It's tempting to send new recruiters to work at fairs, but the expertise of experienced recruiters is needed as recruiters have a very short time to catch an applicant's interest. Recruiters should develop a rough rating system, so they can record immediate impressions of candidates to help in follow-up. It's important to reach interesting candidates as soon as possible after the fair, as good candidates have spoken with representatives from a lot of companies, and the company who contacts them first will have an edge.

Even if no one is hired because of the fair, recruiters can benefit from networking with recruiters from other local companies. Job fairs are not as popular as they used to be as recruiters have found other sourcing methods to be more effective. Factors to consider when deciding to participate in a job fair are:

> cost (fairs can be quite expensive)
> services provided by the host
> history of effectiveness of other fairs conducted by the host
> number of present job openings the company needs to fill
> the identity of the other companies who will be participating.

See: *Career Fairs* on page 181.

Open Houses

An open house could be described as a job fair with only one company participating. This would be a minimal description, as companies usually go all out for open houses. Some set up elaborate displays in a cafeteria; some arrange for continual tours of the facilities; some provide complete buffet meals. Many more people are involved in open houses as the open house presents not only technical jobs, but all openings throughout the company. The main problem with open houses is getting potential candidates to come. A job seeker might be willing to spend time at a job fair because many companies are represented, but must be interested in the specific company to attend an open house. Therefore, good advertising for the open house is critical. Usually only large consulting firms would hold an open house, and this is not a technique that employment agencies use.

College Recruiting

Information Technology is a field that needs entry-level talent. The technology is such that education or training can only do so much, actual expertise must be learned on-the-job. There are some tasks that require little knowledge beyond what is learned in school, so the ideal staffing is to have entry-level people to handle the basic tasks, and grow to more complex assignments through work experience. New entry-level people are hired on a regular basis to take over the basic tasks as existing employees move on to more senior positions. A college degree is a common requirement for both applications and technical developers, so college recruiting is used in these areas. It is not used to fill entry-level support jobs, because these jobs don't require a degree and usually don't pay enough to entice college graduates. Because the recruiting process is somewhat different for college recruiting, companies usually have special college recruiters. College recruiting is discussed separately in Section 10.

Cold Calling

A cold call is a call to a potential candidate who has no idea that a recruiter even has his or her name. Usually this potential candidate is passive, meaning the person is not actively job hunting. Recruiters get names from many sources, including mailing lists, technical organization membership lists, and simply phoning companies that are using targeted technologies and asking for "your DBA." Currently the Internet is being used to find passive candidates. Recruiters use techniques such as monitoring technical discussion groups and getting e-mail addresses of people who answer technical questions. "Calls" can be made by phone, but candidates found on the Internet are usually contacted by e-mail as the e-mail address is the available contact information. Internet "cold calling" is discussed in Section 5.

Cold calling is a controversial recruiting technique and one that takes a lot of time for limited results. It can be effective if the recruiter plans it well. The purpose of the call is to quickly determine if the prospect can become a valid candidate and, if so, obtain a résumé. The most critical part of the cold call is the planning. A script should be written for these calls, and the recruiter should practice until he or she is comfortable with the script. Write a script based on the following points:

- A cold call is not a single call. Several calls are usually made so it's important to build a relationship from the very first call.
- Be honest and specific throughout the conversation. Don't make grand but vague claims eg., "the best opportunity in your career."
- Let the potential candidate do most of the talking. The purpose of the call is to determine base qualifications, so let them talk.
- Ask if this is a good time to talk and, if not, try to set a phone appointment.
- Don't expect potential candidates to return calls (and don't bother leaving messages on voice mail).
- Get to the point quickly by appealing to the candidate's interest.
- Technical people most often change jobs for technical opportunities and technical growth.
- Ask about sending a job description. If permission is granted, follow up within in few days.
- Even if no job description was sent, follow-up. Be sure to mention something personal about the candidate that was determined from the first phone call.
- Call before and after hours—before nine and after five.
- Cold calls should be short—no more than five minutes.
- If the candidate does not have basic qualifications, end the call quickly.

Cold calling is not an easy technique and takes practice. The most common reaction to a cold call is irritation, but this doesn't have to be true. People shouldn't be irritated when someone shows an interest in them and is impressed by their qualifications. A well-prepared call from an honest, respectful, and friendly recruiter can be the start of a relationship that can definitely lead to a job change—if not right now, sometime in the future.

Networking

Although listed last, networking is the most important sourcing technique for all recruiters. Recruiters can take advantage of every interpersonal interaction to add to their personal network of contacts. During every interview, they ask if the applicant knows anyone he or she could refer as a potential employee. They send thank you letters to anyone who does refer an applicant, and keep in touch with good applicants who were not hired. Recruiters also keep in touch with employees who leave the company. These are excellent people to ask for referrals, because they know the company. Recruiters network on college campuses, with alumni associations, and at job fairs.

If a recruiter interviews a good candidate that just doesn't fit the job, he or she doesn't want to lose touch with this person. Recruiters build a personal "keep in touch" file and use it to send birthday cards, or notes "I saw an article about {hobby…}." This shows candidates that they made a positive impression and builds a relationship that might result in a later hire, but at the least will probably result in references for other jobs. Once the relationship is built recruiters can call and ask if they know anyone for other openings. Names are often provided because the person is talking to a friend, not a headhunter. IT people within a local area know each other and are happy to help each other find good jobs.

> **See: *Networking Information* on page 137.**

A major opportunity to network with other recruiters is provided by associations. There are general HR associations, recruiter groups, and even specific associations for technical recruiters, and the major reason to join one of these groups is the opportunity to network. Regular meetings allow recruiters to hear about new ideas and recruiting tools and to build relationships with fellow recruiters. Through networking, recruiters actually swap candidates. If a recruiter gets a résumé that looks good but doesn't fit any of his or her present needs, that résumé can be shared (with the applicant's permission) with a recruiter in another organization who might need that particular skill set. Perhaps a recruiter has two good candidates for a job and only one can be hired. The recruiter can build a positive relationship with the rejected candidate by using a network to let them know about other jobs. The favor will be returned later on, perhaps doubly so, as the candidate is likely to contact the original recruiter when again job hunting, and the second recruiter will call with a good, but unusable, candidate at some later date. Recruiters not only build networks at regular meetings, but also attend conferences and conventions where they exchange ideas and information.

> **See: *Associations* on page 180.**

5. Recruiting on the Internet

▰▰▰▰▰ Recruiting on the Internet ▱▱▱▱

The Internet is a valuable resource for many jobs, including technical recruiting, and is used in many ways. For example, Web-hosted recruiting systems are now available on a subscription or license arrangement, so many recruiters now use the Internet for complete applicant tracking. The Internet contains regional and metropolitan information, so a recruiter can find out about hotels and available transportation for an out-of-area interview, and then access information about schools and housing to help the candidate decide whether to accept an offer. Recruiters visit Web sites of similar companies to be prepared to answer competitive offers, and they read online salary surveys to know what their industry and region is currently paying technical people. The Internet is mostly used, however, during sourcing (finding possible candidates).

The Internet has become one of the most important sources for recruiters and should always be used in technical recruiting. Sourcing should never be limited to one technique, but because technical recruiters are looking for people with computer-related skills, and these people naturally use the Internet for many things (including job hunting), it definitely should be one of the options. Richard Nelson Bolles (author of *What Color is Your Parachute*) estimates that only 2% of people looking for non-computer related jobs will find them on the Internet—but that's how 45% of technical applicants find jobs.

The pros and cons of Internet recruiting are highly related. Pro: the Internet reaches a vast number of people, many more than any other source, or even combination of sources. This makes it easier to find applicants for new, unique, or even legacy skills that make jobs hard to fill. Con: the Internet reaches a vast number of people, which means there can be many many unqualified résumés to read through. Pro: the Internet runs 24 hours a day and is quick, as soon as job ads are posted applicants can electronically respond, even in the middle of the night. Con: the Internet is quick, recruiters have very little time to move through the recruiting process. Sometimes hiring decisions must be made too quickly because of the intense competition for good candidates. Pro: recruiters don't have to wait for résumés to be sent, they can go to résumé banks or even basic searches to find applicants with important qualifications. Con: there are so many résumés available on the Internet that recruiters spend way too much time on this single source. Pro: the Internet is constantly changing, which means there are constantly new and better Internet tools for recruiters. Con: the Internet is changing daily, which means recruiters constantly have to learn new techniques and tools.

There is one Pro that stands on its own, and that's cost. Internet sourcing is very cost-effective. A job posting can run for a month on a major job bank for one to two hundred dollars—a similar ad in one Sunday's classified section could cost ten times as much. There's one con that stands alone too, and that's how much time is wasted using the Internet. It's important that companies build an Internet strategy that defines how they use this resource. Recruiters could spend 100% of their time on the Internet, and they could spend the entire recruitment budget posting ads. Developing an Internet strategy is discussed later in this section.

Posting Jobs on the Internet

Posting a job on the Internet is advertising, and the recruiter has to do two things—design the ad and decide where to advertise. While designing a job ad for the Internet is similar to designing a print ad, there are differences that should be clearly understood. Internet postings have two parts: a one or two line banner that leads potential candidates to click to the second part—the full ad. Job ads can be posted to different sites, and most do run in several places.

Designing an Internet Job Ad

All Internet ads, or postings, should be as carefully designed as print ads. In fact, a good place to start is with print ad standards:

1. All ads must still clearly state how an applicant can respond. A recruiter's name, fax number, e-mail address, or regular address, (or any combination) can be included. The "recruiter's name" can still be a dummy name, and unique e-mail addresses are often set up for each ad. One difference from print ads is that phone numbers are not included as a contact option. Because the response to an Internet job posting can be overwhelming, companies don't take a chance on having a phone line—and the person on the receiving end—continually busy.
2. All ads should have a focus. Advertising is used to sell things. Decide what's being sold—is it the job, the company, or the opportunity? Concentrate on one of the three.
3. Identify the potential respondent. Make sure the ad clearly identifies the person who could fill the job, or jobs, currently open. Most ads use a job "title" that really isn't a title at all, but is rather a short description of the job. This is usually included in both the banner and the full ad.
4. Indicate the employment status of job, whether it's permanent, contract, part-time, intern, etc.
5. Always state the location of the job. Internet ads are global, so it's important for applicants to know exactly where the job is.

ONLINE JOB AD

TITLE
Short description of job

LOGISTICS
Location
Start date
Ad identifier

HOW TO RESPOND
Recruiter's name
E-mail address
Fax number
Street address

CORE JOB DESCRIPTION
Background
Experience level
Environment

TECHNICAL SKILLS
Key skills
Technical "plusses"

ADDITIONAL SELLING POINTS
Corporate benefits
Training Options

The banner part of an Internet ad is usually limited to 65 to 150 characters. It's difficult to write a good banner, as it should be as specific as possible within the allowed characters, yet include information that will entice an applicant to read the full ad. Many banners simply state "C/C++ Programmer." A banner that went a little further and said "C/C++ Programmer. Stock options" would get more response. A banner ad that said "C/C++ Programmer. Minimum 3+ years experience" would cut down on responses from college seniors and junior programmers. Most job sites have a standard format for these banners, and the recruiter fills out a form when he or she posts the job. The banner is set up with a link to the full ad, which contains the detailed information.

Print ads are limited in size and larger ads cost more. Ads, or job postings, in the electronic world are much longer because size doesn't matter and lengthy ads cost no more to run than short ones. This means electronic ads can contain more details. These details accomplish two things. They limit the number of unqualified responses by being very specific about the job requirements, and they help entice applicants to respond by including positive points about the job and the company. The full posting includes many things including how to respond, logistical information, the core job description, technical skill requirements, and additional selling points.

Logistical information includes the title of the job, location, start date, salary information, and an ad identifier. Whenever possible the ad should link to the corporate Web site. The title is usually taken from the banner and is a short description of the job. Location should be as specific as possible, eg. stating "downtown Chicago" rather than "Chicago." The start date does not have to be specific, but should indicate how quickly the company wants to fill the job. Salary, usually expressed as a range, does not have to be included but often is. With technical jobs, salary is often an important part of the job description, as salary identifies the status of the job. The ad identifier is used to track responses to evaluate the effectiveness of the ad and many ads contain a response code for easy tracking. Others simply use the recruiter's name or e-mail address from the "how to respond" information.

The core job description contains information on the background required, the technical environment, and the experience level. The background describes the job (and thus the candidate) as an applications developer, a technical developer, or a support position. The technical environment is either large computers, midsize or desktop systems, and the experience level is either junior, mid, or senior. This information is covered in Section 3, Technical Job Descriptions.

Technical skill requirements should state both what is required and what "would be a plus." Technical jobs really have only one to four key skills, even though it often seems there are many more. Specifically state what the required skills are, and then list other skills as additional plusses. An online ad can list experience requirements on specific skills in addition to stating an overall experience level such as junior, mid, or senior. For example, a job for a senior developer could require strong expertise and over five-years experience in Oracle, but realistically ask for only six months experience in Java.

The online ad can include other selling points that would make a print ad much too long. Internet ads can contain information about the company including advertising popular benefits such as subsidized, or even free, day-care, an on-site gym, laundry, and barber/beauty shop facilities and extra vacation or comp days. Companies could also include a corporate description including information about their status in the industry, advancement policies, location of branches and transfer possibilities. Information about the community can attract some candidates. This includes information about schools, recreation options, and cultural and sport's events and organizations. One of the most important benefits to technical people is training, and it's always a positive to mention training options.

Job-Posting Sites

Jobs can be posted to many different sites, starting with the Corporate Web site. Other sites to be considered include job banks, specialty sites and publications, and newsgroups (message boards).

JOB-POSTING SITES

Corporate Site   Posting jobs on the corporate site can attract passive candidates. Every visitor is someone who is interested in the company.

Job Banks   Some are free, some charge monthly fees, some charge by the number of postings.

Portal Sites/Search Engines   Most portal sites allows job postings or have partnerships with a major job bank.

Specialty Sites   Many technical specialty sites, such as sites for Oracle developers, accept job postings. So do most alumni groups and special interest groups.

Newsgroups   There are many newsgroup job-posting sites. Be sure to post on a site that allows postings.

The Corporate Web Site   Every corporate Web site should have a section for job postings, and this section should be highly visible and easily accessible from the home page. There should, in fact, be links to the job postings from every page in the site. Candidates who have reached a Web site because they are interested in the company or the company's products are already showing an interest. The overall job section should be attractive and contain positive information about the company that would apply to all jobs. Include pictures—people like to know where they would be working! Individual job postings should contain reference to all selling points about the specific job and can be a copy of what's posted in job banks. Make sure that job ads posted in job banks link back to the corporate information (candidates have already read about the specific job).

Include an online application that can be e-mailed when filled out. Keep the application simple and make it as easy as possible to fill out by already including the job information and using selection lists as much as possible (address information, years of experience, etc.) Ask for a résumé, but make sure candidates can e-mail résumés. If possible let them attach the résumé to the application. Because a corporate Web site can attract passive candidates who usually don't have current résumés, make sure they can respond without a résumé. Suggestions have been made that as more and more job placement is done over the Internet, a complete résumé will become rare, and instead online applications that allow interested parties to fill in experience and skill information next to each job requirement will be used.

Job Banks   Job banks are sites that contain databases of job postings, and there are thousands of them. Some job banks are free, but most charge companies for posting. General job banks accept job postings for any kind of job, while others specialize in a job category such as technical jobs. Some are regional and some are global. Most also post résumés, but some only post jobs. There are, of course, separate résumé banks. Most provide some assistance beyond just accepting postings. Two things to consider when choosing a job bank are the traffic to the bank, and the extras provided.

See: *General Job Banks* on page 162.
Technical Job Banks on page 163.
Technical Specialty Banks on page 164.

Traffic is the most important measure of effectiveness as job hunters must visit the site to find the job postings. There are several measures of traffic. One is the number of hits or visitors. A hit does not equate to a person visiting the job bank as a hit includes every access to the site. There could be two or three hits from one person looking at one job posting if the system had to access the site multiple times to retrieve graphics and text. Visitors is a more meaningful number as hits that occur very quickly together are assumed to be one person moving through the site and are counted as "visitors." It still is not exact, as a user who, eg., stops to answer a question and then returns to the site will be counted as two visitors because of the elapsed time during the interruption. Most sites will provide information on the number of hits or visitors. Another measure of traffic is the number of links to the job site. A link is established when a different site includes the job bank's URL as a link (meaning a click will take the user to the job bank). Job banks actually establish thousands of links to their sites, so it is easy for job hunters to access them. Yet another measure of potential traffic is advertising. Job banks will advertise with a link on many sites, such as search engine sites and university and college sites.

The extra services often provide much of the value that comes from using a job bank. Some job banks provide assistance in developing ads and often have software that builds the posting with a "fill in the blanks" interface. The fill-in forms are easy to work with and provide a standard look, but a free-form job ad will usually display at least a logo and often additional graphics to make the ad more attractive. Some will link a job posting to the corporate Web site which allows each company to use its own site to reinforce selling points and perhaps collect information from interested candidates. Getting information about job openings to potential applicants quickly is important, and some job banks will automatically send information on a job opening to applicants who are looking for that opportunity (push technology) as soon as the job is posted. Others will "push" information about appropriate candidates to the company as soon as a résumé is posted. Another extra provided by some job sites is faxing or mailing a printed résumé in addition to the electronic one. Electronic résumés are difficult to read, and having a more attractive résumé to take to job requestors can be a big plus. Any of these extras can enhance the value of a job bank.

Other things to consider:
• How many jobs are posted, and does this job bank specialize? There are many sites for technical jobs only. If it is a general site, how many of the job postings are for technical jobs?

- Find out how matches are made with the job postings and applicants. Do job seekers contact the company directly, or does the notification come from the job bank? If the databank includes résumés, how many résumés are posted? Do companies have free access to the résumé database or are they just notified of matches?
- Check the logistics of using the databank. How are job postings entered? How long does it take to post ads in the job bank? How are they updated and deleted?

Finally, calculate the cost. Some job banks allow free job postings, but most charge a fee. The fee can be annual or monthly (usually monthly) and most have different rates based on the number of jobs posted at any one time. When determining the actual cost, be sure to estimate how much time a recruiter would spend working with this databank each month and add salary costs for that time.

Specialty Sites and Publications   Job banks are not the only sites that post jobs. Specialty sites can be very valuable, especially in niche situations. Technical specialty sites have been established to provide a forum for special interest groups, and there are many for IT specialties. Many of these sites post jobs and/or résumés. Alumni sites can be very valuable as many accept job postings (in fact, so do some university sites). Specialty sites include online industry or trade journals, and also include regional and professional sites. Sites for women, ethnic groups, and even special interests can attract people who want to work for a company that shows concern in a particular area. Many specialty sites actually are publications—magazines and newspapers that have an online version on the Web. *ComputerWorld* and *Java World* are technical publications and *The Black Colle:gian Online* and *Women in Technology* are examples of special interest publications. Most accept job postings.

See: *Technical Special-Interest Sites* on page 166.

Newsgroups (or Message Boards)   A newsgroup is a collection of computers and networks that share news articles and is located on Usenet. These newsgroups are organized topically and are often called "the world's largest bulletin board!" Newsgroups exist for anything from hobbies to issues of public debate to business topics and one of the busiest is misc.jobs. To access this newsgroup, type news:misc.jobs as the URL. This accesses a long list of job-related topics. Use the newsgroups set up for job postings, not the informational newsgroups.

Newsgroups are free and can be valuable as several services retrieve job postings from them and place them in other sites.

Job-Posting Software

There are several different types of job-posting software and services available. With most of them, the recruiter enters a job once and that posting is automatically submitted to multiple sites. Most post to multiple free sites, but some also post to the major fee-based job banks. Posting fees, if any, are passed on to the company. Some of this software will also post to the corporate Web site. In fact, some of this software actually helps create the job posting part of a corporate Web site. If a company does post jobs on several sites, using these products can save a lot of time.

See: *Job-Posting Services* on page 172.

Searching for Candidates

The Internet has even more places to look for résumés that it has places to post jobs! Recruiters could actually spend all day on the Internet working with résumés.

Responses to Job Postings

Candidates searching the Internet for new jobs answer job ads and/or post résumés, although not everyone who posts a résumé is an active job candidate. People do post résumés just to see what's out there, or to get offers to use in negotiating with their present employer, but most of the time the presence of a résumé identifies an active candidate.

The first source of candidates is the matches to job postings supplied by job banks. This is an excellent source of good candidates, because these people are considering a job change and have at least some of the necessary job qualifications. Job postings also bring résumés of candidates who saw the ad and are interested in the opening. These candidates are definitely looking for a new job, are interested in this specific job, and also have basic qualifications. Proactive recruiters, however, do not work only with the responses to job postings. They also conduct an online résumé search.

Résumé Searches

Technical applicants don't necessarily search job banks. Many of them simply post their résumé on the Internet and wait until companies respond. If a candidate has good qualifications, this technique works well with minimum effort from the candidate. This means the recruiter has to do the work to find the good candidate.

There are hundreds of thousands of résumés available on the Internet, and finding good résumés without spending too much time is the challenge. Recruiters can find résumés in all the same places used to post job ads, and then some. First of all, there are résumé databanks that aren't associated with job banks. Some résumé databanks allow free postings and others charge a fee. Many people feel that the quality of résumés in the free databanks is not as good as the quality in the ones that charge. Too many people post a résumé just to see what's out there, and people who pay to post résumés are usually serious job hunters.

Recruiters first search résumé banks and portal sites which either contain résumé postings or link to a major job/résumé bank. Job seekers also post résumés in alumni group's sites, special interest sites for ethnic groups, women's groups, and college placement sites. Newsgroups contain résumés and many individuals post a résumé on their own site. The major ISPs (Internet Service Providers such as AOL) host individual Web pages so this is easy to do.

RÉSUMÉ SEARCHES

Alumni Groups   Most allow alumni to post résumés and these sites can be a good source of experienced candidates looking to progress in their careers.

Ethnic Groups   A job could require fluency in Spanish, for example, so ethnic sites are a resource for candidates with this type of skill.

Job/Résumé Banks   Most job banks include résumés, and often companies have free access to the résumés, if they post jobs. Companies also can pay to search other banks they don't use for job posting.

Newsgroups   There are many newsgroup résumé sites.

Portal Sites   Most portal sites allow candidates to post résumés. Some have partnerships with a major job/résumé bank.

Résumé Banks   These banks post résumés only. They are valuable because many candidates simply post a résumé and wait for responses (including those with valuable skill sets).

Technical Interest Sites   Sites for specific technologies such as ERP technicians often post jobs as one of the services supplied to members.

The Web   IT people often keep an updated résumé on their own Web sites (many IT people have their own sites).

Virtual Communities   These are general sites that millions of people belong to and create their own home pages. Many people store résumés and/or job information on these home pages.

Women's Groups   These sites are valuable if women's issues, talents, or interests would be an asset.

Résumés are found on the Internet by providing keywords to a search engine. The job and résumé banks have their own search tools, and recruiters are prompted on how to specify keywords. To search for individually posted résumés, the search engines (or portal sites) are usually used, but other tools are available including meta-search engines and spiders (also called robots and bots).

Search Tools

Search Engines/Portal Sites   A search engine is a program that builds an indexed database of Internet Web pages, and later returns a list of Web sites from this database that match a search's keywords. These databases can be huge. Altavista's database has over 150 million pages. Search engines don't really search the Web; they search this index database (also called a directory). The directory can be generated by hand or by spiders, or bots. A spider is a search-engine program which surfs the web and builds index entries according to predefined algorithms. Because each search engine builds its indexes differently, using different search engines for the same keyword search will get different results. There will, of course, be some overlap, but listings of results from different search engines will generally return around 60% identical sites and 40% unique sites.

Search engines work with a list of keywords which can be single words or phrases. The keywords are connected with Boolean logic which has rules such as "both must appear" "either can appear," and "the word or phrase must not appear." Each engine has its own methods of expression—some require the use of "AND", others require "+". Remembering the notation can be confusing when using different engines, which is often done to get broader results.

A portal is a Web site that offers a broad array of resources and services starting with a search engine. The portal then adds such functions as e-mail, forums, and online shopping malls. While the first Web portals were ISPs such as AOL, now most of the traditional search engines have been transformed into Web portals to attract and keep a larger audience. A portal is built to simplify an Internet search by building a hierarchy of links to point the user through ever-narrowing categories of information. The major portals link to sports, shopping, life styles, etc. All the portals contain a link to "jobs" or "careers," and recruiters find résumés here. If the portal doesn't post résumés itself, it links to one of the major job/résumé banks. These original information portals work with general information categories, and their success has led to the development of specific portals, such as business portals, government service portals and, recently, recruiting portals.

See: *Search Engines* on page 171.

Metasearch Engines   Metasearch engines take the provided keywords and submit the search to multiple search engines. The response varies. Most integrate search results and merge duplicate findings from different search engines into one entry. Most rank the results according to various criteria; some allow selection of search engines to be searched; and some eliminate dead links. All of them work with the major search engines, some also search Newsgroups and e-mail lists. The meta-search engine must have permission to use the search engines' databases, and none, in fact, search NorthernLight or FastSearch. Time is a problem, so meta-search engines are given a limited time on each database, and this limits the thoroughness of the search.

Some search engines limit the number of sites they will return on a single search, and meta-search engines definitely do in order to return results quickly. In fact, meta-search engines usually look at only 10% of the entries in each database. Also, because the various search engines have different notation requirements, complex searches are often misinterpreted, or even ignored. A meta-search engine will not return as many finds as any single search engine, and recruiters must balance retrieving the top ten matches in many search engines against retrieving the top 100 matches from a single source.

See: *Metasearch Engines* on page 168.

Spiders, Robots, Bots   Another category of search tools are programs called spiders, robots, or simply bots. A spider is a program that prowls the Internet, attempting to locate new, publicly accessible resources such as WWW documents and files available in public archives based on keyword criteria or a starting URL. Spiders go to one site and then follow all the links in that site. Each link takes them to new pages with new links. Spiders then store the information they find in a database or catalog, which Internet users can search by using an Internet-accessible search engine. Spiders are used in search engines to build the appropriate databases, and there are several spider programs available that search for résumés.

See: *Résumé Spiders* on page 170.

Building a Keyword List

The Internet is searched for information by keywords, and whether the recruiter is searching résumé banks or the Web in general for individual résumés, the keywords are critical. Recruiters should build a keyword list for each job, or job type, they are currently trying to fill. After this is done, a keyword list should be built for each job or job type the recruiter can realistically expect to fill in the future. Obviously, this is easier for the corporate recruiter who can get a fairly complete picture of corporate IT jobs. Even though they work with many companies, recruiters in consulting and placement firms can build keyword lists for typical, or standard, jobs.

The recruiter must identify keywords that should appear in résumés appropriate for each job opening and build a keyword profile. Titles don't work very well for technical jobs because everyone uses different titles and the most effective keywords identify specific skills. Pick general terms, eg. "MVS" not "MVS/XA" to get the broadest response. Also, include both product and vendor name, eg. "NetWare" and "Novell" when people in the industry refer to either. The type of job, or employment status, can be a good keyword and be sure to include all overlapping job types such as "free lance" "contract" and "consulting." Background expressed as "applications," "technical" (also include "systems"), or "support" can also be used. Job functions such as "coding" and "data modeling" are also good keywords. Once the list is built, prioritize it and start the search using only those words that absolutely must appear in a résumé for it to reflect a viable candidate. List the most important keywords first and add more words to limit the search when too many résumés are returned.

Résumé banks and Web searches all have their own way of specifying keywords and recruiters have to know whether to use "+" or "AND" (whatever the rules are) in order to conduct the search. This can make Internet searches time-consuming and confusing, so it's important to carefully handle the responses to get the most out of every search. When searching the Web for individual résumés, make sure that the word "résumé" is included as a keyword. It's also a good idea to state you want sites that don't contain the word "jobs" so you won't get job ads returned.

Handling the Résumés

Standard e-mail templates should be prepared ahead of time, so good candidates can be contacted immediately by filling in the specifics and sending the mail. While one of the benefits of the Internet is its speed, that also means that many recruiters see résumés as soon as they're posted. Use the e-mail to express interest in the candidate, state high points about potential jobs, ask for a current résumé if the one on the Internet is old, and ask to be contacted. Also include any nonnegotiable factors. If the job will definitely require wearing a pager and providing weekend support, make sure that's clear so candidates can self-select out of the recruiting process if this can't be done. E-mail good candidates, print the résumés, and copy them to an internal database.

Actually, two standard templates should be prepared, as recruiters will have access to many good résumés that just don't fit this specific job opening. These résumés are also saved in an internal database, and an e-mail establishes initial contact with good candidates that might fit later job openings.

Finding Passive Candidates

Passive candidates are people who are not looking for jobs at all. In fact, they are quite happily employed. The best way to find passive candidates is through referrals, but the Internet does contain information that recruiters can use to entice people with a good offer. People belong to technical discussion groups, visit technical sites, and post messages on newsgroups and listservs. Virtual community sites contain millions of personal Web pages, and many IT people identify their technical background on these personal pages. Corporations often maintain lists of employees on Web sites for internal use. There are tools and techniques that can be used to find these people.

See: *Virtual Communities* on page 167.

One way to look for passive candidates is to find people who have participated in discussions on a technology you are interested in. You can read through the discussion threads and identify people who "talk" knowledgeably about the topic. Newsgroups have many of these discussion groups, and Deja News (www.deja.com) is the most popular search tool for searching newsgroups. Technical sites such as Brainbuzz (www.brainbuzz.com) also host discussion groups as do many of the technical specialty sites. These sites also permit job postings, so jobs posted here can attract passive candidates. Finding passive candidates takes a lot of time, and recruiters can spend hours identifying a single potential candidate. Identifying an individual with pertinent skills is only the first step, now the candidate must be contacted—very carefully. Highly skilled technical people get multiple e-mails each day from recruiters, and most simply delete the e-mail unread. Phone calls work better for recruiters who have a prepared script that will not take much of the potential candidate's time. The goal of the phone call is to get a résumé, and the recruiter should be prepared to accept an old résumé through e-mail.

Another way to find passive candidates is through site flipping, and this technique is very controversial. Flipping a site means accessing a corporate site to find information such as employee lists, e-mails, and employee résumés. This and other techniques are fairly well known and are taught in Internet training seminars. Flipping a site does get names, but this is information that the company did not intend to be accessible to anyone on the Web, and many don't like it This technique also takes a lot of time, not only to do the searching but also to work with the results. The recruiter ends up with a broad list of names that now must be qualified.

Internet "Cold Calling"

Once names are found, the recruiter is now really "cold calling" these potential candidates. The recruiter usually has an e-mail address and must prepare a carefully thought out letter. The most important part of the e-mail is actually the subject line, as many people delete e-mails from unknown sources without even reading them. It also looks like a good idea to attach a job description, but don't—people definitely delete e-mails with attachments if they're not expecting them.

The e-mail should stress strong selling points, and most often mention the company, the location, or something like "We provide three weeks of technical training for every IT person—every year." It can also explain how the recruiter learned of the candidate mentioning, eg., "the comments you wrote about installing Oracle8i." Many e-mails include a link to the corporate Web site. Most of the time the link is to the job opening page, but some recruiters link to a page advertising the benefits of the location, if this is a big plus, or information about the company, if the company name is a big selling point. All this is not necessarily done in one e-mail, the original message can be followed up. Often response comes after several contact attempts.

The e-mail should contain the recruiter's name, e-mail address and a phone number to allow the candidate to respond in the way that is easiest for them. Ask for a résumé, but don't insist, as passive job seekers usually don't have current résumés available. Linking to an application form that is easy to fill out can get more responses than an open-ended "please contact me."

Developing an Internet Strategy

The Internet is an invaluable tool for recruiters, especially during the sourcing phase of the recruiting cycle. It can be, however, the biggest waste of time possible. Recruiters can literally spend all day surfing the net and end up with nothing. An Internet strategy controls the time spent on the Internet and makes sure it is time well spent. Internet usage is part of the overall recruiting strategy, and companies must decide how much of their recruiting time and budget should be spent on the Internet. A strategy is really a plan, and like all plans the Internet strategy must be revised based on actual experience.

Overall Strategy, or Plan   Even before defining a plan, it is important to realize that whatever strategy is used, it must be regularly evaluated and refined. In fact, because the Internet is so dynamic and new features and sites appear daily, a review and revision schedule is the most important part of the plan. Every activity (every job posting and every résumé search) must be evaluated for effectiveness and a regular review schedule (every three or four months) should be implemented.

INTERNET STRATEGY	
Schedule	Evaluate Internet usage
	Record each activity
	Hold scheduled reviews
	Annual decision making review
Post Jobs	Corporate site
	Job banks (fee or free)
	Others (newsgroups, listservs)
	Build evaluation procedures
Search	Job/résumé banks (fee or free)
	Others (Web, newsgroups, etc.)
	Search tools (portals, spiders, etc.)
	Build evaluation procedures
Who	Internal recruiters
	Internal sourcing specialists
	Contract sourcing specialists
	Outsourcing firms

The overall strategy also defines exactly how the Internet will be used, and who will be using it. Some companies post jobs, others only search for résumés. Some use it as a major source, others use it sparingly or only for certain jobs. Who uses the Internet also varies. Companies have many options including outsourcing the entire operation, contracting Internet sourcing specialists, training internal sourcing specialists, or having each recruiter do Internet sourcing. Usage is defined in two ways—amount of time and amount of money. Both are often expressed as percents; eg., a company will spend x% of its recruiting budget in posting job ads on the Internet, and will allow recruiters to spend 50% of their sourcing time on Internet searches.

Internet Usage—How   The Internet can be used to post jobs and to search for résumés. For job postings, the Internet plan must include what sites will be used. The sites used, however, should be one of the most dynamic parts of the strategy, as they can vary depending on the type of job. For example, there is a technical specialty site that can be used when looking for an Oracle DBA, but not for every technology. There are job banks that specialize in IT jobs, but the major general banks also post many of these jobs. A good plan is to decide on several job banks to use, then decide *for each job* which bank to use. Posting sites can originally be picked by reputation, and there are numerous references that evaluate these sites. The sites being used can then be changed through experience.

Whatever decisions are made, every posting site should be evaluated every time it's used. The technical specialty site looks like a good place to post an ad for the Oracle DBA, but there actually might be more résumés on one of the major job banks. Free job postings look good, but in fact might fall in the "waste of time" category because they don't get responses. Keep records not only of how many résumés were received from each job bank, but track each résumé through the entire recruiting process. The most important statistic is how many people were hired from this source. It might take a year to really know how effective this job bank is (the fee-based job banks often require a year's contract anyway), but regular reviews will establish the facts needed to decide whether to continue with this bank. As new job banks are added to the Internet on a daily basis, the effectiveness of each constantly changes.

See: *Job-Posting Record* on page 135.

Searching for résumés starts the same way—by deciding on what sources will be searched. For searching, however, the entire Web is a source as many people post résumés on individual home sites. Searching job banks is easily done through each bank's search options, but searching the Web requires search tools such as meta search engines and spiders. Most search tools are free, and the ones that are purchased are not expensive, but this is not the true cost of searching. The true cost of Internet searches is time. To ensure that recruiter's spend time effectively on the Web, some training should be provided, and the training can be quite expensive. Every search should be evaluated by recording the searcher, the area being searched (job/résumé banks, the Web, newsgroups, specialty sites, etc.), the search tool used, the keywords used, and the résumés returned. Every search should be assigned an identifier which should then be used to track an applicant through the recruiting process. Again, it's not the number of résumés received that's important—it's the number of hires made.

See: *Résumé Search Record* on page 145.

Internet Usage—Who   Because sourcing is such a critical and time-consuming activity, many companies have already implemented the use of sourcing specialists and the move to Internet sourcing specialists is natural. Other companies have each recruiter doing his or her own sourcing. Training must be considered when deciding who should do the Internet work, as some training is necessary. Training every recruiter in Internet sourcing techniques might not be desirable. Also, keeping up with new features and sites can take a lot of time. If sourcing is done by internal staff, someone must have the responsibility of knowing what's new for recruiters. Sourcing is one phase where contract recruiters can be used. Companies can contract for specific jobs or projects, or can use a contract recruiter (or sourcer) on a part time basis. Finally, companies can outsource the entire Internet operating to firms that offer many options ranging from simply finding résumés to also doing screening, or qualification, of candidates.

6. Screening

**Requirements screen
Technical screen**

Screening

The screen phase of the recruitment cycle, which is often called qualifying, is selecting the viable candidates from the large (hopefully) pool of résumés collected during sourcing. Tracking candidates starts at this point. If a candidate looks good enough to screen, this should be recorded. Screening chooses what résumés will be forwarded to the job requestor and determines what candidates will continue on to be interviewed, so it is a critical function. Screening has two parts, an initial requirements screen of logistical, technical and personal requirements, and the technical screen, which ensures candidates meet the technical job description. Résumés and applications contain a lot of information and the recruiter matches the résumé with the job requirement. When there is a good match, the screening is used to verify that what's on the résumé is true. This is not to say that applicants lie on résumés; it is to say that they put their best foot forward and it's often easy to read better or stronger experience than really exists. Most of the time screening, at least checking the requirements, can be done over the phone. The technical screen can be done by phone or in person.

See: *Pipeline Report/Candidates* on page 139.

Requirements Screen

The requirements screen ensures that the candidate meets the job requirements. Job requirements are those specifics that are an absolute must and are not necessarily technical. Requirements fall in three areas: logistics, personal and technical. Logistical requirements could cover required hours, travel, or even a requirement that the person who takes this job must carry a beeper for 24/7 support. Personal requirements can be varied and range from requiring applicants take a drug and/or polygraph test to needing fluency in a second language. Technical requirements can include insisting on a college degree and/or technical certifications such as Microsoft or Novell network certifications. Information pertaining to technical requirements usually does appear on résumés, but most of the other information does not. The recruiter must tell the candidate of the requirements and make sure the candidate can meet them, or, as in the case of drug testing, is willing to be tested. This should be the first thing done during the screen because requirements are nonnegotiable. If the candidate doesn't meet them, there's no sense in proceeding with the recruiting process. This does not always mean that the résumé should be discarded. If a company requires a college degree for all IT positions and a candidate doesn't have a degree, there's no reason for a corporate recruiter to keep this résumé. However, a recruiter for a consulting firm who works with multiple companies will have openings with different requirements, so the résumé should be stored in an applicant database.

Technical Screen

The technical screen is a critical part of the recruiting process, and it's the most important part of the process in terms of building credibility with hiring managers. Hiring managers quickly lose faith in a recruiter if they read résumés or interview candidates who don't have the basic qualifications. Recruiters do not have to conduct technical interviews, which are discussed in Section 7, but they do determine if the technical interview should even take place! The most common complaint of technical managers is "why did you send me this résumé (or person)—they're obviously not qualified." The job requestor is frustrated and blames the recruiter for wasting his or her time. The recruiter is frustrated because the résumé looked good! It had all the same words on it that were in the job request. Technical recruiters must know how to screen candidates to build credibility with hiring managers. The comment everyone wants to hear is "I always get good people from…" Basic technical screens can be conducted prior to an in-depth interview and are often done over the phone. This is done to keep from even scheduling a in-depth interview with a recruiter if the candidate does not have basic skills.

The technical screen works with the job requisition to make sure the candidate fits the basic profile. It's important to work with the entire requisition and a common mistake new technical recruiters make is to screen only the technical skill set. Because the same skills and products are used by juniors and seniors, and by mainframe developers and support personnel, having the right skill experience is not enough. Recruiters should first make sure the candidate's background fits the core description.

Core Description

Checking Job Type   IT jobs fall into three basic types: applications development, technical development, and support. Skill set does not define the job type, people in all three areas can use the same skill. One job needs someone to develop a checking account system that uses Oracle for data storage (application developer), another opening requires tuning Oracle systems (technical developer), and a third describes running standard systems and handling the backups of the Oracle data (support). Résumés for people performing all three types of jobs will say Oracle, but that just isn't enough information.

See: *Job Type Distinctions* on page 155.

Distinguishing the job types can be difficult, and while sometimes it can be done from the résumé, often the recruiter will have to get further information from the applicant. Whether used in a résumé, or during a screen, certain words do indicate what job type a candidate is.

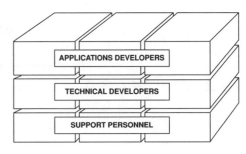

Checking Technical Environment   Job requestors want to see applicants who have worked in the appropriate environment (or platform), be it the mainframes, midsize, or desktop systems. Software is developed differently for the three environments.

This does not necessarily mean that the skills are different and, in fact, some skills are used everywhere, eg., developers in all three environments write programs in the C language, and Oracle databases exist in all three areas. Other things are specific though, such as communication with the operating system and program design.

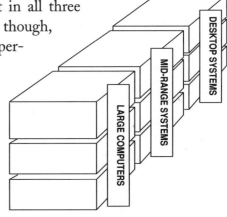

The technical environment is easily found on résumés, so all the recruiter has to do is verify that the applicant has actual on-the-job experience working in the desired environment. Everyone in IT has experience with desktop systems, so expect to see this on all résumés. Experience on midsize systems might be from training, and while training is valuable, it cannot duplicate actual work experience. Recruiters can trust that mainframe experience occurred on-the-job, as neither training schools nor homes are likely to contain mainframes.

Checking Seniority Level   As in most fields, jobs in IT are for junior-, mid-, or senior-level people. Often job requestors will use years-of-experience to specify seniority level. As a general guideline, juniors have from zero to two years, mids have from two to five, and seniors have over five years of experience. Simply working with years doesn't give a com-

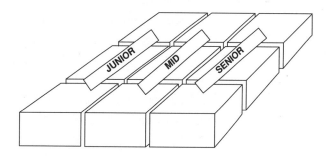
plete picture, however. Especially in IT where new technologies appear almost daily, a "senior" developer in a particular technology might only have two or three years of experience because that's as long as the technology has been used. To help categorize the applicant's experience:

Juniors: During the first year or two in an IT career, an individual is concentrating on developing and adding new technical skills and this is usually all that counts. Junior jobs are often described as "entry-level" and can sometimes be filled by people straight out of training programs. This includes both college and technical school graduates.

Mids: At least some work experience is required. Technical skills are important, but additional job functions are usually expected. Applications developers are starting to develop industry or application experience, and job requests will ask for such things as "experience with manufacturing systems." Interpersonal skills start being required and résumés will reflect some user-contact. Technical developers are starting to specialize in the operating environment, database management systems, or networking area. Support personnel are starting to troubleshoot problems and schedule job functions. In all three areas, the IT people are working more independently and require less supervision.

Seniors: Senior personnel are the most critical people in any IT operation. They have all the skills that mids have, and can be described by two additional words: responsible and supervise. Responsible is the key word for all senior jobs, and must appear on the résumé or come up during the screening. Most applications developers work in teams so supervision is definitely part of the job of senior application developers. Technical jobs, however, are often "loner" jobs where only one person is doing this particular work, so there is no one to supervise. "Responsible" is still part of the identity of a senior, but "supervise" is not always part of technical development or support jobs.

Technical Skill Set

Once the recruiter determines that the candidate fits the core description of the job request, the next step is to check the technical skill set.

Many recruiters consider this the most difficult part of the job, as most recruiters don't have a technical background and asking questions about technology often results in sitting quietly while the applicant responds in what sounds like a different language. Technical screening takes preparation and requires some technical knowledge. Each recruiter must determine how much technical knowledge he or she needs, as different recruiters are comfortable with different amounts of knowledge. Technical skills fall into four categories: platforms, development, data management, and communications (online); and most IT jobs can be described by a skill in each area. A fifth area, applications, must also be considered. Sometimes one skill is so important that it's the only one necessary, especially with new technologies. Usually though, the job requestor will identify several skills. The skill set of the job being done by more applications developers than any other is COBOL (development), DB2 (data management), CICS (communications), and MVS (platform). All descriptions don't fall as nicely, however. Recruiters can ensure they have a complete description by building a picture from the four or five skill areas.

The purpose of the screen is to make sure that the candidate has work experience in the skills requested. There are several ways to do this. Technical recruiters do not have to have a technical background, but they do have to know enough to be able to tell if the candidate can talk knowledgeably about a skill. Recruiters can work with a list of topic points for each technical area. For example, a topic list for Unix could include: operating system, shell (Bourne, C, Korn), shell scripts, Perl, AWK, SED, C, commands, kernel, GUI, MOTIF, Open Look, pipes, and device drivers. If a recruiter wants to know if someone has worked with Unix, they can ask questions about familiar terms from this list. All applicants won't know all the terms, but each candidate should know some of them, so the recruiter should be prepared to work with four or five terms. Questions can be very basic, "Tell me about the Unix shell" and should be open-ended. Recruiters do have to know enough about the technology they are discussing to evaluate the correctness of the response, but the questions asked don't go very deep into the technology. If the answers get too technical, simply move on to another question. Although if an applications developer candidate gets too technical, it's a good opportunity to check interpersonal skills. Ask them to try again, and tell them that interfacing with users (nontechnical people) is part of the job. Getting an understandable explanation also helps recruiters to increase their own technical knowledge.

See: *Technical Skills* on pages 156–158.
Topic Points on page 159.

One way of screening an applicant's skill knowledge is by verifying pertinent job experience with that skill. Job requisitions don't just say they want someone with a particular experience, but ask for a level of experience by specifying junior, mid, senior, or years of experience. Years of experience can be a valid measure, but be careful how the questions are asked. Asking "how long have you been working with Oracle?" will get you an answer, but it might be misleading. Someone might have worked with Oracle for four years, but only on one project, and it might be a project they only worked on once or twice a week. A completely true answer of "four years" makes the candidate look like they have strong experience, but in actuality their experience is limited. Using a skill on more that one project would also show stronger experience, as it's likely that only a subset of a particular skill is used on any one project.

Another way of checking strength of knowledge is by asking applicants to rate themselves in the key skills. Ask them to rate on a scale from one (light) to four (expert). Don't give them an odd number of choices as too many people will pick the middle (average). Make them commit to above or below average. Two things to remember about self-ratings: One is that IT people tend to rate themselves low. They've put everything they can on their résumé to look good, but during questioning will be very careful not to oversell. These people don't want to be hired into a job they're not ready to do. If someone rates themselves a two, they're average. If the rating is a four, hire them! There are, of course, exceptions to this. Every technical recruiter has met the two-year hotshot who knows everything about everything. Asking this candidate for self-ratings will get nothing but the highest possible—at least a four plus, if they can't come back with a five.

General Screens

Screening is often done without a specific job in mind. Job fairs and open houses can find many applicants who need to be screened to see which of many jobs might be appropriate. Recruiters, especially from consulting firms and agencies, are constantly screening applicants in order to build a base of applicants as more jobs open up. These general screens are used to build an applicant profile, which can then be used for many jobs, not just one.

Checking requirements in a general screen is somewhat different, because now the recruiter is determining whether the applicant has any personal requirements that must be met. Requirements in a general screen fall into just two areas, logistical and personal, and these two areas do overlap—many logistical requirements exist because of personal circumstances. Some logistical requirements could be:

REQUIREMENT	EXPLANATION/EXAMPLES
Job logistics	As an example, the applicant might need to work part-time or at home. This is usually because of child, or elderly parent, care.
Hours	Perhaps the applicant can only work third-shift, or needs flex hours that allow him or her to take a day off in the middle of the week and make up the time on Saturday. Again, this is usually for child, or elderly, parent care.
Travel	How much travel can the applicant do? Could be none.
Location	Basically, this refers to the applicant's willingness to relocate. This is especially important for recruiters from consulting firms and agencies, who are likely to work with multiple regions, but corporate recruiters dealing with many branches also need to know if a particular location is a requirement.
Salary	Some applicants will be very definite about the minimum salary they will accept.
Other financials	The most common "other" in the financial area comes when an applicant is expecting a bonus from their present employer and requires that the bonus be matched as a hiring bonus from a new employer.
Vacation	Some applicants insist that their existing earned vacation time be matched.
Green Card	Alien applicants can have legal requirements that a new job must meet.

This is, of course, not an inclusive list as each individual can have specific requirement that no one else does.

The recruiter should also screen for personal circumstances that might affect an applicant's ability to accept a job or a consulting assignment. This could include such things as physical handicaps that require wheelchair access, a sick spouse that requires medical insurance, or an ill parent that could require time off on a fairly regular basis.

The technical part of a general screen is different only in checking the skill set. The recruiter still must determine the core description of job type, environment, and experience level, but there are no specific technical skills to screen for. Recruiters, however, know what skills are "hot" and can usually determine the applicant's key skills from their own personal knowledge of the types of job openings that are common. The recruiter can pick one or two skills from each technical area (platforms, development, data management, communications, and applications) and question the applicant on these skills. Recruiters often simply ask the applicant what his or her strengths are, and work with the skills the applicant chooses. More time is spent on specific skills during a general screen because the applicant will be matched against many jobs.

> See: *Technical Skill—Summary* on page 158.

The applicant profile should be in writing, because it is very likely that a different recruiter will work with the applicant at a later date. If a thorough screen is conducted and documented, it will not have to be repeated.

> See: *Applicant Profile* on page 119.
> *Applicant Control* on page 115.

7. Interviewing

Interview Types
Technical Interviews
Interview Preparation
Interview Structure
Questioning

Interviewing

Interviewing is an integral part of recruiting and occurs throughout the entire process. Screening sessions are interviews, whether they are conducted over the phone or in person. These screening sessions are then followed by one or more in-depth interviews. Hiring, or placing a person in a consulting assignment, is a situation where everyone is trying to find the best match between an open job and the available candidates. The more information that is exchanged, the better the chances are of making a good match. Interviewing is actually an exchange of information: The candidate is getting information about the job opening and the interviewer is getting information about the candidate. Interviewing is also a sales effort, again by both parties. Candidates are selling themselves, and interviewers are selling jobs. The formal, or in-depth, interview is where most of the interaction and selling takes place. Interviewers often prepare a guide for each interview to ensure nothing is left out.

See: *Interview Guide* on page 129.

Interview Preparation

One thing that all interviews have in common is that their effectiveness depends upon the amount of preparation done by the recruiter. The importance of preparation cannot be overstressed, and the in-depth interview requires preparation in two areas. The recruiter must prepare statements covering the information the candidate should have and also prepare questions to extract the information the recruiter needs. One of the most expensive mistakes businesses make is wrong hires. And, wrong hires occur because either the hiring manager or the new employee expected something different.

Recruiters usually prepare questions to ask, but often don't spend enough time preparing the presentation of information to the candidate. The better the candidate understands the job opening, the less likely it is that he or she will be unhappy if hired. Providing information to the candidate is also an opportunity to sell the job, and this can only be done if the recruiter knows what he or she is working with. In a corporate setting the recruiter can usually get detailed information on the exact job requirements, the hiring manager, and corporate policies and benefits. Agency and consulting recruiters must work from generalities about the "typical assignment" or "most of our clients," but still can provide positive information about the opportunity. Technical recruiters can work with the knowledge that most IT candidates have at least two goals in common: Virtually all of them, regardless of the specific job they do, want to work in state-of-the-art technology. And, they want all want to grow technically. Technical recruiters use this knowledge to include information about technical training and hot technologies that the company uses when making the presentation.

All aspects of the job should be presented, and the recruiter should be ready for any objections the candidate might have. A requirement of 24/7 beeper support could easily be a negative, yet that must be part of the information conveyed to candidates. If the candidate objects, or even just looks away, the recruiter can balance that by stressing that the job has a four-day workweek and three-weeks vacation to start. Preparing information for contract assignments can be more difficult, as the recruiter probably doesn't know as much about the assignment, but the recruiter needs to find out as much as possible and work with the positives. Interviews for consulting assignments often require the most preparation.

Preparing questions is the other half of preparation, as the recruiter must complete a picture of the candidate. First, questions are used to fill in holes in the résumé and clear up confusing items. Educational background is often confusing. It seems that technical candidates often obscure whether a degree was granted from a college or university, and a recruiter should prepare a question to clarify this. Résumés often have missing time periods of work experience, and the recruiter must ask what was done during this time. If the recruiter gets satisfactory answers to these questions, the next thing to do is to determine whether the candidate looks like a good fit with the job, the company, and/or the hiring manager. The recruiter works with what is known about all three areas and asks questions to determine the intangible aspects that enable a person to fit into a new job situation. For example, one job might provide little supervision because the current manager firmly believes that people work best when left alone. Asking the candidate how much time was spent with their last supervisor and how comfortable they were with this arrangement can help find the right person. This question would not be used with another opening, even in the same department. Each job, each company, and each hiring manager has unique specifics that determine who will best fit the opening.

This "fit" is the most important thing in recruiting, and it's most often up to the recruiter to look for it. The final hiring decision belongs to the technical manager, but usually he or she needs guidance from the recruiter. Technical managers tend to fall in love with technical skills. Recruiters hear "they've got all the skills I need, make them an offer," and know this would be a mistake because of a personality mismatch with eg. the manager. For example, one question that can be used to determine interpersonal skills is "What form of communication do you prefer?" This simple question really does tell a lot about how a person likes to interact with others. It can also show what kind of a work environment the candidate prefers. If a candidate basically answers "everything should be in writing," they shouldn't be hired to work for a very gregarious manager, or in a volatile job where requirements change daily and there's no time to write everything down.

See: *Sample Questions—Traditional* on page 192.

There actually is a third area of preparation, but it's general preparation for all interviews. Recruiters should be prepared for questions they might be asked. Every recruiter has at one time or another been completely stumped by an unexpected question they don't know how to answer. Some of these questions can be startling and, while the recruiter doesn't have to know the answer, he or she can't blurt out, "Are you kidding?" Which might be a natural answer to a question like "Will I be paid royalties if the company sells software that I write?"

See: *Questions Candidates Might Ask* on page 189.

Types of In-depth Interviews

One-on-One Interview   The one-on-one interview is the most common and is conducted by one interviewer with one candidate. The interviewer can be a recruiter or someone from the IT department. Most of the time this interview is done in person, but sometime is done over the phone for logistical reasons. The interview usually takes from 30 to 60 minutes. In a one-on-one interview, it has been established that the candidate has the necessary skills for the position, and the interviewer wants to see if there is a fit with the company, job, the manager, and how this candidate will complement the rest of the department. Rapport building is very important, both for the candidate and the interviewer. This is the most common interview type used by technical recruiters.

Panel, or Board, Interview   This setup consists of many interviewers and one candidate (and, as would seem obvious, can be very difficult for the candidate). Usually the panel has prepared questions and each person knows what they will ask. Often the panel has agreed on what are acceptable answers. These interviews also take between 30 to 60 minutes. These interviews are conducted by the IT department, and recruiters would probably not be involved, but in actuality formal panel interviews are rarely used in technical recruiting.

In technical recruiting informal panel interviews are used to introduce a candidate to the team he or she would be working with. There is little, if any, preparation by the existing employees, and they tend to ask any questions that come to mind. These questions are often technical to make sure the potential hire can effectively do the job. This kind of panel interview can indicate how the person will interact with the existing team, and team members are asked for their opinions after the interview.

Group Interviews   This is an "interview" where a group of candidates is evaluated. The group is given a problem to solve, and the "interviewers" evaluate how well each candidate works in a team environment, and what role each takes on: leader, conciliator, problem solver, worker. Usually there are at least two people supervising the activity. A group interview can take a couple of hours, and some even take all morning or afternoon. Group interviews are not common in technical recruiting.

Sequential Interviews   Sequential interviews are very common in IT, especially with more senior positions. A sequential interview consists of a number of one-on-one interviews, starting with the most junior person and working up to the hiring manager. In these interviews potential seniors are actually interviewed by people that would be reporting to them, if hired. In some cases, each interviewer has the authority to refuse to pass the candidate on to the next level, but usually these interviews are not scheduled until the recruiter has thoroughly screened and interviewed the candidate, so all the interviews are held. There are at least three, but no more than six, interviews. The interviews take place on the same day, and it is an exhausting day for the candidate. Each interviewer is required to fill out a standard form, and all interviewers meet to discuss the applicant when the interview series is completed.

See: *Applicant Evaluation* on page 117.

Impromptu Interviews   As the name implies, impromptu interviews are unplanned, and no specific preparation has been made. These interviews often occur at job fairs and sometimes occur at social events. An impromptu interview is usually a screening and is followed by an in-depth interview. These interviews usually do not take over 30 minutes.

Second Interview   For very senior positions, a series of interviews is scheduled and the candidate must progress through each. These interviews are called second interviews even though there might be three or four of them. Each interview concentrates on a different aspect of the job or the candidate and one of the interviews is usually in a social setting—often dinner with the hiring manager, spouses included. This series of interviews is similar to a sequential interview except the interviews do not take place on the same day and each interview can result in an end to the application.

Stress Interview   A stress interview is well named, as it is an interview designed to see how the candidate handles himself in an uncomfortable situation. Any of the above interviews can be stress interviews, and many people definitely put panel interviews in this category! Usually though, the stress interview is a staged setup. The interviewer may be sarcastic or argumentative. Tricks are used to make the candidate uncomfortable—such as giving them a chair with uneven legs or coffee in a cup with a slow drip. Candidates are often made to wait for a long time, or the interview is interrupted by someone who comes in and whispers to the interviewer. Another common technique is the use of silence. The interviewer does not say anything after an answer to a question and waits to see how long the candidate will let the silence last, and what the candidate will say to break it. These techniques might be used for jobs that require a lot of interpersonal interaction with possibly unhappy users, but are not too common with IT jobs. They are, in fact, most commonly used for sales jobs.

Structured vs. Unstructured Interviews (also called Directed vs. Undirected)   A structured interview is both systematic and standardized. The interviewer prepares a set of questions that are used with every candidate. This gives a basis for comparing candidates, but limits the interviewer's ability to gather in-depth information. Completely structured interviews aren't really possible, as each résumé and each candidate introduces different traits, but building a structured interview with room for personal questions is often done. Structured interviews are excellent for initial screenings and very useful for inexperienced interviewers, since it helps guide the interview and ensures that all relevant factors about the candidate's qualifications and the open position are covered. One problem is that it's possible for the interview to become mechanical and, unfortunately, boring. The interviewer must make sure the interview stays personal and interesting.

An unstructured interview is free-form and is used to get the candidate to talk about a variety of topics. Consequently, these interviews tend to be informal and undirected. They frequently begin with the interviewer's asking the candidate to, "Tell me about..." Although this type of interview can ask for detail on any topic, it does have shortcomings. The first is that because questions for each interview are different, there is no basis for comparing one candidate to another. The second, and most important shortcoming, is that this approach often doesn't let the recruiter obtain necessary information because too much time was spent on a sideline. An unstructured interview can also open the door for discrimination charges. There is no objective basis for comparing candidates because each was asked different questions, so unsuccessful candidates can feel they were unfairly rejected.

The best interview is a combination of both techniques. The interview should be well planned with prepared questions. Most questions can be used with all candidates. For example, every candidate should be asked, "What form of communication do you prefer?" if this is the question the recruiter chooses to start a discussion on interpersonal skills. The answer to the question might then lead to other questions that are not asked of every candidate, but are used to get more information from a specific candidate. Once the recruiter is satisfied on interpersonal skills, he or she returns to the list of questions that everyone is asked. This builds a basis for comparing candidates, but keeps each interview fresh and unique.

Traditional vs. Behavioral   A traditional interview typically asks questions about hypothetical situations, and a behavioral interview asks questions about actual situations. An example of a traditional question might be: "How would you handle an angry user?" It isn't difficult to figure out what the interviewer wants to hear and answers are usually something like, "I would politely ask them to tell me the problem, then I would offer my assistance in solving the problem." A behavioral interview would ask a different question, such as "Tell me about a specific instance in your past where you had to handle an angry user." It is often easy to turn a traditional, or hypothetical, question into a behavioral one by simply stating "Tell me about a situation when…" rather than asking "What would you do if…?"

Behavioral interviews are presently very popular. The interview is based on the premise that past behavior will be the best predictor of future behavior. The interviewer determines what nontechnical skill traits are most important to the job, or the hiring manager, and then builds a question list checking for behavior indicating the candidate has that trait. These traits include such things as assertiveness, decision-making ability, interpersonal skills, and leadership. A behavioral question for interpersonal skills could be "Give me an example of when you mediated a conflict." The interviewer does not stop with the single question, but follows up with questions such as "What did you say?" "What were you thinking?" and usually, "What was the result?" The interviewer will establish specifics and will sometimes verify the situation during a reference check. Another characteristic of behavioral interviews is that many of the questions are negative: "Tell me about an instance in which you missed a deadline," or "Tell me about a time when you made a mistake that cost your company time and money." Either of these questions can be followed up with "Is that the worst mistake you've ever made?" Behavioral interviews must be thoroughly planned and are usually structured interviews with each candidate being asked the same questions.

Just as most interviews are partly structured and partly unstructured, most interviews contain both traditional and behavioral questions. Some traits are more easily examined by one method over the other. For example, if a recruiter wants to verify organizational skills, a traditional question asking what scheduling tools the candidate uses can be simpler than asking for specific instance examples. When the recruiter is looking for leadership ability, a behavioral question that asks for a specific instance gets more accurate results than a hypothetical asking what the candidate would do in a leadership situation. Behavioral questions, if not complete behavioral interviews work very well with IT candidates.

See: *Sample Questions—Behavioral* on page 190.
Sample Questions—Traditional on page 192.

Writing Questions for the Interview

The first recommendation is that most questions should be open-ended. An open-ended question is one that requires a full, multiple word response. This gives the candidate a chance to talk openly, and gives the recruiter time to listen to the answers, assess verbal communication skills, and observe the candidate's poise and self-confidence. Closed, or Yes/No, questions are often easier to develop, but can be turned into open-ended questions with a little work. Different types of questions used during an interview and are used at different times and for different reasons.

Opening Questions   These are nondirective questions intended to see where the applicant will go with an answer. They are used to see what's important to the candidate. The most common example is "Tell me about yourself." Other opening questions could refer to hobbies or interests such as "I see you enjoy theater. Please tell me about your involvement." Knowing whether the candidate is a participant, an observer, or a supporter tells the recruiter a lot.

Rapport-Building Questions   These questions are a subset of opening questions and are used at the beginning of an interview to put the candidate at ease. They tend to be more personal and, when possible, use both of the words "you" and "I". For example, "I enjoyed reading your résumé and am looking forward to our interview. May I get you coffee or tea?" Or, "I see you list snow boarding as one of your hobbies. I've never tried it although I ski; would you tell me a little about it?" In addition to putting the candidate at ease, these questions help to build a personal relationship between the recruiter and the candidate. For

OPEN-ENDED QUESTIONS

Closed Question	Open-Ended Question
Are you a good leader?	Tell me about an instance where you became the leader of a group? How did the situation end?
Are you pleased with your career so far?	What are your eventual job goals? What do you see as the next step? How do you plan to accomplish this?
Do you think you can handle this job?	How do you feel your talents, experience, and education prepare you for this job?
Do you work well with people?	Tell me about a problem you had in a work relationship you had to maintain. How did you handle it?
Can you take criticism?	Tell me about an instance when you received negative criticism. How did you handle it?
Are you a good decision-maker?	Describe a situation in which you had to make an important decision. What did you do?
Did you work well with you boss?	In what ways did you and your boss think alike? Think differently?

permanent positions, taking the time to chat also indicates that the company cares about individuals and their interests, so this could be a good place to work.

Clarifying Questions   Often candidates are too nervous to think of all the details the recruiter wants to hear, or they give simple answers waiting to see if the interviewer wants more detail. These questions can be fairly simple and always open-ended. Examples: "Why do you feel that way?" "Anything else?" "What do you think causes that?"

Another reason technical recruiters use clarifying questions is because the answer didn't tell them anything! They really need to clarify the answer to get the information they're looking for. A recruiter might ask "In what ways did you and your boss think alike, or think differently," to see how well the candidate worked with his or her boss. An answer might be, "He and I both think that Cold Fusion is the only way to go, although basic ASP might be needed sometimes. I like VBScript and he likes Perl, so I guess we disagree there." This answer needs to be followed up with "How did this affect your working relationship?"

Editorial Questions   Editorial questions are a form of clarifying question and are used when the recruiter wants more specific detail. Many questions need to be expanded and often a candidate does not understand what kind of information the recruiter wants. Editorial questions use the words who, what, where, why, when, and how. For example, asking "Who else from programming was in user meetings?" can tell the recruiter more about whether the candidate was a participant or a leader in meetings with the users.

Laundry List Questions   In many cases, asking for a list of information is a quick way of getting good information. Instead of "Tell me about your most influential boss." The recruiter asks "Tell me about your most influential teachers, bosses, and mentors." The recruiter doesn't really care about one influential boss, the recruiter is trying to find out what management style the candidate responds to, and can get more information by allowing a broader response. Laundry list questions can also speed up the interview. "Tell me about your electives, special activities, and work experience while you were in college" will get a shorter response than asking three questions. The candidate will automatically edit his or her response and provide only the most important detail.

Non-question Question   Some recruiters feel that making statements is a better way of putting candidates at ease than is asking questions.

"Please describe a situation when you had to discipline a subordinate" can be easier to answer than "When and how did you last discipline a subordinate?" Most behavioral questions tend to be non-question questions.

Parrot Questions   A parrot question is another form of a non-question question. The recruiter encourages the candidate to go into more depth by simply repeating the last statement in an answer. For example, if a candidate states "I like working with the user" the candidate can repeat "You like working with users" and wait for more information. People in general don't like silence, and the candidate will almost always provide more information.

Problem-Solving Questions   These questions are also called situational questions and are used to see how the candidate would approach problems. Technical recruiters often use them, as Information Technology is problem solving! A typical example is "Your're writing a program and it's past the due date and the user is irate. How would you handle this?" Problem solving questions can easily be turned into behavioral questions—"Tell me about a time when you were late with a project and the user was irate. How did you handle this?"

Leading Questions   It's easy to ask leading questions, even though they're not effective. "Don't you think that getting along with subordinates is necessary to good management" is obviously looking for an "Of course" type answer. Simply turning the question to "Do you think getting…" doesn't let the candidate know what the recruiter believes. This question is still a poor one, because it is a closed (yes or no answer), not an open-ended, question. Getting rid of closed questions also eliminates most of the leading ones.

Legal Issues

The best way to win a legal dispute is to avoid it in the first place! Unfortunately, discrimination claims are not rare, and it's up to recruiters to avoid ending up in court. Discussions usually concentrate on what questions can be asked, but actually it's not the questions that are illegal; it's making an employment decision based on discriminatory elements that sends a company to court. Of course, the discriminating decision was based on the answers to questions that were asked during the interview, so the questions are important. The discrimination laws leave room for interpretation, so no definitive list of good and bad questions exists, but the summary effect of the laws is that all questions must relate to the candidate's ability to do the job in question. Basically, personal questions should be avoided. Avoid questions on: citizenship or national origin, race, color, ethnicity, sexual orientation, gender, marital status, disabilities, economic status, religion, health, and arrest record.

Some people say the only really illegal questions are "How is your health?" and "Have you ever been arrested?" Health issues are very touchy. It is illegal to ask someone if there is any health-related issue which would prohibit them from performing the job. It is legal to state the job requirements and ask if the candidate can do this job (The second question is legal because it does not specifically ask about disabilities, and there could be other reasons for being unable to perform the job.) It is illegal to ask if the candidate has ever been hospitalized, treated by a psychiatrist or psychologist, or been treated for drug addiction or alcoholism. The other specific "don't ask" is arrest record. Recruiters can ask about convictions, but not about arrests.

LAWS ABOUT INTERVIEWING/HIRING

Title VII Civil Rights Act (1964)	Forbids employers from discriminating on the basis of sex, race, age, national origin, or religion.
Age Discrimination in Employment Act (1967)	Prohibits discrimination against workers age 40 or greater.
Title I Americans with Disabilities Act (1991)	Prohibits discrimination against persons with disabilities in all areas of employment including hiring.
State laws	Vary from state to state.

Because the illegality enters in when the hiring decision is made, conducting structured interviews where all candidates are asked the same questions helps. If a recruiter can show that the person who was hired was asked the same questions and gave similar answers, there is no discrimination.

See: *Legal Issues* on page 186.

The Interview Itself

All interviews are unique. Even if the same questions are asked, the answers are always different. There are, however, several basic points that apply to all interviews.

INTERVIEWING

1. Do not send someone to bring a candidate to the interview, escort them personally. An interview should be an exchange of information between peers, and it looks like the recruiter feels he or she is too important, or too busy, to greet the applicant when someone else is sent.

2. Make the interview comfortable. Learn the candidate's name and use it during the interview. Describe the interview process and define everyone's role. If behavioral questions are going to be used, tell the candidate exactly how this type of questioning works. At the end of the interview ask if the candidate would like to use a rest room before proceeding to the next step.

3. Allow plenty of time for the interview. Interviews typically last between 15 and 50 minutes. Make sure there is enough time to conduct a proper closing.

4. Develop good listening skills. Let the applicant do the talking. It's very easy to set a conversational mode and end up chatting about mutual work experiences, but that's not a good interview. A guideline to follow is that 70% of the interview should be the candidate talking. Silence is a good technique to encourage candidates to talk. Most people feel they have to fill the void if no one else is speaking and will keep adding details as long as the interviewer is quiet.

5. Control the interview. Turn the phone off and shut the door if people might just walk into the office. Have business cards and company brochures on hand. Many candidates don't really know much about the company and/or the available job, so have material ready.

6. Take notes, but don't lose eye contact. This is a compromise. Taking notes shows an interest, but eye contact is necessary to keep the interview personal.

7. Don't make judgements. Be aware of typical judgement errors so they can be avoided:

Halo effect	Interpreting one or two strong characteristics as a strong candidate (or the reverse).
Contrast effect	Judging any candidate that follows a weak one as strong.
Similarity effect	Rating candidate similar to oneself as strong.
First-impression	Making a judgment early in the interview.
Stereotyping	Self-explanatory, probably the most common, definitely hard to avoid.

8. Watch body language. A basic knowledge of body language signals can give a recruiter additional information in interpreting answers. This knowledge can also be used to control the body language signals the recruiter sends out!

BODY LANGUAGE SIGNALS

CONFIDENCE
Leaning forward in chair
"praying" or "steepling" with hands
Hands behind back when standing
Good eye contact

OPENNESS, WARMTH
Open-lipped smiling
Open hands with palms showing
Talking with hands
Unbuttoning coat when seated
Humor

NERVOUSNESS
Fidgeting
Jiggling pocket contents
Running tongue across teeth
Clearing throat
Playing with hair
Running fingers through hair
Biting fingernails (or evidence of)
Twiddling thumbs

DEFENSIVE
Squinting
Frowning
Tight-lipped grin
Arms crossed in front of chest
Touching nose or face
Darting eyes
Avoiding eye contact
Clenched hands
Gestures with fist
Rubbing the back of the neck
Clasping hands behind head

BORED
Staring into Space
Slumped posture
Doodling
Foot tapping
Fidgeting
Leaning on elbow with chin in hand
Yawning

Parts of an Interview

All interviews have a definite sequence of parts, and questions for each part should be developed to build an interview guide, which can then be used with every candidate. As long as open-ended questions are used, the interviewer will be able to explore individual experiences and skills with each candidate when appropriate, and return to the guide to ensure nothing is omitted.

PARTS OF AN INTERVIEW

Interviews can be broken down into parts, and the recruiter should spend the bulk of his or her time on Past Job Specifics.

OPENING	5%	Put the candidate at ease; build rapport Overview of job or job opportunities Overview of company
GENERAL FACTORS	25%	Personal characteristics Educational background Goals and motivation
JOB SPECIFICS	60%	Non-technical work skills Work experience Technical screen (if not already done)
CLOSING	10%	Prepping the candidate Benefits (selling the job) Candidate's questions

---

Opening The opening of the interview is often called the rapport-building section. During this part, recruiters use standard social skills to put the candidate at ease and start building a relationship. While this part of the interview should not take more than five minutes, it creates the candidate's first impression of the company and the job. Even in general interviews that are not focused on a single specific job, the candidate still builds an impression of the company which will influence his or her decision if an offer is made later on in the recruiting process. One or two basic questions such as "Did you have any trouble finding us?" Or, "The weather's supposed to be wonderful this week-end; what do you think would be a fun outdoor thing to do?" usually start an interview. These questions have nothing to do with any job, but just break the ice (in fact are called ice-breakers). The job, or type of job opportunities, is presented during the opening section. Some recruiters go into detail but most feel that too many details will lead the candidate to slanted answers during the interview, so they only give an overview at this point. Finally, recruiters explain how the interview will go, how long it will be, and what format it will take, if applicable. For example, it would be appropriate to explain that behavioral question will be used, and tell the candidate that these questions look for answers from actual experience. Notes are generally not taken during the Opening part of the interview.

General Factors   General factors are usually covered next. These include intangible factors such as leadership ability and interpersonal skills, educational background, and goals and motivation. If a job, or perhaps a client company for a consulting assignment, has specific non-technical requirements, the recruiter would verify that the candidate meets them at this point. Each job requires different general skills, so recruiters must build a different interview guide. Asking about the candidate's goals and motivation is very important. First, it shows the recruiter cares about the applicant and second, it gives the recruiter information to be used during negotiation if a job offer is made. Interviewers do take notes during this part of the interview.

Job Specifics   The third part of the interview, Job Specifics, is over half of the interview. This is where the recruiter verifies that what's on the résumé actually reflects actual knowledge and experience. During this part of the interview the questions relate to performance, not potential or interest. General job skills are discussed at this time, and recruiters ask about a variety of things including career progress, promotions, work relationships, and supervisory experiences. Questions cover both performance and attitude. Interviews also contain technical questions, and the technical portion of the interview could even be the first technical screen. Technical screens are discussed in Section 4 and technical interviews are discussed later in this section.

Closing   The closing section of the interview takes less time, but is not less important. Interviews are used to obtain and impart information, this is the time to impart information. Recruiters are advised to do no more than 30% of the talking during an interview, and this is where most of that 30% occurs. One of the most critical parts of any interview is ensuring that the candidate understands all aspects of the specific job, or general job-type, openings. The interviewer presents detailed information and even repeats information that was provided earlier in the interview. Questions by the candidate are encouraged, and the questions can be about anything (although it seems that more questions are asked about benefits than anything else). Recruiters must be prepared to answer anything, and it's important to be completely truthful about all aspects of the job and not exaggerate or oversell. Every job, every company has negative aspects and the recruiter should be prepared to present these in a positive way. For example, if the company had a bad year last year and an applicant asks about the corporate financial health, a truthful answer like "We've had a bad year, but things are improving since we released …" leaves a positive impression.

A candidate's questions are often a way of stating objections, or negatives, that he or she has, and the recruiter must recognize and handle these objections. Candidates aren't always direct about their feelings. If a candidate asks "How permanent are the development teams," they could be really asking "Am I going to get stuck on a project for a long time?" as that is the picture they have gotten. When a recruiter thinks there might be an underlying reason for a question (or just doesn't understand why it was asked), he or she should probe, eg. "Why are you concerned?" Silence can be another indicator of an objection, and again the recruiter must probe to be able to know what the candidate is thinking. The more the recruiter finds out about the candidate's desires and worries, the easier negotiation will be if an offer is made.

Be very careful at this stage of the recruiting process to not say anything that could be construed as a job offer. Answer all questions with "If an offer were made…" or some comparable disclaimer.

This is also a chance to prepare the candidate for the next step, which could be a technical test, a technical interview, an internal interview within Information Technology, an interview by a client company's recruiters, or an interview by a client company's IT people. In other words, it's important to let the candidate know what comes next, and prepare him or her for that step. Preparation can include telling them references will be checked and asking for permission to do so. Have a prepared form for the candidate to sign authorizing these and any other background checks that might be made. It could mean telling the candidate something about the personality of the next person who will be interviewing them, or telling them an Account Manager will contact them to set up a client interview. Be very specific about the next step whatever it is. Especially let the candidate know time frames—when the next interview would occur, or when they should expect to hear from you.

> See: *Authorization for Reference Check* on page 121.

Finally, the best way to end an interview is to escort the candidate to the door or perhaps to the next interview. It takes just a moment and adds a touch of courtesy that candidates remember.

The Technical Interview

A technical interview is used to determine the depth of a person's skills in one or more technical areas and should be conducted by technical people. The information that is being exchanged is the interviewer telling the candidate what work he or she will be doing if hired, and the candidate telling the interviewer he or she has the necessary skills to accomplish those tasks. A recruiter can do a technical screen to determine that the applicant has actually worked with specified skills, but it is very difficult for someone who does not know the subject matter to determine a candidate's technical proficiency. In a corporate environment, technical interviewing is usually done by the IT staff. Consulting firms often do not do technical interviewing at all and count very heavily on the technical screen. The client company can then choose to do a technical interview or not. This is usually the case where the consulting firms deal only with contract workers and have no permanent consultants on staff. If the firm does have permanent consultants, often the recruiters can use these people to conduct technical interviews.

Technical interviewing often includes technical testing. There are three basic sources of technical tests. Companies have their own technical people write technical tests. Vendors write and sell tests. Other vendors provide testing services with a range of test logistics that varies from buying tests and returning them to be scored, to having the candidate log onto a Web site that will administer and score the test as it is being taken. Any of these methods can get good results by following three principles: (1) the test should not require a single specific answer to each question, (2) the test should be scored by someone who knows the technology, and (3) the test is verified within the corporate environment using it. Information Technology has few absolute answers to anything, so in any skill area most questions have several correct answers. The problem with many tests is that the answer key has only one correct answer to each question. If the applicant has to come up with the exact answer that's on the key, the test will eliminate skilled applicants who do things differently from the test creator. Because of this, it's important to have a technical person who can give credit for the "different-but-correct" answers score the test. Ideally, technical tests would be administered by a technical person and scored in front of the applicant, so the applicant has a chance to explain his or her answers. Finally, tests should be validated within a single company. Testing vendors and services provide statements about the accuracy of their tests, but these statistics can mean very little to any one specific environment. A company cares only if a test is a good evaluator of skills as they will be used internally, and average results might not mean anything.

See: *Technical Testing Products* **on page 196.**

8. Post-Interview Processing

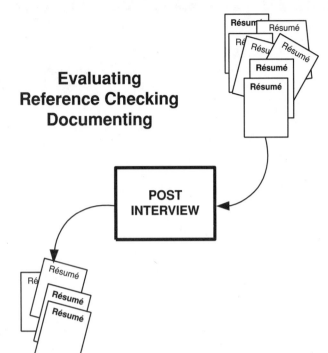

**Evaluating
Reference Checking
Documenting**

When an interview is over, there's still work to be done. Post-interview processing starts with evaluating the candidate. During the interview, the recruiter is intent on listening to the candidate, so it is important to record an evaluation as soon as the interview is over. The evaluation will help decide whether this candidate still looks good for the open job. Continuing with the candidate usually means doing reference checking and sometimes other background tests. Finally, the interview process could end with a number of things including scheduling another interview, preparing to make an offer, or writing a reject letter.

Evaluating the Candidate

At the end of each interview, the recruiter needs to record his or her impressions, and at least 15 minutes should be left between interviews for this purpose. Most interviewers take notes during the interview, but the notes are sometimes scattered and sparse. Often they're just key words that won't really make sense in a day or two, especially if the interviewer sees four or five more people for the same job. Therefore, it's important to formally record the evaluation of the candidate. The easiest way to do this is to use a standard form which has a listing of typical performance characteristics such as initiative, relevant technical experience, and interpersonal skills. The form should have plenty of room for notes, and often recruiters are asked to write explanations of any characteristic that was rated either very high or very low. In addition to a standard check list, overall impressions about strengths and weaknesses should be recorded. Each entry here should refer directly to something that was said during the interview.

See: *Applicant Evaluation* on page 117.

Standard forms are especially critical when the applicant has been interviewed by more than one person. If everyone is using the same form, there is a basis for collating and comparing appraisals. Sometimes the forms are simply collated, and other times the interviewers get together to discuss the candidate(s). Often candidates are ranked in order of preference.

Sometimes hiring decisions are not made until background tests, especially reference checks, are conducted. More often, the decision will be made and conditional offers extended.

Background Checks and Testing

There are many different background checks that can be made and companies decide which ones to use. Some companies do checks prior to making an offer, others make conditional offers depending upon satisfactory completion of the checks and/or tests. Still others don't make any checks until after the person is hired knowing they can release the person for providing false information if any check shows the applicant

BACKGROUND CHECKS AND TESTS	
CHECK	COMMENTS
Identity	Can check by name, SSN, or both.
Finances	Check credit history for debt loads (must state check is for employment). Check public records for financial liens, bankruptcy, etc.
Criminal History	State, County and/or Federal. Felony and/or Misdemeanor. Necessary to avoid legal liability from Negligent Hiring.
Motor Vehicle History	Current motor vehicle records in any state or states. Used to determine if person is "responsible."
Previous Employment	Confirm employment, dates, salary. Done by recruiters with reference checking. Done to check employment when no reference was provided for that company.
Education	Confirm college attendance, number of years, degree granted (if any). Often done by recruiters.
Worker's Compensation	Review of compensation claims and disposition by state (only some states provide). Can only be requested after a conditional offer has been made (per ADA).
Military Service	Check service branch, date, type, and date of discharge.
Drug Testing	Pre-employment drug testing is legal.
Physical Exams	Can have pre-employment physicals but only if all employees are required to take them.

wasn't truthful. Drug testing is fairly common and employment and educational verifications are usually done. Different companies have different policies on other checks, but only financial institutions will do financial checks unless the position requires bonding (rare, but occurs sometimes with technical jobs). Looking at motor vehicle records would only be done if the job required driving, which is extremely rare with technical jobs. The most common check is, of course, the reference check.

Reference Checking

It's long been thought that reference checks are very difficult and the most anyone will ever verify is dates of employment, job title, and salary. Companies could be sued for keeping someone from getting a job if they give negative references. It is illegal to say anything false about a past or present employee, but the laws do allow telling the truth about negative behaviors. References can tell a prospective employer any information relating to the individual's job performance as long as it's documented in the personnel file. And, in fact, if companies do not conduct reference and background checks, they could be liable under negligent hiring suits if, for example, an employee demonstrates violent behavior that was apparent in prior employment.

Some recruiters don't even bother to check references because they assume people won't talk to them, and this really isn't true. Several things can be done to encourage references to talk. The first is to assure them that the applicant gave permission for them to be contacted. Use a form signed by the applicant and fax a copy of the form to the reference, so they can see exactly what the applicant said they could respond to. Forms can be sent to get written references, but actually phone calls get better information, so the best technique is to fax the signed form and then follow up with a phone call asking the questions. Questions asked should only relate to job skills, general work ethic, ability to work with others, and attendance. Do not ask any personal questions. Assure the people you call that what they tell you is confidential and will be used only to make a hiring decision. Assure them that no hiring decision will be made on the basis of a single reference check. People want to give realistic references and most will do so. In fact, recruiters are often startled by how many negatives will be offered by references, even though questions very carefully ask only about job factors.

> See: *Authorization for Reference Check* on page 121.

The best references are not just former employers, but also peers and even sometimes subordinates. When asking applicants for references, ask for specific names "your former immediate supervisor," or "someone you worked with on project xxx." Ask for at least three or four names, because some of the references provided will not be available, or won't provide pertinent information. Try to get names from the last two jobs, not just the last one. Of course, if the applicant is currently employed, no one can be contacted from that company without explicit permission. Call or write every reference you get, and document both the attempts you made to get references and any information you got. Document refusals to supply information. Finally, be sure to get the same number of references for each applicant.

Reference checking is difficult and time consuming, but it's well worth it. Persistence will pay off, and getting valid references is a matter of making enough phone calls and writing enough letters. The information provided by references is a valuable piece of input to the hiring decision, but it should not be the major determining factor. When a recruiter is really positive about a candidate and gets a negative reference, additional reference checks should be made. It's important to realize that the number one reason people leave jobs is because of a personality conflict, and that conflict is usually with their immediate supervisor who is probably the person giving the reference. When an applicant gives you a name, he or she will often volunteer that this person will not give a good reference. If this happens, ask for detail and see if the reference confirms the applicant's description of the problem or problems. If other references are good, this is probably a classic example of a personal problem.

Recruiter Evaluation

Another type of evaluation should be done on at least a periodic basis, and that's an evaluation of the interview and the recruiter's performance. Recruiters will get formal performance evaluations, but in addition can do self-evaluations or ask peers to sit in on an interview to evaluate them. If someone is sitting in on an interview, the applicant assumes they are in training and doesn't pay attention to them. A simple check list can be used to make sure all parts of the interview are covered and nothing was left out.

> **See: *Interviewer Evaluation* on page 127.**

In addition the recruiter should consider the following questions:

1. Did the interview follow the prepared guide?
2. Were the right people interviewed?
3. What went well—what part of the interview went best?
4. What went poorly—what part of the interview was the worst?
5. Was the correct information obtained?
6. Were the applicant's goals clearly determined?
7. How did the interview end?
8. Was the applicant relaxed, and did he or she smile?
9. Is it clear whether to recommend the applicant for a job?
10. What additional preparation should have been done?

The Decision

After an interview one of four things can happen: (1) the recruiting process can continue, (2) the candidate can be rejected, (3) the application could be put on hold, or (4) an offer can be made.

Continuing the recruiting process means different things. It might mean scheduling another interview, this time with the hiring manager or client company. If there are no other interviews, then various checks might need to be made. Eventually the process concludes with either an offer or a rejection.

If it's decided that the applicant is not qualified for the job, he or she should be advised of that. While it's not easy to tell anyone that they have been rejected, it's only fair to the applicant to do so as soon as possible. Recruiters have standard letters for informing candidates they will not be offered a job, but it's common to revise and personalize these letters, especially for candidates that have good qualifications—just not for this job or at this time. In fact, most recruiters will personally inform these candidates of the decision in addition to sending a letter. This keeps the door open if an opening that's a better match occurs later on.

It also ends the recruiting process on a positive note. Information Technology is a relatively small community, and programmers in a local area know each other. They quickly tell each other of both good and bad interviewing experiences, and anything that can be done to ensure "good press" is worth doing. In addition to telling the candidate of the decision, the recruiter has to document it. Companies have different requirements and forms for doing this, but it's necessary for legal reasons.

Probably the hardest decision to manage is putting someone on hold. Obviously, they are qualified or they would be rejected. The most common reason to put someone on hold is that there is a stronger candidate in the pipeline. Holds are also started, however, because of budget problems or a personal issue such as a sudden illness in the hiring manager's family. While the only thing that has to be done is notify the candidate, this can be difficult because the recruiter wants to keep the candidate interested knowing he or she is undoubtedly interviewing with other companies. A letter should be sent, but a personal phone call is important. Remember, these are good candidates.

Employment offers are most often made by phone with a follow-up letter. The recruiter goes over the basic job factors and looks for an oral acceptance. This way, if there are any objections, the recruiter can start negotiating. Because IT people often have several good jobs to choose from, negotiation is a very important part of the recruiting process.

9. Negotiating

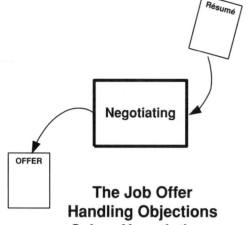

The Job Offer
Handling Objections
Salary Negotiations
Technical Candidates

Making an offer, or negotiation, while formally listed as a last step in recruiting, actually depends upon the exchange of information between the recruiter and the candidate throughout the entire process. Much of the actual negotiation is done during interviews, and many objections have already been answered. The recruiter prepares a job offer that includes the job title and a description of the job, start date, salary, location, benefits, and any conditional requirements. The information in the offer varies in depth from job to job. Job title and description can be very brief at this point, and a detailed job description can be provided when an offer is accepted. The job description should state whether the job is full- or part-time, a permanent position or a contract (and if so, for how long), and whether there is a probationary time period. Salary includes the annual salary and usually mentions how long it will be before a salary review. Location is important because so many companies have multiple locations. Benefits are often stated as "standard benefits package" but offers can specify unusual benefits. Finally, many job offers are conditional until certain requirements have been met. This can include educational verification, reference checking, drug testing, and passing a physical. Offers are often made over the phone, but should be confirmed in writing. Many times the confirmation is not sent until the candidate has informally accepted. Finally, all offers should have a deadline for acceptance.

Working with Offers

A job offer sounds definitive, but in fact everything in it is negotiable, and recruiters must know how much leverage they have in each area. Smaller companies really have an advantage here because their policies usually aren't as strict as those of larger companies, and it's much easier to negotiate by trading one benefit for another. Every offer does have some room for negotiation; it's important for the recruiter to be aware of what objections might come up, and know how to handle them. There could be room to change the specific factor causing the problem, but equally often the recruiter has to accept the negative and point out how it is balanced by another factor in the offer.

> **JOB OFFER**
> Job title and description
> Start Date
> Location
> Benefits
> Salary
> Conditional Requirements

Handling Objections

Even job title and description can create a difference of opinion that must be negotiated. If a candidate is questioning a job description when an offer is made, not enough information about the job has been provided throughout the recruiting process. After all the screens and interviews have been completed, there should be no questions about the job itself. Questions about the job title are often legitimate, because so many IT titles are inaccurate and really say nothing about the actual job. This is especially true with newer technologies such as the Internet. Webmaster is an ill-used title, as the people who use it have an incredible variety of skills. It started out as an expert title, and people seeing it assumed they were looking at a senior position or person. More recently the title is used for junior developers and Web support personnel, and a senior Web developer might not want to take a job with that title. It is usually seniors that question a title. Someone who has earned the title "Senior Programmer" might balk at accepting a job with the title "Programmer/Analyst." A nice solution to this objection is to change the title, but that's usually not an option. Admit that the title really isn't representative of the job and explain that job descriptions and titles are being reviewed (if true). Point out that the more junior title leaves room for promotion (if true). Or, most commonly, agree it's a bad title and point out that the salary is definitely a "senior" salary. This does assume that the title is indeed a problem, and the job really is a senior job. If the title accurately reflects the job level and the candidate thinks they are senior to it, better to find that out now.

Start date is sometimes firm, but usually jobs can be held for a length of time to allow people time to give notice at a present job, perhaps take a vacation between jobs, or even move if relocation is involved. Present the offer with the shortest time period between the offer and actual start. "We'd like to have you start tomorrow, but realistically can you start in two weeks?" is a good way to introduce the start date. If the candidate needs more time, the recruiter can give in gracefully and allow an additional week or two. In negotiation, every concession the recruiter makes contributes to making the candidate feel important and desired, and the start date is usually negotiable. Do be careful of how much time is allowed. Hires aren't complete until the candidate actually shows up for work, and the number of "I changed my mind" phone calls increases in direct proportion to the amount of time between the acceptance and the start date. Good candidates will be receiving other offers until they actually start work.

Training and orientation programs sometimes establish a final start date that is nonnegotiable; at least it seems that way. For the super candidate, anything can be worked out. Maybe the training can be accomplished over the Internet—or part time—or even waived (orientation type information) and replaced by a company information book and a really good mentor. Good technical candidates have no shortage of offers. Those with hard-to-find skills can write their own ticket and will simply go someplace else if their desires aren't met.

Location really can't be changed, so recruiters have to be prepared with every positive: good schools, close to skiing, little traffic (instead of "in the middle of nowhere"). Be sure to offer information on benefits such as telecommuting, job sharing, flex hours, and on-site gyms, dry cleaners, convenience stores. All these can balance an out-of-the-way location, but recruiters must be reasonable and cannot expect someone who loves city life to accept a job in the country. In fact, this would probably end up being a bad placement and the person would leave fairly soon.

Benefits are a highly competitive area and play a major part in negotiation. The usual objection is, of course, a missing benefit. For example, some companies offer dental insurance, others do not. Recruiters should know their own company's benefit package inside and out, but also know how it compares to competitors' packages. They don't need to know exactly what each competitor offers, but they do need to know if their own company plan is above or below standard. In addition, they need to know other corporate assets that can be used during negotiation. For example, many young people are concerned about the environment and knowing that a company sponsored a local river clean-up program is a definite selling point. Corporate recruiters have to work with their own company, agency recruiters often have to work with many clients. The easiest way to collect benefit information is by filling out a standard form early in the recruiting process. Corporate and consulting firm recruiters should get this information during their first week of work, and agency recruiters should fill out a form with each job requisition.

See: *Company/Client Analysis* on page 125.

Most companies offer the same fringe benefits—health insurance, life insurance, retirement plans, paid vacation, overtime pay, paid holidays, and regular salary increases. Benefit plans differ on exactly what is offered in each area, how much the company pays for, and how much the employee has to contribute. Different candidates will want different benefits. A parent of three school-age children wants a dental plan, a college graduate wants a quick salary increase. The parent wants life insurance, the college graduate wants more vacation. No plan is perfect for everyone, and the recruiter has to be able to point out the positives for each individual candidate. Explaining that the benefit plan is a flexible, or cafeteria, plan is a plus. With this type of plan, each employee has some choice among the benefits.

Often a "missing" benefit has to be balanced by some other factor in the job. Large companies have better benefit packages than do smaller ones; that's a known fact. Smaller companies give new hires more responsibility and independence. Not as well known, but that's also a fact. Many technical people would rather have the less-controlled work environment than the extra benefits.

Salary is undoubtedly the most negotiated of all job factors, and there are salary surveys available to help ensure an offer is in line with the standard wages. Given that, there is a big range of acceptable salaries for most technical jobs. And, the company wants to start the candidate at as low a salary as possible while the candidate wants to get as much as possible. Both the company and the candidate usually have a range in mind, and the best results occur when the company pays less than they were willing to pay and the candidate gets more than they were willing to accept. As long as the two ranges overlap, negotiation should be successful. If, however, the candidate's lowest figure (I'll accept $70,000) is higher than the job maximum (company's range is $50,000 to $64,000), chances are not good. The most important thing to realize when negotiating salary is that there's much more to consider than just the annual figure.

See: IT Salary Surveys on page 185.

Salary includes fringe benefits, bonuses, stock options, profit sharing plans, tuition reimbursement, and often-ignored benefits such as daycare facilities, a corporate gym, and early salary review. Many recruiters talk about the corporate cost of the benefit package (typically it's 35% of salary), but this is not really an effective negotiating tactic. Candidates know that they'll get these basic benefits in all but the smallest companies, so they're not impressed. What *is* effective is pointing out that day care for a single child would be $100 a week, so the corporate sponsored day care for the candidate's one-year-old twins is really an additional

$10,000 annually for the next three or four years. Concentrate on the financial value of the benefits that are unique to the company and are not likely to be matched by every other offer.

Many salary objections are a reaction to the starting salary and often result from a realistic look at expenses that might result from a job change. If the new job is in a different city, relocation expenses are quite obvious, but there are other new expenses even when the locality doesn't change. The candidate might lose vacation time, might have to cancel a planned event and lose deposit money, could have higher commuting costs, or even have to purchase a different wardrobe. A few questions can usually find the concerns and the recruiter can try to work with the problem. Most companies will allow a sign-on bonus for a good candidate. Another way to deal with objections to the starting salary is to point out a frequent, and substantial, salary review plan, completion bonuses, access to a corporate car for personal use—each company has its own pool of financial plusses.

See: *Negotiating Leverage* on page 188.

Counteroffers

Job changes are so common in Information Technology, that counteroffers seem to have become the norm rather than the exception. Companies are realizing the cost of replacing employees and are willing to spend at least the amount recruiting a new employee would cost on retaining the old one. This means that one of the last obstacles a recruiter might have to overcome is a counteroffer from the candidate's existing employer. Counteroffers can be very successful, because the company knows the other offers and always comes up with more.

Counteroffers seem to be common when the candidate was never really serious and was "testing the waters." The candidate is looking for ammunition to use in his or her next salary negotiation, but will stay where they are if possible. Recruiters agree that it's valid to be suspicious when the only reason given for leaving is salary. IT people are well paid, and, in fact, rarely leave a job simply to get more money. One way to thwart this behavior is to send acceptance rather than offer letters. Make offers over the phone, and do not confirm the offer in writing until the candidate has accepted. The letter now states very clearly that the individual has accepted another offer and cannot easily be brought back to the present company to use as leverage since it would be obvious that the candidate was playing one company against the other.

Recruiters simply ask the candidate how he or she would react to a counteroffer. It's an opportunity to discuss why the person is planning to leave and to point out that a counteroffer won't change the basic job environment. In fact, by initiating a discussion of counteroffers, recruiters can point out the negatives. Employers mentally start replacing the person who has submitted a resignation, even if the counteroffer is accepted. Trust is gone, and companies use counteroffers to build a transition time and no longer consider the person a valued member of the team. Even if the employee accepted the offer in good faith, the employer expects them to be gone within a year anyway. Tell your candidates that before they accept a counteroffer they should get the offer in writing with a one-year "no fire" contract. Most companies will refuse to do this, and the candidate will have a good idea of where they stand. Estimates have been made that over 80% of people who accept a counteroffer will leave the company within a year.

When candidates come back with counteroffers, remind them of their reasons for interviewing. Ask them if they think things in their present company have changed. Some counteroffers are valid, and these usually include a formal promotion or transfer to a different assignment. Companies do lose track of good employees, especially the quiet ones, and sometimes it takes a resignation to correct the situation. At any rate, if a good candidate honestly accepts a counteroffer, wish them the best and keep their number at hand. Call them when you have another opening they could fill, as few people accept counteroffers more than once.

Successful Closing

Some recruiters consistently get acceptances to their offers, while others frequently lose good candidates to other offers. The reason is simple. The successful recruiters spend time listening to the candidates and learning what is important to each individual. They get to know Information Technology people and learn how to communicate with them.

Generalizations can be dangerous, but there are a few that can be made about IT people. These are based on personality tests such as Myers-Briggs, analysis of computer jobs, and plain observation. First, and really undisputed, over 70% of IT people are thinkers, not feelers (Myers-Briggs). This means that they base their decisions on logic and fact, not value and feelings. The general populace is over 50% "feelers" so communicating with people who always find a logical answer to situations can be frustrating. This "logical approach" can cause interpersonal problems, and technical recruiters know that. Another indicator on the Myers-Briggs scale is extroverted/introverted. Again, while the general populace is almost evenly split between the two, over 70% of IT people are introverted and focus on ideas rather than people. Technical recruiters quickly learn that they must carefully develop questions that draw out introverted applicants. Usually giving them a chance to explain an intricate problem they worked on can break the ice.

Understanding computer jobs helps recruiters understand what will appeal to IT people. The word programming is often defined as "problem solving," and that's what attracts many people to an IT career. Problem solvers are attracted to the challenge, and also to the solution. They get completely caught up in what they're doing and will work day and night until they're finished. But finishing is important. IT people want to get an assignment, complete it, and move on to something new. IT is also a creative field where programmers and designers create a specific solution to a problem. Like all creative people, technical people want to share what they've done, and want appreciation for the uniqueness or originality of the finished program or system.

Simple observation points out some other generalizations. One, these people love their work! They love to do it, and they love to talk about it (although they prefer to talk to other computer professionals who will understand them). Next, they're focused and don't like to waste time. The typical IT department is from three to ten years behind in its work, which means that everyone on staff has a lot to do. They'll spend hours analyzing a new testing product, but don't ask them to go to lunch with the software salesman.

Finally, IT people aren't necessarily motivated by money, as strange as that sounds. Remember these people make a lot of money. There are other things that are more important. In general, IT people's goals according to experience are:

Juniors: (1) Money, and (2) Technology
Mids: (1) Technology, (2) Growth and (3) Money
Seniors: (1) Technology, (2) Growth, (3) Respect, and (4) Status

The most important thing to an IT professional is the technical environment. Second most important is the opportunity for technical growth—which translates to learning new technologies. A book allowance and/or paid-for technical magazine subscriptions is a strong selling point. The biggest concern of IT people is getting stuck working with systems and falling behind technically. While recruiters must be completely honest in describing the work environment, whatever can be presented that is state-of-the art helps. Even if the specific job that is being offered does not include Internet applications, promising an applicant that there is an excellent chance that will be the next assignment is a plus—just make sure it's true. IT people expect training, and growth opportunities can best be proven by telling applicants about training that typically is provided. A company with a good training program definitely has a hiring edge. Because training is so expensive, and computer people change jobs so often, many companies make employees sign a contract to repay the cost of the training if they leave within a year. Recruiters must be open about this, but this rarely is a negative. People who accept a new job aren't thinking about leaving, so they won't be worried about such a contract.

All of these points are used by technical recruiters in describing the jobs they are offering, and by mentioning any of them the recruiter shows that he or she understands the needs of technical people. It is still most important to listen to the individual. Everyone has his or her own hot button, and only by listening can a recruiter find out what an applicant wants. For some it might be having an office. Most IT people work in cubicles, and some reach a point in their careers where they just want an office to themselves with no "cube-mate." A programmer might be really pleased with getting business cards. There's probably no real use for them and the cards end up dropped in restaurant fish bowls to win a free lunch, but the cards indicate that the company thinks of the programmer as a professional, and this is important to everyone. The successful recruiter listens to everything to find the one thing that will make a candidate accept this offer.

10. College Recruiting

Technical jobs require initial training; and Computer Science, MIS, or Information Technology graduates are attractive candidates for entry-level positions. Many companies and consulting firms have specific recruiters who handle college recruitment because of its specific processing requirements. First of all, college recruiting is incredibly competitive, especially in the field of Information Technology. Large companies, especially technology companies, have been active on campus for many years, and college recruiters must compete with the best-known companies in the country. Another part of a college recruiter's job is the travel. College recruiters visit schools—they go to the applicants on a regular schedule, while most other recruiters don't travel at all. The next specific for college recruiting is that "job requisition" is the same for all applicants, but questioning is different. College recruiters fill two jobs; they look for entry-level applications programmers and entry-level technical programmers, so recruiters don't have to spend as much time understanding the job requisition. They do, however, have to spend time developing different questions. While general recruiting concentrates on work experience, college students have very little work experience to offer. Therefore, questions must be developed that probe an applicant's abilities—not experience. Finally, college students and recent graduates tend to have different interests than people who have been in the work force for a few years. Recruiters must learn what is important to each student so they can present their opportunities positively.

> **COLLEGE RECRUITING**
> Highly Competitive
> Travel
> Entry-level Positions
> Campus Interviews
> Interests and Problems

Competition for College Graduates

The first thing college recruiters learn is that they are in a highly competitive environment. The average college graduate receives 2.5 job offers, and IT graduates often receive offers from a dozen different companies. Specifics about the company, its image, and its reputation are determining factors in whether an applicant will consider an offer. The jobs tend to be very much alike as all entry-level jobs are, so graduates make job decisions based on other factors. Therefore college recruiters are often more involved in marketing-type activities when building materials and information to take to the schools.

The usual printed corporate brochures are used, of course, but they all tend to look alike, and many companies are using technology to create a more interesting look. They are creating CD-ROMs that describe the company, its products and services, list its customers, and describe the work environment and culture. Many of these CDs contain FAQ (Frequently Asked Question) sections, and all contain complete information on how to contact the company for job opportunities. In addition to having the CDs to hand out, companies can also have a running video to attract students who didn't sign up for an interview, and enough CDs on hand to accommodate new interest. CDs work the other way too. The vast majority of college students are used to the Internet, and use e-mail as their favorite means of communication, so recruiters should establish e-mail as the methodology for all further communication. In addition, many, if not most, students will present a résumé on disk or CD, and recruiters have to be able to handle any electronic résumé.

While recruiters might not be involved in building the corporate Web site, it is important that a company doing college recruiting have an attractive, functioning and informative Internet presence. College students are Internet-savvy and most look up companies on the Web to decide whether to interview or not. A running video might attract a student who had not considered this company, but if he or she goes to a Web site that is slow or has errors, interest will quickly disappear. Students will conclude that a company that has trouble with its Web site is not a good place for a technical person to work.

Travel

Unlike most recruiting which consists of an applicant coming to the recruiter to be interviewed, with college recruiting, the recruiter must travel. Most schools have published schedules for campus visits, and companies send representatives on the appropriate days. Colleges run their own version of a "job fair" with companies setting up booths or tables and students roaming from table to table asking questions and taking literature. This is, however, only part of a college fair. When scheduling corporate visits, most schools publish a list of attending companies, and students schedule interviews ahead of time. These interviews are short, usually fifteen to thirty minutes in length, and both interviewers and applicants schedule one interview after another so these interviews don't run long.

It's important for the recruiter to make contact with the school's placement office, and this can usually be done sometime during scheduled events. It's important to build a personal relationship with the people in the placement office, as they regularly recommend companies to students. The office should have appropriate information, including CDs and video tapes, if available. Recruiters can also work with local alumni associations, sororities and fraternities. These organizations often provide job placement and career counseling services to graduates and most will post job openings in newsletters and at meetings. The alumni associations provide a source of experienced, as well as entry-level, technical candidates.

Job Requisitions for Entry-level Positions

Entry-level positions really have very standard requisitions since every college graduate that is hired will start as an entry-level developer—either applications or technical. Logistics can be more complicated than with general recruiting, as many companies have a special training program for entry-level IT hires. These programs include corporate orientation sessions but also may include additional technical training. Some of these programs are months long and are conducted at a different location from the actual job so the recruiter must know specific details about both the training program and the actual job. Job requirements are usually simple and most insist that the applicant actually graduate, as the job offers are usually made before the school year is over.

The other part of the requisition, the technical skill set, is usually quite flexible. Recruiters will have a set of skills covering the major technical areas (development, platforms, data management, and communications), but rarely insist on a specific skill. C/C++ is the most common development language, but Java is gaining in popularity on campuses, so most recruiters will accept either. Companies know they will have to provide some training for entry-level hires because skill sets vary so much.

College recruiters quickly know the jobs they are filling and the type of person to look for. All they are usually given in terms of a requisition is the number of people required.

Campus Interviews

Interviews set up on campus last from fifteen to thirty minutes and are really quite different from regular employment interviews. The purpose of a campus interview is to select and entice students to come on-site for an in-depth interview. The questions that are asked are different, because the applicants have lots of training, but little to no experience. College recruiters must develop questions to determine what educational behaviors will be indicative of a good employee. Behavioral questions are rarely used for two reasons. First, they're harder to develop because the candidate cannot answer with examples of instances from work, so the recruiter has to make sure that the question creates a situation that would be meaningful at work. It certainly can be done, a question like, "Describe a time when you had a group project to be completed and one of the group members was holding the rest of the group back," can give a good picture of interpersonal skills that will carry into the workplace. The second reason is even stronger. Behavioral questions can be difficult to answer and often make applicants uncomfortable. College recruiting is so competitive that an uncomfortable question will be enough for the student to scratch the company off his or her list.

See: *College Interview Questions* on page 182.

In traditional interviews, the interviewer is gathering information to see if the person is qualified while providing information to interest the candidate in the job. Most of the interview is spent qualifying the person; less time is spent selling the job. The reverse is true in campus interviews. Most of the interview is spent answering the student's questions, and the recruiter has to be thoroughly versed in the company's benefits and policies. The recruiter must also know what the competition is offering in order to make the best presentation possible. Recruiters should be prepared to answer questions about how other graduates have progressed within the company and should have names and histories of previously hired graduates—and permission to use them as contacts!

Interests and Problems

College students and recent graduates can have different interests and problems than experienced people, and learning their needs and responding to them is important. They are often very interested in career paths, but unconcerned with most standard benefits. Talking to college students about retirement accounts is a waste of time, as they don't think that far in the future. Students are also aware that changing jobs is the norm and assume that they will be working somewhere else when retirement comes around. Some graduates want international work and/or travel, and others who are financially astute want real equity in the company. Microsoft has attracted top talent for many years by offering stock options—and lower salaries.

Students are also concerned about the work atmosphere. They generally want an informal atmosphere, and dress codes will cause an immediate lack of interest. They are very interested in whom they will be working with and are looking for an exciting, creative environment. A mentor, or coach, program is a big plus as it shows corporate interest in the individual. Some graduates want to be assured that they will have at least some control of their assignments and can make decisions while others are idealistic and will take a job with a company that is active in the community or proactive in helping the environment. Another major interest is training, and students will accept an offer because of the training opportunities. Companies who have internal training programs or can show a strong training budget definitely have an edge.

Students also have unique problems. Many are nervous about leaving home for the first time and will be attracted by the possibility of business trips or extra compensation that can make visits home possible. One of the most common problems is getting an apartment in a new city, and the company that offers assistance in finding apartments and a "sign-on" bonus that will cover first month's rent and security deposit is way ahead. Many students are seriously involved with someone, and will only accept an offer if their significant other also has a job.

Each company has a different way of responding to these interests and the college recruiter has to know what every company offers. When asked what the most important facet of a job was, computer science graduates listed enjoying what they did as most important, followed by the opportunity to use their skills and abilities, and third, opportunity for personal development. Companies can use these facts to build a recruitment package focusing on college students and graduates.

11. Recruiting Software and Services

There are many services and software packages available to assist recruiters throughout the entire recruiting process, and more is available on an almost daily basis. Products range from simple scheduling programs to complete HRIS (Human Resources Information System) packages that interface with the corporate ERP system. These systems also operate in many ways. First, software can be purchased and then installed on in-house systems. These products usually have a unique interface and often require training. Many products are now offering a Web-based option, which means any Web browser can be used to access the system, so at least there's no training needed to learn the interface. This software can be installed on a corporate intranet, or often is available as a Web-hosted service. Web-hosted systems are really services in that the software runs on the vendor's systems and is accessed through the Internet. Companies purchase memberships, subscriptions, or licenses on a monthly or annual basis. Vendors who provide such services offer a range of support, varying from providing access and technical support if problems occur, to establishing an account with personal service on any number of functions. Companies can use these services to outsource most of the recruiting process, up to and including in-depth interviews.

> See: *General Recruiting Software* on page 183.
> *Web-Hosted Systems and Services* on page 174.

Recruiters use the standard software provided by the company including organizational tools, database, and word processing software. Organizational tools are included with each personal computer, but companies often provide additional software which recruiters use to keep their schedules, address books, and reminder notes. Database software is very important as technical recruiters keep their own personal database of contacts for networking. Even though information is entered into a departmental or corporate applicant database, a personal database is used to keep track of personal relationships that the recruiter has built. Personal information such as birthdays and hobbies can be recorded to personalize contacts, and this database is the first place recruiters look when receiving a job requirement. Recruiters usually use whatever database the corporation provides, and Microsoft's Access is most common. And finally, recruiters write a lot! They send thank you letters, offer letters, reject letters, etc. etc. etc. Even though more and more correspondence is sent via e-mail, recruiters write sample letters that can be revised for the individual situation and mailed or copied into an e-mail message. Again, most recruiters simply use the available word processor and Microsoft's Word is the most common.

In addition to the standard software, there are many recruiting packages which offer a range of capabilities.

Staffing Industry Software

There are many software systems that have been written for the staffing industry—employment agencies and consulting firms. These systems usually work with the entire recruiting process, and include additional functions particular to dealing with third party recruiting. That is, recruiting for a different company. In addition to dealing with permanent hires for a single company, staffing industry software must work with different companies, multiple contacts, and short term assignments. Employment agencies and consulting firms can, of course, use the general recruiting software written for all companies.

See: *Software for the Staffing Industry* on page 194.

Résumé Processing

Résumé processing software is used to handle and standardize the résumés received. These packages usually offer a scanning capability, and most of them will work with e-mail, fax and scanned résumés. The software stores and indexes the résumés for later searching. Some of these systems will also send acknowledgement letters or e-mails when résumés are received. Additional functions that might be included are skills analysis, statistical analysis for EEO reports, and résumé routing to hiring managers and other interested parties. Many of these systems will interface with, or input information, to applicant tracking or complete HRIS systems.

Applicant Tracking

Applicant tracking systems start with résumé processing functions, but continue providing support through the entire recruiting process. These systems are database systems, and applicant information is entered when the résumé is received. This then provides the basic information necessary to track the applicant through screening, interviewing, and reference and background checking. These systems have communications features and provide letters or e-mails for many recruiting functions, eg. An automatic "thank you" letter or e-mail will be sent to applicants when a résumé arrives. These systems also track the job requisition, and provide information on the history of each opening by noting the number of résumés received, the number and dates—and results—of interviews. A complete applicant tracking system records information until the applicant is either hired, rejected, or turns down a job. Many applicant tracking systems will interface with HRIS

(Human Resource Information System) and/or ERP (Enterprise Resource Planning) systems.

Applicant tracking systems are available in any format. Systems can be purchased and run in-house on corporate systems. Another options is purchasing a system that is Web-based, which can be run on a corporate intranet. Companies can outsource recruiting record-keeping by subscribing to Web-hosted systems. And, finally, companies can outsource much of the recruiting process by hiring companies to not just track information, but actually do the screening, interviewing, and reference and background checking.

Web Posting

Software is available to post jobs to the Internet. Recruiters define jobs through a standard interface, and the software then formats and posts the job. Some of this software simply posts the job to the corporate Web site and is used simply because the standard interface makes job posting simple and this task can be done even by administrators. In addition to posting to the corporate Web site, some posting software also posts to other sites, mostly free job banks. This software gets more sophisticated, and some will also post to fee-based job banks that you have an account with, and charge you accordingly. Most of this software is both Web-based and Web-hosted.

See: *Job-Posting Services* on page 172.

HRIS Systems (Human Resources Information Systems)

These are complete packages that cover all human resources functions including such things as benefits administration and attendance processing. Some of these systems even include payroll processing. Recruiting function are not always included, but many of the available applicant tracking systems will provide interfaces. Also called HRMS (Human Resource Management Systems).

Part Two

Forms

This section contains forms, in alphabetical order, used throughout the recruiting process. Accompanying each form is an explanation of its purpose and uses. Also provided is instructions for filling out the form and explanations of the data that is recorded. Forms can be used "as is" or modified for individual use.

Overview and Instructions

OVERVIEW

This form is used to summarize information about a candidate, record any activity with the candidate, and provide a history of that activity. The top of the form provides a quick reference to the candidate's availability and logistical considerations. This information can be obtained from the résumé, phone screens, or interviews. The Applicant Tracking section is used to show where in the recruiting process the candidate is and to provide a history of the recruiting activity on each candidate. Recording the date of each activity provides this information. This form always shows where in the process a candidate is, and it can be used to review the recruiting process for any candidate.

INSTRUCTIONS

1. Candidate's name.
2. Date form is filled out.
3. Position applied for, if known. If application is not for a specific position, use N/A or a job type (eg., "programmer" or "support").
4. If permanent hire, use the department to which the candidate will be applying. If consulting or contract, use the client's name, if known.
5. What is the main thing the candidate is interested in (eg., technology, flex time, training)?
6. When will the candidate be available?
7. Is candidate willing to travel? If yes, how much of the time? Include any restrictions.
8. Is candidate willing to relocate?
9. Is candidate looking for overtime pay, or comp time for overtime?
10. Does candidate have a present employment agreement that must be considered? Include non-compete considerations.
11. How long is a current contractual obligation, if any?
12. Current salary.
13. Desired salary.
14. How interested is the candidate?

APPLICANT CONTROL

1. Applicant:_____ 2. Date: _____

3. Position applied for: _____ 4. Department: _____

5. Goals/looking for: _____ 6. Availability: _____

7. Travel: _____ 8. Relocation: _____

9. Overtime:_____ 10. Employee agreement:_____

11. Contractual obligations: _____ 12. Current salary: _____

13. Desired salary: _____ 14. Interest level: _____

Comments:_____

_____

_____

APPLICANT TRACKING

ACTIVITY	DATE
Résumé received	
Phone call/screen conducted	
Visual interview scheduled	
Visual interview conducted	
Offer/reject determined — letter sent	
References checked/received	
Hire negotiations started	
Offer accepted/declined	
Relocation approved	
Follow-up administration completed	

▰▰▰▰▰ APPLICANT EVALUATION ▰▰▰▰▰

Overview and Instructions

OVERVIEW

This form is used to summarize an interviewer's impressions of a candidate after an interview. It is usually used after an in-person interview, but can be used at any time. If used after a phone interview, that should be indicated on the form. The form should be filled out by each interviewer including the managers and/or technical people also doing interviews. The form can be used as the basis for a discussion about the candidate.

INSTRUCTIONS

1. Circle one for each factor.
2. Note what you felt were the candidate's strengths. This could be one of the factors from question #1, but could be something completely different (eg., Candidate is immediately available).
3. Concerns could also reflect a factor in #1 or be completely different. Also, concerns could simply be nonspecific (eg., I think candidate is hiding something).
4. Circle one.
5. Circle hire or reject, or state a referral. The candidate could be referred for another job, a different department, or a different client.

APPLICANT EVALUATION

Applicant: _____   Interview Date: _____

Position/Title: _____   Department: _____

1. Please circle the appropriate rating where:

5 = Excellent	2 = Below average	
4 = Very good	1 = Unacceptable	
3 = Average	N = Not observed	

Relevant experience	5	4	3	2	1	N
Attention to detail	5	4	3	2	1	N
Required technical skills	5	4	3	2	1	N
Interpersonal skills	5	4	3	2	1	N
Enthusiasm	5	4	3	2	1	N
Initiative	5	4	3	2	1	N
Integrity	5	4	3	2	1	N
Interest in travel	5	4	3	2	1	N
Interest in relocation	5	4	3	2	1	N

2. Strengths: _____

_____

_____

_____

_____

3. Concerns: _____

_____

_____

_____

_____

4. Overall impression (Circle one):

Exceptional   Strong   Capable   Weak   Very Weak

5. Recommendation (Circle one):

Hire   Reject   Refer: _____

Signed: _____   Date: _____
    (Interviewer)

APPLICANT PROFILE

Overview and Instructions

OVERVIEW

The Applicant Profile is used when doing a general screen, which is screening an applicant without a specific job in mind. Its purpose is to build a profile so the applicant can be considered for many jobs, and the form is filled out during, or immediately after, the screening.

INSTRUCTIONS

BACKGROUND

1. Applicant's name.
2. Home phone, work phone (only if it's okay to contact applicant at work).
3. E-mail address.
4. Location of résumé. Possibilities include: don't have, being sent, in file (state what file), in database (state what database).
5. How the applicant's name and/or résumé was obtained. Date the contact was made.
6. Name of person doing the screening, since different recruiters might work with this applicant as different jobs come up. Date of the screening.

REQUIREMENTS

This section is used to record those things the applicant says are critical in order for them to consider taking a job. Not all fields will be filled out, as each applicant has different requirements, if any. This information can be determined by asking if there are any restrictions in the following areas:

1. Job type means full-time, part-time, work-at-home, etc.
2. Some applicants can only work certain hours because of, eg., child care.
3. State the maximum travel the applicant will do, including "none."
4. Fill in "no" if the applicant will not relocate
5. Often this is not determined during a screening, but if it is, state the absolute minimum salary.
6. Often there are additional financial requirements, eg., some candidates require that an expected performance bonus be matched as a hire bonus if they are to change jobs. Another example is insisting that relocation expenses be paid.
7. Applicants often insists that a job offer must match existing earned vacation time.
8. State any legal requirements for aliens.
9. Personal circumstances might require medical coverage.
10. Anything else the applicant might have stated.

"Personal circumstances" is used for anything that might affect the applicants ability to take a given job. This includes such things as physical handicaps that require no stairs and personal responsibilities such as child or parent care requiring flexible hours.

TECHNICAL DESCRIPTION

Core Description   Technical Skills
1–3. Check one.   1–5. List the key skills in each area.

NOTES

Use for anything that came up during the screen that would be part of a placement decision. Continue on back if necessary.

SemCo Enterprises, Inc.

APPLICANT PROFILE

BACKGROUND

1. Applicant: _____   2. Phone: _____

3. E-mail: _____   4. Résumé: _____

5. Contacted: _____   Date: _____

6. Screened by: _____   Date: _____

REQUIREMENTS

Fill in only if applicant has nonnegotiable requirements in the following areas:

1. Job type: _____   2. Hours: _____

3. Travel: _____   4. Relocation: _____

5. Minimum salary: _____   6. Other financial requirements: _____

7. Vacation: _____   8. Green card: _____

9. Medical Insurance: _____   10. Other: _____

Personal Circumstances: _____

_____

_____

_____

TECHNICAL DESCRIPTION

Core Description:

1. Job Type: Application developer ○   Technical developer ○   Support ○

2. Environment: Large ○   Midsize ○   Desktop ○

3. Experience: Senior ○   Mid ○   Junior ○

Technical Skills:

1. Platforms: _____

2. Development: _____

3. Data Management: _____

4. Communications (Online): _____

5. Applications: _____

NOTES:

_____

_____

AUTHORIZATION FOR REFERENCE CHECK

Overview and Instructions

OVERVIEW

This form can be mailed to candidate's references or filled out during a phone reference check. Phone checks usually get better results, but the written form has the candidate's signed release. Recruiters can fax the signed form to the reference, but gather the information during a phone reference check.

INSTRUCTIONS

Have the candidate fill out the top, or authorization, part of the form. If the form is mailed, be sure to include a stamped, self-addressed, return envelope.

1. Often this information is obtained from the Human Resources Department. You might have to make two calls.
2. Get as much information as you can. If you can, determine whether termination was voluntary or not.

(continued on page 123)

SemCo Enterprises, Inc.

AUTHORIZATION FOR REFERENCE CHECK

To: _____ (Individual name)

_____ (Company name)

I am applying for work at (your company name) and authorize you to provide (your company name) with information concerning my employment with you, including, but not limited to, the questions on this form. I release you from any liability for damages regarding this information.

Information about my employment with you:

Name: _____

Position: _____ SSN: _____

Employment dates: From _____ To _____

Signature: _____ Date: _____

Any information furnished about the above applicant will be treated with strict confidentiality. No applicant will be accepted or rejected based on a single reference. A self-addressed, stamped envelope is enclosed for your convenience.

Thank you.

(your name)
(your company)

1. Date of hire: _____ Date of termination: _____

   Beginning salary: _____ Ending salary: _____

   Beginning position: _____ Ending position: _____

2. Reason for termination: _____

   _____

   _____

3. Please rate the applicant in the following areas:

	Unacceptable	Substandard	Standard	Very good	Excellent
Attention to detail					
Technical skills					
Interpersonal skills					
Cooperation with supervisors					
Cooperation with co-workers					
Enthusiasm					
Willingness to assume new responsibility					
Ability to work under pressure					
Initiative					
Learning ability					
Overall evaluation					

4. Would you rehire this person? _____   If not, please explain. _____

_____

_____

_____

_____

_____

_____

_____

_____

Comments: _____

_____

_____

_____

_____

_____

_____

_____

Signature: _____ Title: _____ Date: _____

AUTHORIZATION FOR REFERENCE CHECK

Overview and Instructions

INSTRUCTIONS (*CONT.*)

3. Check the appropriate response to each factor. Use the comment area to record any specifics or extra information on any factor that the reference offered.
4. Yes or No to rehire. The explanation might also be positive information about rehiring.

Overview and Instructions

OVERVIEW

This form is used to provide an overview of a company or a client in order to be able to positively appraise candidates of assets the job offer will include. Used to negotiate a hire.

For permanent hires, it should be filled out for the company doing the hiring and perhaps for a branch, if specific branches have different things to offer. This information can then be used to explain why the candidate should choose your company over other offers.

For consulting and contract jobs, it should be filled out for each client company. When dealing with client companies, often the best place to get this information is from Human Resources, not the Technical Department. This information can be used both to help convince a candidate to take an offer and also to fit the candidate with the best company.

INSTRUCTIONS

Company Data
1. Company or client company name.
2. Industry such as banking, manufacturing, government, etc.
3. Check one to indicate the operational range of the company or client company.
4. Fill in either, or both, if known.

Assets
1. Check yes, if the company name is a selling point.
2. If yes, write in specifics.
3. Yes or No.
4. Check yes for on-site child care. Jot down particulars (eg., ages, times).
5. If yes, write down particulars (eg., doctor or nurse, hours).
6. If yes, write down particulars.
7. If yes, indicate required core hours.
8. If yes, who is eligible, specifics about dates, times, routes?
9. If yes, what are requirements to report to the office, if any?
10–11. Yes or No.
12. If yes, what are the rules? Check for casual Fridays only.
13. This covers both technical training and tuition reimbursement plans. Indicate if technical training must be paid back when employee doesn't work for a stated length of time.
14. If yes, which ones? What are qualifications?
15–16. Yes or No.
17. If yes, what are the rules, monetary limits?

Salaries/Benefits Package
1–7. Check off appropriate level for each factor. Write in what makes an item above or below standard (eg., must work five years to reach three-weeks vacation is below standard). Standard means local standard.

COMPANY/CLIENT ANALYSIS

Company Data

1. Company Name: _____

2. Industry: _____ No. of branches: _____

3. Location (check one):   Local _____ Regional _____ National _____ International _____

4. Size: Annual revenue: _____ No. of employees: _____

ASSETS	YES	NO
1. Known company name/reputation (eg., Microsoft, IBM)	____	____
2. Ethical, moral issues (matching charity contributions, environmental concerns)	____	____
3. Involvement in local community	____	____
4. Child-care provisions	____	____
5. On-premises nurse/doctor/health care	____	____
6. Physical training options (on-site gym, corporate subscription to a gym)	____	____
7. Flex hours	____	____
8. Company-owned van/bus service	____	____
9. Work-at-home option	____	____
10. Allow you to network your home computer system with work	____	____
11. Provide you with a computer system to use at home	____	____
12. Casual dress code	____	____
13. Provide training	____	____
14. Send employees to technical conferences	____	____
15. 401k plan	____	____
16. Supply business cards	____	____
17. Supply credit card	____	____

SALARIES/BENEFITS PACKAGE	STANDARD	BELOW STANDARD	ABOVE STANDARD
1. Salary levels	_____	_____	_____
2. Increase policies	_____	_____	_____
3. Vacation policy	_____	_____	_____
4. Overtime/comp time	_____	_____	_____
5. Retirement plans	_____	_____	_____
6. Life insurance	_____	_____	_____
7. Health insurance	_____	_____	_____

INTERVIEWER EVALUATION

Overview and Instructions

OVERVIEW

This form can be used for both self-evaluation and by a second party. It can be used for self-evaluation at the end of any interview. The recruiter runs through and does a quick check reflecting the parts of the interview he or she felt either went well or not. Recruiters can invite a peer to sit in on an interview and conduct a peer review using this form. (Don't worry about the candidate thinking the recruiter is being reviewed—the candidate typically thinks the second recruiter is in training and is simply observing.) A review of this form prior to an interview also reminds recruiters of what to concentrate on.

INSTRUCTIONS

None.

 SemCo Enterprises, Inc.

INTERVIEWER EVALUATION

Interviewer: _____   Date: _____

Evaluator: _____

	NEEDS WORK	SATISFACTORY	EXCELLENT
INTRODUCTION			
1. Establish rapport	_____	_____	_____
2. Move smoothly past introduction	_____	_____	_____
OBTAINING VALID INFORMATION			
1. Ask open-ended questions	_____	_____	_____
2. Follow through on answers	_____	_____	_____
3. Avoid leading questions	_____	_____	_____
4. Avoid telegraphing own feelings	_____	_____	_____
5. Control the interview	_____	_____	_____
6. Get applicant to speak freely	_____	_____	_____
7. Listen carefully	_____	_____	_____
8. Obtain adequate job information	_____	_____	_____
9. Obtain adequate other information	_____	_____	_____
PROVIDING INFORMATION			
1. Describe job adequately	_____	_____	_____
2. Provide company's background	_____	_____	_____
3. Present job and company positively	_____	_____	_____
4. Encourage applicant to ask questions	_____	_____	_____
CLOSING THE INTERVIEW			
1. Control when the interview ended	_____	_____	_____
2. Inform applicant of next step	_____	_____	_____
3. Leave applicant with positive feeling	_____	_____	_____
4. Make appropriate notes afterwards	_____	_____	_____

▰▰▰▰▰▰▰ INTERVIEW GUIDE ▰▱▱▱▱▱

Overview and Instructions

OVERVIEW

This four-page form acts as a guide to conducting the interview. It breaks the interview down into six areas. Each area should be covered during interviewing, but often different areas are covered during different interviews; therefore, the form has room to indicate interviewer and date on each page. For example, some of the questions could be asked during a phone screen by one interviewer, who then turns the form over to another recruiter, who conducts the in-person interview. The second recruiter can see exactly what the phone interview covered. The actual questions listed on the form are samples of questions that fit in each area and in all cases there are many questions that could be substituted.

INSTRUCTIONS

I. Opening

Nothing need be recorded here as the opening of the interview is used to put the candidate at ease. Room to record information about hobbies and personal activities is provided, because often answers here can provide information about managerial or leadership talents.

II. Education

The specific educational information can be obtained from the résumé, but questions about educational performance and decisions (eg., Why did you choose that school?) can tell you a lot about a candidate's approach to learning. As Information Technology is a field that constantly requires learning new things, a candidate's attitude towards education is important.

III. Intangible Factors

Personal characteristics: Questions here are intended to determine such things as a candidate's drive, sense of responsibility, and initiative. You should have an idea of what personal qualities are most important based on your knowledge of either the person the candidate would report to if hired, the company the person would be working for, or the other people you know that are working in that situation. If you are doing general interviews and have no specific knowledge of the job the candidate would end up doing, record this information so you have it when a specific job is being considered.

Goals and motivation: Questions here are to both determine the candidate's level of ambition, organization and personal planning, and also to find out what is most important to the candidate. This information is very important, as it will be used during negotiation, if you decide to make a job offer.

(continued on page 133)

Interview Guide

Date: _____ Interviewer: _____

Applicant Information

Name: _____

Phone: _____ Fax: _____ E-mail: _____

Position: _____ Department: _____

I. OPENING

Rapport building:

1. How were your directions, did you have any trouble getting here?

2. Would you like coffee, water, etc.?

3. What do you think of the weather? What do you do when the weather turns nice/bad?

4. I see you listed _____ as a hobby. Would you tell me something about it?

   _____

II. EDUCATION

High school and technical school graduates:

1. How were your overall grades? _____

2. In what extracurricular activities did you participate? _____

3. Have you acquired additional education since leaving high school? _____
   What? _____

4. What was the first significant job you held after leaving school? _____

Some college and college graduates:

1. What school did you attend? _____
   Why did you select that school? _____

   _____

2. What was your major? _____
   Why did you choose it? _____

3. What were your overall college grades? _____

4. In what types of extracurricular activities did you participate? _____

   _____

5. What were your vocational plans when you were at college? _____

6. If they are different now, when did you change your thinking? _____
   Why? _____

   _____

Date: _____ Interviewer: _____

III. INTANGIBLE FACTORS

Personal characteristics:

1. Describe a situation when you had to make a quick decision:_____
   _____

2. How do you keep track of the projects you are working on? _____
   _____

3. What have you done to prepare yourself for a better job? _____
   _____

4. How do you handle fault-finders? _____
   _____

5. Describe a situation when you felt like giving up on a task and what you eventually did: ____
   _____

6. What did you do to prepare for this interview? _____
   _____

Goals and motivation:

1. What aspects of a job are most important to you? _____
   _____

2. What are your career goals, short-term and long-term? _____
   _____

3. What factors in the past have contributed most to your growth? _____
   _____

4. What factors do you believe may have handicapped you from moving ahead more rapidly? __
   _____

5. When did you decide to enter this field?_____

6. What influenced you to make this decision? _____

7. How would a job with our company meet your career objectives? _____
   _____

8. What are your present earnings expectations? _____
   How did you arrive at this figure? _____

9. How likely are you to make a move at this time: ____ Somewhat ____ Possibly ____ Extremely

10. Are you interviewing with other companies? _____ Who? _____
    _____

Date: _____ Interviewer: _____

IV. GENERAL JOB FACTORS

Complete Section IV for as many jobs as you feel should be covered.

1. You worked for: _____

   For how long? _____

2. Responsibilities and duties at this job: _____

3. Major accomplishments: _____

4. Biggest setback/disappointment: _____

5. Describe your progress at this company: _____

   If progress was significant: To what do you attribute this? _____

   If progress was not impressive: How did you attempt to overcome this? _____

6. What was the most valuable experience you obtained in this job? _____

7. Why did you leave (plan to leave) this company? _____

8. Would you return to work for them if asked? _____

9. If you could change one factor about the job, what would you change? _____

   _____

V. JOB PERFORMANCE AND ATTITUDES

1. How would you describe the most effective superior you have had? _____

   _____

   What were his or her strengths? _____

   Limitations? _____

2. Tell me about a significant problem you encountered on the job: _____

   _____

   How did you approach it? _____

   _____

3. What do you like best about your work? _____

   What do you like least? _____

4. How do you motivate yourself? _____

   _____

5. How would you describe your energy level? _____

Date: _____   Interviewer: _____

VI. TECHNICAL ISSUES

Technical strengths:

1. Please explain the following skills (skills listed in the résumé that you don't recognize): ____
   _____

2. Which of the skills listed on your résumé would you list as your four main skills?
   A. _____ B. _____ C. _____ D. _____

3. For each of these, please rate yourself on a scale of 1–4 where:

4 = Superior	2 = Below average
3 = Above average	1 = Light

   A. _____ B. _____ C. _____ D. _____

4. For each of these, what project(s) did you work on that required use of the skill?
   A. _____ B. _____ C. _____ D. _____
   A. _____ B. _____ C. _____ D. _____

Specific areas:

1. Systems analysts: How much client contact did you have? _____

   Describe your client meetings including identifying other participants from IT: _____

2. Programmers: How independently did you work? _____
   _____

   What proportion of your time did you spend on analysis _____, design _____,
   programming _____, testing _____, implementation _____?

   Which of the above aspects of programming do you like best and why? _____
   _____

   Which do you like least and why? _____
   _____

   How do (or would) you like working in a team setting? _____

3. Project Managers: Describe your personnel management duties and responsibilities: _____
   _____

   Are you responsible for maintaining a project budget? _____ If yes, how much? _____

   How many direct reports do you have? _____

   Describe how you scheduled a project including what tools you used: _____
   _____

   What do you like most about management? _____
   _____

   What do you like least? _____

Overview and Instructions

INSTRUCTIONS (*CONT.*)

IV. General Job Factors

This section records information about specific jobs and job performance. Use extra paper to repeat the section for as many jobs as you feel are important. As a general rule, experience over five years old is not important, and nontechnical experience is only important if it shows initiative, managerial traits, etc.

V. Job Performance and Attitudes

This section is still asking questions about job performance, but these questions do not necessarily relate to a specific job but instead are general questions. These questions also refer to personal characteristics and the information obtained here should be used to help find the best candidate/position fit.

VI. Technical Issues

While a recruiting interview is not a technical interview, one of the things it provides is a technical screen to determine if the candidate should be passed on to the next step—which usually includes the technical interview. The technical questions should be based on the résumé and are used to determine the candidate's key skills and experience. Candidates list many skills on résumés and one of the purposes of the interview is to determine the candidate's technical strengths. When interviewing for a specific job, have the candidate talk about the required skills. For general interviews, ask the candidate to identify his or her strengths and talk about those. Technical jobs rarely require more than four key skills, and those are the ones you want to talk about.

▰▰▰▰▰▰ JOB-POSTING RECORD ▰▰▰▰▰

Overview and Instructions

OVERVIEW

This form is used to record and evaluate Internet job postings. It's used to evaluate the effectiveness of job posting sites, and one form is filled out for each job posting so a single job would have several of these forms used if the job is posted to multiple sites.

INSTRUCTIONS

A record is kept for each job that is posted to the Internet, and for each posting site. The job title, an assigned ID, the site (job bank) and the date of the posting are filled in. Then, every response to the posting is entered with the name of the applicant (Résumé Received) and the date of the contact. As candidates progress through the recruiting process, this form is updated so the final evaluation can be people hired from job postings.

          SemCo Enterprises, Inc.

Job-Posting Record

Job Title/Description: _____

Job ID: _____

Job Posting Site: _____   Date Posted: _____

ACTIVITY

Résumé Received	Date	Screen	Date	Interview	Date	Hire	Date

Overview and Instructions

OVERVIEW

This form is used to record information about candidates whose names you have gotten via networking. It is filled out when you get the name. Information is recorded about both the contact who is giving you the name and the person they are referring.

INSTRUCTIONS

1–5. These questions refer to the person who is giving you the reference.

6–11. These questions refer to the referral.

Networking Information

Contact Name: _____ Date: _____

Contact Title: _____

1. Current Employer: _____

2. Work Telephone: _____

3. Home Telephone: _____

4. Thank You Sent: Yes _____ No _____

5. Résumé On File: Yes _____ No _____

6. Person Referred: _____

7. Title: _____

8. Date Contacted: _____

9. Initial Phone Screen Date: _____

10. Current Employer: _____

11. Salary Range: _____

Comments: _____

_____

_____

_____

_____

_____

_____

Overview and Instructions

OVERVIEW

This form provides an overview of the position in the recruiting process of all current candidates. This report does not tie candidates to specific jobs.

INSTRUCTIONS

Enter the candidate's name when you receive the résumé. Put the appropriate date in each column as the candidate is processed.

PIPELINE REPORT/CANDIDATES

Name/Telephone/ Source	Résumé Received	Phone Screen Conducted	Interview Scheduled	Interview Conducted	Offer/Reject Letter Sent	References Received	Negotiations in Progress	Offer Accepted or Rejected	Follow-up Admin Done

PIPELINE REPORT/OPEN JOBS

Overview and Instructions

OVERVIEW

This form is used to keep track of all the current open jobs. It is used to give an overall picture of the total candidates for a given job and the position of each in the pipeline. This way a recruiter can report on how close (or far away) a job is to being filled by looking at this one form.

INSTRUCTIONS

Enter jobs in the left-most column when the job requisition is received. Enter the date for sourcing. As you work with candidates for each job, write their names in the appropriate column showing exactly where they are.

SemCo Enterprises, Inc.

Pipeline Report/Open Jobs

OPEN JOBS	Résumé Received (Names)	Phone Screen Conducted (Names)	Interview Scheduled (Names)	Interview Conducted (Names)	Offer/Reject Letter Sent (Names)	References Received (Names)	Negotiations in Progress (Names)	Offer Accepted or Rejected (Names)	Follow-up Admin Done (Names)
Job Title: Date Received: Sourcing Done:									
Job Title: Date Received: Sourcing Done:									
Job Title: Date Received: Sourcing Done:									
Job Title: Date Received: Sourcing Done:									
Job Title: Date Received: Sourcing Done:									
Job Title: Date Received: Sourcing Done:									

REQUISITION FOR TECHNICAL POSITION

Overview and Instructions

OVERVIEW

Ideally, recruiters would receive this form from the job requester, who could be an internal manager for a permanent hire, an account executive for a consulting assignment, or a request from a client company for a contract assignment. In actuality the recruiter fills the form out and often has some difficulty in getting this information. Fill in as much of the information as possible from the original job request, then go back to the job requester with questions.

INSTRUCTIONS

1–6. Fill in.
7. Date, if known. Or put open.
8. Fill in.
9. Fill in for permanent hires.
10. Fill in.
11. Circle appropriate entry for each factor.
12. Fill in, if required.
13–18. Rarely will all these categories be filled in.
19. This can be a specific application (eg., SAP, Oracle Financials) or industry experience (eg., banking, manufacturing).
20. Fill in, if required.
21. Could be personal characteristics (eg., strong interpersonal skills), nontechnical skills (fluent in Spanish), logistical specifics (eg., 50% travel required), or anything else the job requester asked for.
22. For permanent hires, list possible in-house candidates.

SemCo Enterprises, Inc.

REQUISITION FOR TECHNICAL POSITION

1. Department: _____ 2. Date:_____

3. Position/title: _____ 4. Number of jobs: _____

5. Will report to: _____ 6. Phone: _____

7. Requested start date: _____ 8. Salary or rate range: _____

9. Addition to staff: yes _____   no _____

   If no: Name of person being replaced:_____

             Date leaving: _____ Final salary: _____

   If yes: Authorization for staff addition(s): _____

REQUIREMENTS

10. Position description:_____

11. Circle One: Background: Environment: Level:
                   Applications – Systems   Mainframe – Midsize – Desktop   Junior – Mid – Senior

12. Degree: _____ Required   _____ Preferred   _____ Not a factor

    Major (If required): _____ Level (BA/BS, MS, EE, etc.): _____

13. Computer systems: _____

14. Operating systems: _____

15. Programming languages: _____

16. Development tools: _____

17. Data management tools: _____

18. Online/network tools: _____

19. Business applications: _____

20. Required certifications: _____

21. Additional requirements: _____

22. Possible in-house candidates: _____

    _____

    _____

Requested by (Authorized signature):_____

Department Head (If required): _____

Overview and Instructions

OVERVIEW

This form is used to evaluate Internet sourcing techniques. Each period of searching is recorded, and the form is updated with any response. The purpose of the form is to make sure that time spent searching for résumés produces results. Information is recorded about each search and the number of résumés found.

INSTRUCTIONS

The description of the open job (if there is one) is recorded, and the search activity is given an ID. The time of the search is important, as recruiters use this form to make sure they're using time effectively.

Throughout the search, entries are made in the table. Each search location is entered and given its own ID. Then the date, search tool, and keywords used give the details of the search. The number of résumés found is then recorded, keeping track of résumés that fit the prime job, and good résumés that might fit other jobs.

Résumé Search Record

Job Description: _____

Job ID: _____

Search Start Time: _____   Stop Time: _____

Total Time: _____

ACTIVITY

Search location (Job bank, Web, Newsgroups, etc.)	Search ID	Date	Search Tool	Keywords Used	Tot.	A1	A2

Tot. = Total résumés saved   A1 = Résumés for this job   A2 = Good résumés for another job

Overview and Instructions

OVERVIEW

This form is used to record information about a remote assignment or interview. It records information helpful when visiting or moving to a new city. The form should be filled out and handed to the candidate. Information for this form can be obtained from Human Resources, if your contact doesn't know.

INSTRUCTIONS

1–7. Fill out with specific information about the interview or job.

8. Check to see if there are small regional papers in addition to the major paper from the closest city.

9. Often major cities have more than one airport and the less well-known one might actually be closer (and have cheaper fares).

10. Fill in, if there is a preferred travel agency the candidate should use.

11. Is there good public transportation—bus, subway?

12. Provide directions to the company site from hotel and/or airport.

13. For interviews, provide a choice of hotels close to the site.

14. List local restaurants. Be sure to include several price ranges. If possible, provide recommendations such as "good for lunch" or "high prices, good for fancy dinners."

15. For contracts, state length.

16. Any contacts in the new city that could be helpful to the candidate. For contracts, include other employees you have on contract in that city. For permanent hires, if you have placed other people in the city, see if they would be willing to be listed here so a candidate would know someone in the new location.

SITE INFORMATION

1. Company:_____

2. Address: _____

3. Phone: _____ 4. Fax: _____

5. Contact:_____ 6. Ext. _____ 7. Dept. _____

8. Local newspapers: _____

9. Closest airport:_____

10. Preferred travel agency: _____

11. Public transportation: _____

12. Directions: _____

_____ *(cont. on back)*

13. Best hotels: _____

_____

14. Restaurants: _____

_____

15. Length of contract: _____

16. Other local contacts:

Company	Name	Title	Relation	Phone

12. (*cont*)

_____

_____

_____

_____

_____

_____

_____

_____

_____

_____

_____

_____

_____

Part Three

Technical Information

Information included here is used by technical recruiters to conduct technical screens.

TITLE	DESCRIPTION
analyst	Developer, usually application. Determines what should be done to solve the problem. Usually seniors, could be mid-level, not a title used for juniors. See systems analyst.
application tester	Application developer. See tester.
business analyst	Application developer. Similar to systems analyst, but business analysts usually do not have a technical background. See systems analyst.
capacity planner	Technical developer. Determines what hardware and software is needed to keep the computer system functioning at maximum capacity. Makes sure the system has enough storage and speed to handle the workload. Senior title most often used in mainframe computer systems.
communications analyst, engineer, specialist	Technical developer. Usually works with WANs and supports the networking for host-based, long-distance systems. Senior or mid-level title.
configuration analyst	Technical developer. Manages hardware and/or software and analyses uses, interactions, and cost benefits. Also called configuration architect, manager. Senior title most often used in mainframe computer systems.
console operator	Support personnel. Person who monitors the daily computer activity and is responsible for making changes, when required, to the production schedule and/or the equipment assignments. Senior level. Title used in mainframe installations.
data, database analyst	Developer, probably applications, but could be technical. Analyzes and defines data usage and groupings. If referring to a technical developer, could also mean defining the physical grouping and storage of the data. Senior or mid-level title. Often interchanged with data or database architect.
data, database architect	Developer, could be application or technical. Designs the database(s) and the interface(s) between the database software and applications. Senior or mid-level title. Often interchanged with data or database analyst.
data modeler	Application developer. Builds a model of the data relationships to be used for enterprise-wide applications development. Often involved in data warehousing. Senior-level title.
data warehouse architect	Database architect that works with data warehouses. See database architect.
database administrator	See DBA.
DBA	Developer, usually technical. Administrates and controls the organizations' database resources. Responsible for performance and tuning of the database. Companies have a DBA for each DBMS (eg., an Oracle DBA). Responsible for security, backups, and accuracy of the data. Usually part of the technical staff, but some mainframe installations have DBAs in both the application and technical areas. Senior title. Stands for DataBase Administrator.

SemCo Enterprises, Inc.

TITLE	DESCRIPTION
e-commerce developer	Application developer. Develops systems to do business over the Internet. Requires Internet skills such as HTML, Java, CGI Script, etc. and business knowledge and skills. EDI knowledge often part of the job. Senior or mid-level title.
engineer	See programmer.
EDI analyst	Application developer. Expert in EDI systems. Senior or mid-level title.
EDP auditor	Not really an Information Technology job, but a financial job reporting to the finance department. Uses computer tools to audit computer systems. Has audit, accounting experience in addition to statistical and financial software packages. CPA often required. SAS software commonly required.
Help Desk personnel	Support personnel. Provides user telephone support for personal computer systems. Some Help Desks also install software and software upgrades and provide training. Can be any experience level.
integration analyst, architect, engineer	Technical developer. Determines what is needed to integrate various software packages such as databases, communications programs, and application software. Usually senior-level title, could be mid-level.
Internet developer	See web programmer.
Internet engineer, Web engineer	Developer, usually technical. Builds the interfaces between the Internet-user and internal corporate systems. Knowledge of TCP/IP and firewalls. Maintains connectivity between Internet and internal networks. Can be any experience level.
LAN administrator	See network administrator.
network administrator	Support personnel. Monitors functioning of networks, usually LANs. Installs networks, adds new users, and troubleshoots network. Title usually indicates experience in midrange, desktop computer systems. Can be any experience level.
network analyst, engineer	Technical developer. Plans, installs, and supports the company's networks including both LANs and WANs. Knowledge of hardware, protocols, LANs, and NOS. Certification available and often required or at least a plus. Senior or mid-level title.
operator	Support personnel. Operates the equipment in a data center. Controls execution of computer programs by providing hardware and software support. Can be any experience level. Title usually means experience in mainframe computer installations.
P/A	See programmer/analyst.

TITLE	DESCRIPTION
PC rehire, PC software specialist	Application developer. Works with word processors, spreadsheets, PC databases, PC programming languages. Used for departmental, small company software development. Can be any experience level.
PC technician	Support personnel. Coordinates, controls, and maintains the personal computers within a company. Installs new hardware and upgrades. Often part of a Help Desk staff. Can be any experience level.
programmer	Developer. Could be either application or technical. Analyzes specifications, designs logic, writes code, tests, debugs, and documents computer programs. Can be any experience level.
programmer/analyst	Application developer. Title should mean experience working with users and indicate mid- to senior-level experience. Check for experience carefully; title often misused. Title is often abbreviated P/A.
project leader, team leader	Application developer. Senior-level supervisory position. Supervises the work done by mid-level and junior developers. Duties may include personnel management and project planning and scheduling. Sometimes acts as analyst or programmer.
project manager, programming manager	Application developer. First-level management. Manages personnel and does project planning and scheduling for a specific application or function area. Other duties could be to conduct performance appraisals, determine salaries and increases, hire and fire staff, and be accountable for the system budget.
senior programmer, developer, engineer	Developer. Could be application or technical. Analyzes systems, designs logic and testing scenarios. May or may not actually write code. Works on systems and subsystems rather than on single programs. Writes specifications and supervises mid-level and junior developers. Responsible for system performance. Senior level.
shift supervisor	Support personnel. Person responsible for the completion of the production schedule in a data center during a shift. Senior level. Title used in mainframe installations.
software engineer	Software developer. Title originally was used in the desktop world and was associated with client/server, GUI and Unix systems, but now is used by developers throughout the industry and has many definitions. Can be any experience level.
software specialist	Developer. Could be application or technical. Used for a variety of job skills and levels, so has no real meaning.

SemCo Enterprises, Inc.

TITLE	DESCRIPTION
systems administrator	Support personnel. Systems administrator is an official title in a Unix environment, but is also used in other midrange and desktop systems. The systems administrator is responsible for such things as installing new software, adapting software to the system, running system backups, recovering lost data, and maintaining security. Monitors functioning of computer systems, hardware, and/or networks. Can be any experience level.
systems analyst	Application developer. Senior person skilled and experienced in the analysis phase of the system development cycle. Strong interpersonal skills are required, as analysts spend much of their time with the users determining needs and processing functions. Business knowledge is also important and often systems analysts are required to know a specific industry, such as banking, or a specific application, such as human resources.
systems architect, designer	Technical developer (occasionally used by application developers). Designs computer systems and handles software integration. Builds infrastructures. Usually a senior title, sometimes mid-level. Title is used in mainframe and midrange systems.
systems engineer	Developer, probably technical. Used for a variety of job skills and levels, so has no real meaning.
systems manager	Technical developer. Manages other technical developers and is responsible for the performance of the computer systems. Title is usually used in mainframe and midrange systems.
systems programmer	Technical developer. A systems programmer maintains the operating system programs and environment. In addition to the operating system itself, systems programmers work with communications systems, DBMS, and operating system enhancements and add-ons. Provides technical support to application developers. Plans and evaluates hardware and software purchases. Ensures system efficiency and security. Can be any experience level.
systems tester	Usually technical developer. *See* tester.
team leader	*See* project leader, team leader.
tech writer	Support personnel. Writes the user documentation for software systems. This documentation explains how to use the programs and defines the user interface. Usually need to know a desktop publishing system. Can be any experience level.
tester, testing specialist	Developer. Could be either application or technical. Designs test data, test scenarios. Conducts system, or integration, testing. Specific skills can refer to such things as regression testing, black box testing, QA (quality assurance). Can be any experience level.

TITLE	DESCRIPTION
WAN analyst, architect, designer, engineer	Technical developer. Evaluates, selects, installs, and maintains both hardware and software for wide-area-networks. Writes middleware, works with protocols. Provides networking support for online application systems. Senior or mid-level title.
warehouse analyst, architect, designer, engineer	Developer. Could be application or technical. Designs the metadata and builds the indexing algorithms. Senior-level title.
Webmaster	Application developer. Does the graphic design, and updates and maintains Web sites. Requires Internet skills such as HTML, Java, Perl, VBScript, etc., and also database and business knowledge. Senior or mid-level title.
Web designer	*See* Webmaster.
Web programmer, Internet developer	Developer, usually applications. Develops interactive programs using Internet skills such as HTML, Java, CGI scripts using languages such as Perl, VBScript, and/or JavaScript. Can be any experience level.
Web specialist	Developer. Used for a variety of job skills and levels, so has no real meaning other than requiring Internet skills such as Java, CGI scripts, HTML, etc.

SemCo Enterprises, Inc.

◢◢◢◢◢ JOB TYPE DISTINCTIONS ◢◢◢◢

IT titles are of limited use as there are no standards at all, but can be helpful in distinguishing between development and support jobs and personnel. As a general rule the following nouns identify job type:

DEVELOPMENT	SUPPORT	USED BY BOTH
Programmer	Operator	Tester
Engineer	Administrator	Specialist
Developer	Technician	
Designer		
Analyst		
Consultant		
Architect		
Modeler		

Note: this is a general rule, and as with all rules, there are exceptions. The most notable exception is DBA, DataBase Administrator. While "administrator" in almost every other case is a support title, DBA is a developer title.

Title can be a good indicator, but the full distinction is made by looking at the type of work the job requires or is specified on a résumé. The following words are indicative of development or support.

DEVELOPMENT	SUPPORT	USED BY BOTH
write	operate	install
code	monitor	test
design	set-up	implement
analyze	run	maintain, maintenance
program	troubleshoot	configure
debug	install	
diagnose		
customize		
life-cycle		

These words are just a guideline. The distinction between development and support is that development is the actual creation or modification of software systems, and support is the operation, or running of the finished product.

Distinguishing between applications and technical developers really depends on the job tasks but there are some words that help identify applications or technical (*note:* more technical than applications):

APPLICATIONS	TECHNICAL	
logical	physical	protocols
functions, functional	hardware	integration
business terms	tuning, performance tuning	infrastructure
user contact	configuration	internals
real time	networking	kernel
online	embedded	

Again, the words are just a guideline. Applications developers work on solving business problems and are mostly concerned with what systems do. Technical developers must make sure these applications systems run efficiently and are concerned with the hardware and software necessary for operation.

Communications Details

APPLICATIONS	OLTP	CICS, TUXEDO
	GUI builder	Visual Basic, Powerbuilder
	EDI	EDI (generic) or Gentran (specific)
	Groupware	Lotus Notes, Workflo
TECHNICAL	OLTP	CICS (INTERNALS)
	EDI	Gentran (internals)
	Groupware	Notes (internals)
	Protocol	TCP/IP, SNA
	NOS	NetWare, NT Server
	LAN	Ethernet
	Hardware	Equipment, Channels
SUPPORT	NOS	NETWARE, NT SERVER
	LAN	Ethernet, Token Ring
	Hardware	Equipment: Routers, Bridges, Brouters, Switches, Hubs, Gateways… CISCO, 3COM, Nortel (Bay) Channels: T1, T3 lines, Twisted pair Frame relay… FDDI, ISDN, ATM, DSL…

Life-Cycle Details

ANALYSIS
Client contact
Interpersonal skills
Business/applications knowledge
Schedule and follow up meetings with users

DESIGN
Write program specs
Supervise juniors
Data modeling
Data dictionaries/repositories
Schemas

PROGRAMMING
Code
Write
Test
RAD

TESTING
Black box
White box
Regression
Test scenarios/schemes

PROJECT MANAGEMENT
Personnel management
Project management
Hire/fire
Project scheduling
Budget responsibility

DOCUMENTATION
Desktop publishers
Graphics packages
Interpersonal skills
Research skills

Summary

OPERATING SYSTEMS

AIX
Guardian
HP-UX
Linux
MACOS
MS-DOS
OpenVMS
OS/390
OS/MVS
OS/X
Solaris
Unix
VMS
VSE/SP
Windows (3.11,95,98, NT)
XENIX

LANGUAGES

Assembler
BAL
Basic
C
C++
COBOL
Focus
Java
Natural
PASCAL
PL/1
QMF
RPG (II, III)
Smalltalk
SQL

COMMUNICATIONS OLTP

CICS
IDMS-DC
IMS-DC
Multics
Tuxedo

COMMUNICATIONS NETWORKS

Appleshare
Appletalk
Arcnet
Banyan (Vines)
EcoSYSTEMS
Ethernet
Lantastic
NetWare (Novell)
Novell (NetWare)
NT Server (Windows)
OpenView
OS/2 Server
Patrol
TCP/IP
Token Ring
Unix Server
Vines (Banyan)
Windows NT Server
X.25

DATABASES

Access
Adabas
Cache
Centura (Gupta)
dBase (III, IV)
DB2
DB2 Universal Database
Gupta (Centura)
IDMS
IMS
Informix
Ingres
Oracle
Progress
SQLBase (Centura)
SQLServer
Sybase

APPLICATIONS

Baan
EDI Systems
ERP
J.D. Edwards
Lawson
MRP
Oracle Financials
PeopleSoft
SAP

INTERNET

ASP
C/C++
CGI (scripts)
Cold Fusion
DHTML
FTP
Java, JavaScript
Perl
Shockwave
Tango
TCP/IP
Telnet
VBScript

DEVELOPMENT

Delphi
EIF
Eiffel
Empress
Forte
JDK
Oracle Reports
PowerBuilder
Rational Rose
SEER HPS
SQLForms
SQLWindows
Visual Basic
VisualAge
Uniface

◢ TOPIC POINTS ◣

While a recruiter does not want to conduct a technical interview, there are some points in each technical area that can indicate knowledge of the area. Points are listed below for the current "hot" areas (Client/server, Data warehousing, Internet, Networking, Object oriented) and some major technical areas (Relational databases, CICS, MVS, Unix). Do not expect applicants to know all the points for a given topic, but they should be able to discuss some of them, either in the résumé or during an interview. This list certainly does not cover everything, but can help confirm that the applicant has knowledge of the given area and can be recommended for the next step in the process — possibly a technical interview.

CLIENT/SERVER
Relational database, SQL, GUI, GUI builder, front-end, back-end, application partitioning, three- or multi-tiered partitioning.

DATA WAREHOUSING
OLAP, data mining, complex queries, metadata, data mart, replication, DSS.

INTERNET
Web, browser, download, Java (applets), Cold Fusion, CGI script, firewall, HTML, DHTML, Perl, JavaScript, VBScript, URL, HTTP, MIME, FTP, intranet, extranet, ASP (Active Server Pages), e-commerce, XML.

NETWORKING
Network, LAN, NOS (server, peer-to-peer), WAN, MAN, middleware, protocol, topology (token ring, bus, star), RPC, SNA, APPN, ACF, VTAM, NCP, SDLC, TCP/IP, X.25, LU6.2.

OBJECT-ORIENTED
Object, class, libraries, C++, Smalltalk, Booch, Rumbaugh, OMT, OODB, inheritance, polymorphism, encapsulation, reusability, MFC, JFC, OWL, components, ORB, CORBA, COM/DCOM.

CICS
OLTP, transaction processing, command level, macro level, BMS.

MVS
Operating system, MVS/ESA, MVS/XA, JCL, JES2,3, VSAM, VTAM, virtual storage (VS), PROC, Linkage Editor, object program.

UNIX
Operating system, Shell (Bourne, C, Korn), shell scripts, Perl, AWK, SED, commands, kernel, GUI, MOTIF, Open Look.

RELATIONAL DATABASES
SQL, tables (rows/columns), tablespace, data modeling, entity-relationship diagrams/models, normalization, referential integrity, data locking, triggers, stored procedures, thread/threading.

DB2   Also: VSAM, cluster.

ORACLE   Also: SQL*Plus, Oracle Forms, Pro*C (etc.) SQL*Net.

SYBASE   Also: Caching, TransactSQL.

Part Four

Internet Sites

The Internet is an invaluable resource for technical recruiters, and there are many sites used throughout the recruiting process. Internet references are heavily used during sourcing, and there are many different locations for posting jobs and finding résumés. The lists provided include the major sites in each category, but are not all-inclusive. While all listed sites have been checked, the Internet changes on a daily basis, so it is possible that sites listed are no longer active, or new sites are not listed.

JOB AND RÉSUMÉ SITES

General Job Banks

These are thousands of Job Sites on the Internet, most of which contain postings for all jobs. These are some of the major sites, and even though they contain all jobs, not just technical, a large number of people using these sites are technical people.

URL	COST BASIS, COMMENTS
www.4work.com	Fee to post jobs, fee to see résumés.
www.ajb.dni.us	Free, America's job bank.
www.careercentral.com	Fee to post jobs, fee to see résumés.
www. careerexchange.com	Fee to post jobs, fee to see résumés.
www.careermagazine.com	Fee to post jobs, fee to see résumés. Pushes jobs to candidates.
www.careermart.com	Fee to post jobs, fee to see résumés. Pushes jobs to candidates.
www.careermosaic.com	Fee to post jobs, fee to see résumés.
www.careernet.com	Fee to post jobs, fee to see résumés. Annual or monthly fees available.
www.careerpath.com	Fee to post jobs, fee to see résumés. Partners with over 58 newspapers.
www.connectme.com	Free for jobs, No résumés.
www.cweb.com	Fee to post jobs, fee to see résumés. Pushes jobs to candidates.
www.classifieds2000.com	Fee to post jobs.
www.gojobs.com	Fee to post jobs, fee to see résumés.
www.headhunter.net	Free for both jobs and résumés, but pay fee to upgrade position in job list.
www.helpwanted.com	Free for both jobs and résumés.
www.hotjobs.com	Fee to post jobs, fee to see résumés.
www.ipa.com	Fee to post jobs, fee to see résumés. Recruiter's Online Network (RON).
www.jobassistant.com	Fee to post jobs, free to search résumés.
www.jobbankusa.com	Fee to post jobs, fee to see résumés.
www.joblocator.com	Employers' membership and credits allow job posting and viewing résumés.
www.monster.com	Fee to post jobs, fee to see résumés.
www.nationjob.com	Fee to post jobs. Pushes jobs to candidates.
www.topjobsusa.com	Fee to post jobs, fee to see résumés.
www.usjob.net	Fee to post jobs, fee to see résumés. Push to employers.

JOB AND RÉSUMÉ SITES

Technical Job Banks

These are job sites that post jobs for technical positions. Some of these sites work with IT jobs only while others include engineering jobs, but all specialize in high-tech. These job sites work with all IT jobs; check Technical Specialty Job Banks for job sites for a specific technology.

URL	COST BASIS, COMMENTS
205.230.23.123	Fees, links to employers. TechJobBank.
www.1-jobs.com	Fees, contact for information.
www.a1acompyterpros.net	Fee, per-job posting.
www.americanjobs.com	Fee, per-job posting. Includes engineering jobs.
www.brainpower.com	Free.
www.careernet.com	Fee, subscription service. Includes engineering jobs.
www.computerjobs.com	Fee, monthly or per-job posting. Also called computerjobsstore.
www.computerwork.com	Fee, monthly charge.
www.computerworldcareers.com	Now called ITcareers.
www.developers.net	Fee for posting to site, includes e-mailing to member companies.
www.ddj.com	Fee, Dr. Dobb's Journal.
www.dice.com	Fee, can choose time-period membership or per job posting option.
www.ggrweb.com	Fee to post jobs. For IT, Geoscience and engineering professionals.
www.isjobbank.com	Must belong to NACCB (computer consulting association).
www.it123.com	Fee, subscription charge.
www.itcareers.com	Fee, subscription or per-job posting.
www.itclassifieds.com	Fees for job postings, separate fees for résumé searches.
www.jobsurfshop.com	Free, paid membership will improve positioning.
www.passportaccess.com	Fees for job postings, separate fees for résumé searches.
www.prgjobs.com	Fees, contact for information.
www.selectjobs.com	Fees, also posts to other job banks.
www.softwarejobs.com	Free job posting, pay if hire someone.
supersite.net/techjobs	Fee, per-job posting plus advertising options.
www.techengine.com	Fee, job postings or subscription service.
www.techies.com	Fee, subscription charge.
www.techjobbank.com	Fee, many choices.
www.techuniverse.com	Free.
www.virtual-edge.net	Fee, per-job posting. Pushes to candidates.
www.witi4hire.com	Fee, unlimited jobs for a time period, Women in Technology, Inc.

JOB AND RÉSUMÉ SITES

Technical Specialty Banks

These are job sites that post jobs and sometimes résumés for a specific technology or technical interest only. Some are free, some charge for job postings and/or résumé access. Also check Technical Interest Sites for job postings for a specific technology, and technical job sites for general IT job postings.

SPECIALTY	RÉSUMÉS	FREE	URL
Access	No	No	www.JustAccessJobs.com*
Adabas/Natural	No	Yes	www.intandem-tech.com/users/sferrell/jobs/
AS/400	No	No	www.JustAS400Jobs.com*
ASP(Active Server Pages)	No	No	www.JustASPJobs.com*
Baan	No	No	www.JustBaanJobs.com*
C	No	No	wwwJustCJobs.com*
C++	No	No	www.cplusplusjobs.com
	Yes	No	www.CplusplusSearch.com
CAD	No	No	www.JustCADJobs.com*
COBOL	No	No	www.coboljobs.com
	No	No	www.JustCOBOLJobs.com*
Cold fusion	No	No	www.JustColdFusionJobs.com*
college graduates	Yes	No	www.collegehire.com
databases	No	No	www.databasejobs.com
	No	Yes	www.Databaseanalyst.com**
DB2	No	No	www.JustDB2Jobs.com*
Delphi	No	No	www.delphijobs.com
developers	No	Yes	www.SoftwareDeveloper.com**
	No	Yes	www.SoftwareEngineer.com**
	No	Yes	www.Programmeranalyst.com**
	No	Yew	www.SystemsEngineer.com**
ERP	No	No	www.erp-jobs.com
	No	Yes	www.ERPProfessional.com**
	No	No	www.ittoolbox.com Home of:
			www.crmassist.com
			www.sapassist.com
			www.erpassist.com
			www.oracleassist.com
			www.peoplesoftassist.com
			www.baanassist.com
FoxPro	No	No	www.JustFoxProJobs.com*
Help Desk	No	No	www.JustHelpDeskJobs.com*
Informix	No	No	www.JustInformixJobs.com*
Internet	No	Yes	jobs.15Seconds.com/default.asp

Category			
Java	Yes	No	www.javajobsonline.com
	No	No	www.JustJavaJobs.com*
	Yes	No	www.JVsearch.com
LAN	No	No	www.lanjobs.com
Lotus Notes	No	No	www.lotusnotesjobs.com
	No	Yes	www.LotusProfessional.com**
	No	No	www.JustNotesJobs.com*
mainframe	No	No	www.JustMainframeJobs.com*
NetWare	No	No	www.JustNetWareJobs.com*
networking	No	No	www.JustNetworkingJobs.com*
	No	No	www.NetworkEngineer.com**
	No	Yes	www.CertifiedProfessional.com**
NT	No	No	www.JustNTJobs.com*
OLAP (warehousing)	No	No	www.OLAPJobs.com
Oracle	Yes	No	www.oracjobs.com
	Yes	No	www.ORAsearch.com
	No	No	www.JustOracleJobs.com*
	No	Yes	www.OracleProfessional.com**
Oracle DBA	Yes	Yes	www.oracledba.net
PeopleSoft	No	No	www.JustPeopleSoftJobs.com*
	No	Yes	www.PeopleSoftDeveloper.com**
Perl	No	No	www.JustPerlJobs.com*
PowerBuilder	No	No	www.powerbuilderjobs.com
	No	No	www.JustPowerBuilderJobs.com*
project managers	No	Yes	www.ProjectManager.com**
SAP	No	No	www.JustSAPJobs.com*
	No	Yes	www.SapDeveloper.com**
seniors –CIOs,VPs	No	No	jobs.cio.com
	No	No	www.6figurejobs.com
	No	Yes	www.MISManager.com**
Sybase	No	No	www.JustSybaseJobs.com*
System Administration	No	Yes	www.Systemadministrator.com**
Systems analyst	No	Yes	www.SystsemsAnalyst.com**
technical sales	No	No	www.JustTechSalesJobs.com*
Unix	Yes	No	www.UnixAdminSearch.com
	No	No	www.JustUnixJobs.com*
Visual Basic	No	No	www.visualbasicjobs.com
	No	No	www.JustVBJobs.com*
	Yes	No	www.VBasicSearch.com
Web developers	No	No	www.JustWebJobs.com*
	No	No	www.webprogrammingjobs.com
	No	Yes	www.WebsiteBuilder.com**
	Yes	No	www.webjobusa.com

* Part of justcomputerjobs.com
** Part of careermarketplace.com

JOB AND RÉSUMÉ SITES

Technical Special-Interest Sites

Special-interest sites offer information and services for people working in specific areas. These sites are often called community sites and function as portal, or gateway, sites for the special interest. The job and/or résumé postings are only one of the services provided. All the sites in this list accept job postings, some also post résumés. Jobs posted on these sites can attract passive candidates who are on the site for other reasons, but check out the jobs just to see what's available.

SPECIALTY	POST RESUMES	FREE JOB POST	URL
AS/400	Yes	Yes	www.news400.com
COBOL	No	No	www.infogoal.com/cdb/cdbhome.htm
DB2	No	No	www.idug.org
Ecommerce	No	No	www.ecommercetimes.com
ERP	No	No	www.erpcentral.com
	Yes	Yes	www.erp-people.com
	Yes	Yes	www.erpfans.com
HPC developers	No	No	www.hpcwire.com
Internet developers	No	No	jobs.internet.com
Java	Yes	No	www.javajobs.com
mainframe	Yes	Yes	www.mvshelp.com
Microsoft technologies	Yes (anon)	Yes	www.ntspecialist.com
	Yes	Yes	www.bhs.com/default.asp
midrange	No	Yes	www.midrange.com
Oracle	Yes	Yes	www.orafans.com
Systems Administrators	No	No	www.swynk.com
Telecom	No	No	www.totaltele.com
Unix	Yes	Yes	www.ugu.com
Visual Basic	Yes	No	www.vbonline.com
Web developers	Yes	No	www.cfadvisor.com
	No	Yes	www.hwg.org
	Yes	Yes	www.siteexperts.com
	No	Yes	www.wwwac.com

Virtual Communities

A virtual community site has millions of members who enter the community by joining a specific part of the community. These communities are organized by regions, interests, or any topic that would bring a group together. Members often put job information on their home pages, so virtual communities can be a source of passive technical candidate.

www.angelfire.com	Contains search/browse link. Does not publish number of members. Part of Lycos. Organized into clubs, which can be started by members.
www.fortunecity.com	Contains search engine. Under a million members, but growing. Organized by themed districts and has an International flavor.
www.geocities.com	Provides a search engine. Contains over 3 million members. Organized into neighborhoods.
www.theglobe.com	No search engine. Over 2 million members. Organized into clubs under interest areas such as shopping, health and fitness, sports, etc.
www.tripod.com	Provides a search engine. Contains over 2 million members. Part of the Lycos network. Builds "pods" under specific interests such as shopping, health and fitness, sports, etc.
www.xoom.com	Search engine to be added. Over 5 million members. Organized by interest areas under typical areas of sports, health, arts, etc.

Metasearch Engines

All4One
Searches Lycos, AltaVista, HotBot, Excite. Free. www.all4one.com

Big Search
Searches user selected search engines from Yahoo, Infoseek, Excite, WebCrawler, HotBot, Lycos, Ask Jeeves, AltaVista. Also searches newsgroups and specialty sites. Free. www.thebighub.com

BullsEye
*Offline. Finds results in over 450 sources including 30 major search engines and 420 sources from the invisible Web. (The invisible Web is comprised of databases and archives which aren't accessible through most search engines.) Eliminates dead and duplicate links and ranks results. www.intelliseek.com

C4
Multiple search engines including AltaVista, Yahoo, InfoSeek, Excite, Lycos, Snap.com, Magellan, WebCrawler, HotBot. Returns only most relevant results. Includes newsgroup search capability. Free. www.c4.com

Copernic
Multiple search engines including AltaVista, Excite, Yahoo, HotBot, InfoSeek, Lycos, Magellan, OpenText, WebCrawler. Retrieves information from the Web, newsgroups, and e-mail directories. Displays results in order of relevancy, and duplicates and unreachable documents are automatically filtered out. Free. www.copernic.com

Debriefing
Searches Lycos, AltaVista, HotBot, Excite, Yahoo and InfoSeek. Merges results. Free. www.debriefing.com

Dogpile
Multiple search engines including goto.com, InfoSeek, AltaVista, Lycos, Yahoo! Returns list of hits from each search engine so duplicates occur. Operated by Go2Net.com. Free. www.dogpile.com

Express
*Offline. Searches seven searches engines and over 300 specialty sites. Free. Express.infoseek.com

Highway61
Multiple search engines including Yahoo!, Lycos, WebCrawler, InfoSeek, Excite. User can indicate number of hits per search. Free. www.highway61.com

Inference Find
Searches AltaVista, Excite, InfoSeek, Lycos, WebCrawler, Yahoo! Removes duplicates and merges the results. Free. www.infind.com

MetaCrawler
Searches multiple search engines including Lycos, InfoSeek, WebCrawler, Excite, AltaVista, Yahoo! Organizes results by relevance. Operated by Go2Net.com. Free. www.go2net.com.

SemCo Enterprises, Inc.

MetaFind	Searches AltaVista, GoTo.com, InfoSeek, Thunderstone, Yahoo! User can specify maximum number of results. Free. www.metafind.com
OneBlink	Searches InfoSeek, AltaVista, Excite, Yahoo, Lycos, HotBot. Users can download code to their own Web site to provide mega-search functions to their visitors. Free. www.oneblink.com
Profusion	Searches up to nine engines (user chooses). Uses artificial intelligence to merge and rank results. Eliminates duplicates and dead links. Free. www.profusion.com
SavvySearch	Searches twelve search engines simultaneously. Also searches newsgroups and offers specialty searches. Free. www.savvysearch.com
Verio search	Searches seven search engines and returns one list with results ranked. Removes duplicates. Free. Search.verio.net
Web Bandit	*Offline. Searches ten search engines. Users can customize search settings. Removes duplicates. www.jwsg.com
WebFerret	*Offline. Searches multiple engines. Evaluation version can be downloaded. www.ferretsoft.com

*Offline product. Purchased and downloaded. Runs on user system, not the Web server.

Résumé Spiders

Flipsearch	Includes 5 distinct tools to improve your productivity: sweepsearch, powersearch, résumé search, flipsearch and super-seek. www.flipsearch.com
Netsurfers	Searches newsgroups hourly and provides information on newly posted résumés. Monthly subscription service. Can use filters for regions, experience level. www.netsurfers.org
Résumé Agent	Searches individual sites and newsgroups. Searches can be scheduled or run on demand. www.personic.com
Résumé Detective	Searches the major search engines, DejaNews résumé archives, and résumé banks. Web site lists résumé banks that will be searched on a weekly basis. Free. www.résumédetective.com
Résumé infoFinder	Simultaneously searches top résumé sources. Résumé infoFinder Gold adds the ability to search fee-based résumé banks. License arrangement. www.infogist.com
Résumé Robot	Searches free and fee résumé banks. Also searches individual Web sites and newsgroups. Searches on a 24/7 basis and returns reports of newly posted résumés. Monthly subscription service. www.prorecruiter.com
RésuméMiner	Finds résumés freely posted throughout the Internet including those on free careerboards and general portals. Allows Web-based search of database of all these résumés. www.ezeenet.com
Résumérobot	Internet-wide search that returns results to recruiter's desktop. Creates and maintains corporate database eliminating duplicates. www.résumérobot.com
SearchStation	Searches not only the major search engines and free résumé banks, but also finds candidates in specialty sites, colleges and organizations, and even in corporate Web pages. Annual subscription service. www.airsdirectory.com
Skillbot	Concentrates on finding résumés in individual Web sites and discussion groups. Does not search newsgroups or résumé databases, but looks for links to résumés. Annual membership. www.skillbot.com

Search Engines

(PORTAL SITES)

www.altavista.com
www.aol.com
www.excite.com
www.explorer.com
www.fastsearch.com
www.google.com
www.hotbot.com
www.infodump.com
www.infoseek.com
www.lycon.com
www.netscape.com
www.northernlight.com
www.snap.com
www.supersearch.com
www.webcrawler.com
www.yahoo.com

Job-Posting Services

These services post jobs to corporate Web sites and to other job banks. It provides an interface so that recruiters, or even administrators, can supply job information and the software will then create the job posting. All these systems are Web-hosted, which means they run on the Internet and companies subscribe, become members, or purchase a license for use of the service.

BestRecruit	Web-hosted job posting system. Posts to major job sites, including OCC, CareerWeb, 4Work, JobBank USA. User charged only job site fees. Responses are stored and organized by Best Recruit. Service provided by Best Software. www.bestrecruit.com
EZwebLink	Web-hosted job posting service. Requires EZaccess and membership in DICE, RON to post jobs there. Jobs are posted from EZaccess to corporate Web site, DICE and RON. Résumés are returned to EZaccess database. Vendor: Personic Software, Inc. www.Personic.com
Go Jobs	Web-hosted job posting service. Automatically takes jobs descriptions from a corporate Web site and posts them to various client requested job banks. Posts to major job banks. Manages the job postings and updates and deletes jobs according to activity on the corporate site. Vendor: Go Jobs, Inc. www.gojobs.com
HireTrack	Web-hosted job posting service. Allows recruiters to instantly post jobs to the corporate Web site. Stores résumés in a private database. Ranks and identifies best candidates. Provides applicant tracking throughout entire recruitment process. Concurrent user license. Vendor: Simpatix. www.simpatix.com
Internet Recruiter	Web-hosted job posting service. Posts jobs to hundreds of job sites and optionally to corporate Web site. Builds private résumé database. Ranks responses against job requirements. Integrates with Resumix and other applicant tracking systems. Vendor: Resumix. www.resumix.com
JobLauncher	Web-hosted job posting service. Posts to over 1,000 job Websites. Tracks responses from each site. Membership program. Commonly called eQuest. Vendor: eQuest, Inc. www.equest.com
Personic WebLINK	Web-hosted job posting service. Requires Personic Workflow and GO Jobs and CareerWeb memberships. Applicants can sent résumé or fill out online application and WebLINK returns information to corporate Personic Workflow database. Vendor: Personic Software, Inc. www.personic.com

SmartPOST   Web-hosted job posting service. Posts to multiple sites including America's Job Bank, Classifieds 2000, and newsgroups. Vendor: SmartPOST Network. www.smartpost.com

WinSearch.Jobs   Web-hosted job posting service for staffing industry. Builds and hosts Web pages that match corporate Web sites and collects electronic résumés which can be downloaded to internal systems. Interfaces with WinSearch. Vendor: Relational Systems, Inc. www.winsearch.com

WEB-Hosted Systems and Services

These systems run on the vendor's systems and companies interface through the Web. They're called by many names including web-hosted, web-based, web-enabled, and outsourced systems. Payment for the systems, or services, is expressed as subscriptions, memberships, and/or licenses. The functions provided range from complete applicant tracking systems to specialized functions such as building an employment Web site.

Alexus	See Networker.
AppTracker	Web-hosted applicant tracking system. Includes job posting functions. Also distributes job information to internal candidates, archived candidates, employment agencies, Web sites, newsgroups, and newspapers. Stores résumés in central database. Sends acknowledgement of all responses. Vendor: AppTracker. www.apptracker.com
BRN (Bridgepath Recruiters Network)	Web-hosted service for third party recruiters and staffing companies. Provides customer-relationship management including sending contacts newsletters, birthday cards, and other personalized communications. Vendor: Bridgepath.com. www.bridgepath.com
CareerBuilder	Web-hosted career site containing job bank and recruiting services. Posts jobs to multiple sites. Applicants fill out short form detailing interests and site pushes jobs that fit to them. Vendor: CareerBuilder, Inc. www.careerbuilding.com
E-Cruiter Enterprise	Web-hosted applicant tracking software. Includes E-Cruiter Express for job posting functions. Express posts to multiple job boards (CareerBridge, Positionwatch, CAREERSpan, CareerMosaic, Internet Job Locator, JobSAT, NetJobs, CareerMagazine, and News Groups) and charges by number of jobs posted. Express can used alone. Vendor: E-Cruiter, Inc. www.e-cruiter.com
e-Recruiter	Web-hosted. Gathers information at corporate Web sites about what kind of jobs visitors would consider—what salary and what regions. Sends the visitor an e-mail questionnaire for further qualification. Profiles and matches applicants with job openings posted to corporate Web site. Will push job information to the now-candidate when an appropriate job opens up. Monthly subscription. Vendor: Hire.com. www.hire.com (formerly World.Hire)
eWorkforce	Suite of Web-hosted applications that handle the entire recruiting process. Handles contingency hires, résumé processing, internal job management. Uses e-mail for communication. Presents different views to recruiters, hiring managers, executive management, etc. Vendor: Icarian. www.icarian.com

EZwebLink	Web-hosted job posting service. Requires EZaccess and membership in DICE, RON to post jobs there. Jobs are posted from EZaccess to corporate Web site, DICE and RON. Résumés are returned to EZaccess database. Vendor: Personic Software, Inc. www.Personic.com
Go Jobs	Web-hosted job posting service. Automatically takes jobs descriptions from a corporate Web site and posts them to various client requested job banks. Posts to major job banks. Manages the job postings and updates and deletes jobs according to activity on the corporate site. Vendor: Go Jobs, Inc. www.gojobs.com
HireSystems	Web-hosted résumé management service. Accepts scanned, faxed, e-mailed résumés and stores them in a searchable private database on the Web. Works with résumés in any format. Vendor: HireSystems, Inc. corp.hiresystems.com
HireTrack	Web-hosted job posting service. Allows recruiters to instantly post jobs to the corporate Web site. Stores résumés in a private database. Ranks and identifies best candidates. Provides applicant tracking throughout entire recruitment process. Concurrent user license. Vendor: Simpatix. www.simpatix.com
Hot Chili	Web-hosted résumé management service. Scanned, faxed, e-mailed résumés are stored in Web-hosted database accessible from any browser. Vendor: Hot Chili Technology. www.hchili.com
HR Smart	Web-hosted résumé management service. Candidates apply for jobs to the corporate Web site and are transparently connected to HR Smart. An online profile can be filled out, or a résumé submitted through cut and paste. Résumés are stored in a database that is accessible over the Web. Integrates with existing HR Software, eg. Resumix, PeopleSoft, Oracle, etc. and simultaneously posts jobs to www.careernet.com. Vendor: Career/Net L.L.C. www.hrsmart.com
IIRC	Web-hosted service that works with many job sites. Builds an Internet recruiting plan for each company and analyses effectiveness of each site so jobs are posted to those that work best. Vendor: International Internet Recruiting Consultants, Inc. www.iirc.com
ijob	Web-hosted recruiting system that lets candidates enter job preferences, résumés. Records interview information online. Vendor: Lawson Software. www.lawson.com
Internet Recruiter	Web-hosted job posting service. Posts jobs to hundreds of job sites and optionally to corporate Web site. Builds private résumé database. Ranks responses against job requirements. Integrates with Resumix and other applicant tracking systems. Vendor: Resumix. www.resumix.com

IRIS (Internet Recruiting Information System)	Web-hosted recruiting system that provides a manager's forum for input from hiring managers, uses agents to find matching résumés on the Internet, and manages the corporate Web site. Vendor: Global Recruiting Solutions (GRS). www.grs-software.com
I-Search	Web-hosted applicant tracking service. Maintains private database of applicants and provides most applicant tracking functions. Allows applicants to quickly fill in online application and verify accuracy. Services include sourcing, tracking, and résumé management. Vendor: iSearch. www.isearch.com
JobLauncher	Web-hosted job posting service. Posts to over 1,000 job Websites. Tracks responses from each site. Membership program. Commonly called eQuest. Vendor: eQuest, Inc. www.equest.com
JobMark	Web-hosted. Builds and maintains a Web-hosted employment site that interfaces with the corporate Web site. Vendor: JobMark. www.jobmark.com
LumiNet	Web-hosted résumé searching tool. Searches free Internet résumé banks, and any paid banks for which a subscription exists, with a single search command. Ranks candidates based on job requirements. Interfaces with Resumix applicant tracking systems. Vendor: Resumix. www.resumix.com
Networker	Web-hosted applicant tracking system. Includes résumé management functions, interview scheduling, interfaces for recruiters, hiring managers. Annual license basis. Vendor: Alexus International, Inc. www.alexus.com
NuWeb Suite	Web-hosted applicant tracking service. Includes MatchMaker, the applicant tracking module of HR:Expert suite. Integrates with corporate Web site. Vendor: NuView Systems, Inc. www.nuviewinc.com
PeopleMover	Web-hosted applicant tracking service for the staffing industry. Works with permanent staff, temporary workers, consulting firms, and free agent contractors. Interfaces with back-office packages like PeopleSoft. Web-based interface. Can be purchased to run on internal systems. Vendor: PeopleMover, Inc. www.peoplemover.com
Personic Résumé Agent	Web-hosted. Searches for résumés almost anywhere on the Internet with any combination of criteria. The searches can be scheduled or made at-will. Résumés can be moved into either EZaccess or Personic Workflow databases. Vendor: Personic Software, Inc. www.personic.com

Personic WebLINK	Web-hosted job posting service. Requires Personic Workflow and GO Jobs and CareerWeb memberships. Applicants can sent résumé or fill out online application and WebLINK returns information to corporate Personic Workflow database. Vendor: Personic Software, Inc. www.personic.com
Pro-Active Recruiter	Web-hosted. Made up of many programs that are available as a subscription service. Includes: Résumé Robot (searches Web for résumés), JobSWEEP and JobPOST (post job information to multiple job banks, newsgroups and listservs), JobBANK (maintains job bank functions), JobREFERRAL (manages an employee referral program). Vendor: ITTA L.L.C. www.prorecruiter.com
Recruiting Center	Web-hosted recruiting package that includes a candidate/résumé database, candidate tracking, and requirement tracking. Provides integration of communications with all parties including recruiters and hiring managers. Variety of subscription services available. Vendor: Recruiting Solutions, L.L.C. www.rsllc.com
Recruitment and Assessment	Web-hosted package that has candidates fill out online applications, take online interviews that include behavioral questionnaires and job specific task assessments. Version available for phone interviews. Vendor: SHL Group, PLC. www.shlusa.com
ReviewNet	Web-hosted screening and interviewing system. Provides testing tools for over 100 different technologies. Companies build tests from a knowledgebase so they can test the specifics important to each job. Also provides online technical interviewer. Vendor: ReviewNet Corp. www.reviewnet.net.
RezKeeper (Corporate)	Web-hosted applicant tracking service. Maintains private database with complete history for every candidate. Provides e-mail communication features such as sending an e-mail "thank you" note to all new applicants, and notifying recruiters through e-mail when a new job order arrives. Subscription service, accessible through any Web browser. RezKeeper is for staffing industry, RezKeeper Corporate is for corporations. Purchased version called RezManager. Vendor: rezLogic, Inc. www.rezlogic.com
SearchAdvantage	Web-hosted applicant tracking system. Works with scanned, faxed, e-mailed and Internet résumés. Includes EEO reporting functions, reference screens to record results of interviews, and job posting services. License arrangement based on number of users. Vendor: SearchAdvantage, Inc. www.searchadvantage.com
Simpatix	See HireTrack.

SmartSearch Online	Web-hosted applicant tracking service. Manages the recruiting process from job requisition, to posting jobs on the Internet, processing résumés, qualifying candidates, and making the offer. Available through subscription; purchased system available (SmartSearch) to run on internal systems. Vendor: APS (Advanced Personnel Systems). www.aps.com
Softshoe	Web-hosted applicant tracking system. Builds customized job boards. Softshoe is the software used by HotJobs.com and can by purchased for corporate use. Vendor: Softshoe. www.softshoe.com
Virtual Recruiter	Web-hosted. Maintains recruiter's data including rolodex, appointment schedule, and activity tracking. Uses e-mail for contacts. Designed for work-at-home. Vendor: The Virtual Recruiter. http://thevirtualrecruiter.com.
Webhire JobPost	Web-hosted job posting service. Automatically takes job descriptions from a corporate Web site and posts them to various job banks. Posts twice weekly. Basic subscription posts to America's JobBank, Excite and Yahoo. Additional fees are charged for additional job banks. Candidates reply directly to company. Vendor: Webhire, Inc. www.webhire.com (formerly called ResTrak)
Webhire Recruiter	Web-hosted applicant tracking system for small to midsize companies. Creates and manages job requisition. Creates and hosts a private database of candidates accessible only to subscribing company. Generates EEO and other reports. Access through a Web browser. Webhire Enterprise version can be purchased to run on internal systems. Vendor: Webhire, Inc. www.webhire.com (formerly called ResTrak)
WebPAS	Web-hosted system for the staffing industry. Presents a personalized screen to each user showing where they were the last time they accessed the system. Provides client, job order, candidate and résumé management functions. Stands for: Web Placement Automated System. Vendor: VCG, Inc. www.c-pas.com
WebRecruiter Outside	Web-hosted. Provides résumé processing, searches and job posting functions. Subscription service for Web host. Uses Oracle databases. Interfaces with HRIS systems. Vendor: COM.sortium LLC. http://com.sortium.com
WinSearch.Jobs	Web-hosted job posting service. Builds and hosts Web pages that match corporate Web sites and collects electronic résumés which can be downloaded to internal systems. Interfaces with WinSearch. Vendor: Relational Systems, Inc. www.winsearch.com

Part Five

Lists

Information lists cover many things used by recruiters. Web addresses are provided for many of these lists, where the information in the list is products and the appropriate vendors have Web sites.

Technical Recruiter Associations

Arizona Technical Recruiters' Association . . . . atra.hypermart.net
Chicago Technical Recruiters' Network . . . . www.trnchicago.org
Colorado Technical Recruiters' Network . . . . www.ctrn.org
Canadian Technical Recruiters' Network . . . . www.ctrn.com
Delaware Valley Technical Recruiters' Network . . . . www.dvtrn.org
Houston High Tech Recruiters' Network . . . . www.hhtrn.org
National Association of Computer Consulting Businesses . . . . www.naccb.org
Minnesota Technical Recruiters' Network . . . . www.mntrn.com
New Jersey Technical Recruiters' Alliance . . . . www.njtra.org
New York Technical Recruiters' Association. . . . . www.nytra.com
Seattle High Tech Recruiters' Network. www.hightechrecruiters.com
Southeast Employment Network (SEN) . . . . www.senetwork.com

General Recruiting Associations

American Management Association. . . . . www.amanet.org
Human Resource Planning Society. . . . . www.hrps.org
International Association of Corporate and
     Professional Resources. . . . . www.iacpr.org
International Personnel Management Association. . . . . www.ipma-hr.org
National Association of Personnel Services . . . . www.napsweb.org
Society for Human Resource Management . . . . www.shrm.org

Career, or job, fairs are held through the country. In addition to companies that operate on a national or regional level, many local fairs are held by local organizations and newspapers. Check your area for local events.

CareerFairs	National	www.lendman.com
Career-Tech	East coast	www.career-tech.net
E*Fair.net	East Coast	www.efair.net
High Tech Career Fairs	National	www.network-events.com
Northwest High Tech	National	www.network-events.com
Personnel Strategies	Midwest	www.psijobfair.com
Senet Career Expo	Chicago, California	www.senetcareer.com
TechExpo	Northeast	www.tech-expo.com
TechFest	National	www.professional-exchange.com
Terrastarr	Chicago, East coast	www.terra-starr.com
WestTech Career Expo	National	www.vjf.com/westech/index.html

COLLEGE INTERVIEW QUESTIONS

What are your future educational plans?

In what school activities have you participated? Why? Which did you enjoy the most?

Why do you think you might like to work for our company?

What jobs have you held? How were they obtained and why did you leave?

What courses did you like best? Least? Why?

Why did you choose your particular field of work?

What percentage of your college expenses did you earn? How?

How did you spend your vacations while in school?

What do you know about our company?

Do you feel that you have received good general training?

What qualifications do you have that make you feel you will be successful in your field?

What extracurricular offices have you held?

If you were starting college all over again, what courses would you take?

How much money do you hope to earn at age 30? age 35?

Do you think that your extracurricular activities were worth the time devoted to them? Why?

What do you think determines a person's progress within a company?

What personal characteristics are necessary for success in your chosen field?

Why do you think you would like this particular type of job?

What kind of boss do you prefer?

How did previous employers treat you?

What have you learned from some of the jobs you have held?

Can you get recommendations from previous employers?

What interests you about our product or service?

Did you ever change your major field of interest while in college? Why?

When did you choose your college major?

Do you feel you have done the best scholastic work of which you are capable?

Why did you choose to go to college?

What do you know about opportunities in the field in which you are trained?

Which of your college years was the most difficult? Why?

What types of people seem to rub you the wrong way?

Have you ever tutored an underclassman?

What jobs have you enjoyed the most? The least? Why?

What are your own special abilities?

What job in our company do you want to work toward?

Would you prefer a large or small company? Why?

Do you like to travel?

What kind of work interests you?

What are the disadvantages of your chosen field?

What have you done which shows initiative and willingness to work?

GENERAL RECRUITING SOFTWARE

This software is purchased and runs on internal systems. Some of it has a Web-based interface, which means it can be accessed over a corporate intranet from Web browsers. This software is used by both corporate and staffing (consultant and agency) companies.

!Trak-It Applicant tracking software. Includes: Scan, which scans faxed, hardcopy, e-mail résumés; AT, the applicant tracking module; HR, which adds other human resource features. Runs on Macintosh systems. Part of Eddon's Advantage Package. Vendor: Trak-It Solutions, Inc. www.trak-it.com

Abra Recruiting Solution Applicant tracking software. Automates entire recruiting process. Works with hardcopy, faxed, e-mailed résumés. Selects the best candidate for job requirements. Includes Abra Applicant and Abra Scan. Runs on PC systems. Part of Eddon's Advantage Package. Vendor: Best Software, Inc. www.bestsoftware.com

Advantage Package Applicant tracking, HR functions, payroll, etc. Includes Abra Applicant and !Trak-it AT. Runs on PC, Macintosh systems. Vendor: Eddon Corp. www.eddoncorp.com

Applicant Tracking (AT) Builds an applicant database that can be shared by all departments within the company. Includes résumé routing and interview scheduling functions. Runs on AS/400 systems. Vendor: Optimum Solutions, Inc. www.optimum-solutions.com

ApplicantSmartware Applicant tracking system. Tracks both internal and external candidates. Generates acknowledgement letters. Manages relationship management for company, hiring manager, and/or recruiter. Runs on Windows systems. Vendor: S. Reynolds & Associates, Inc. www.applicantsmartware.com

askSam Résumé Tracking Includes résumé tracking, contact management, skills database and job requisition tracking. Runs on PC systems. Vendor: askSam Systems. www.asksam.com

CompassSelect Applicant tracking system. Scans résumés, manages contacts, includes accounting functions. Accesses Web-enabled database. Runs on Windows systems. Vendor: HauserTech. www.compassselect.com

Desktop Recruiter Applicant tracking system based on Lotus Notes. Includes: which allows employees to view current job openings from any Web browser; Manager's ViewPoint (MVP) enables hiring managers to track the entire recruitment process from any Web browser; and DataXchange which moves data to internal HRIS systems. Vendor: SkillSet, Inc. www.skillset.com

Employ! Automates entire recruiting life-cycle. Supports collaborative hiring, including access by recruiters, and hiring managers. Web- and intranet-enabled front-ends work with most major legacy systems, browsers and network e-mail. Uses e-mail for communication. Vendor: Deploy Solutions, Inc. www.deploy.com

Greentree Employment System Includes applicant tracking and job requisition management functions. Optional modules include résumé processing, résumé scanning, applicant self-entry (Web interface), and document management. Runs on Windows systems. Vendor: Greentree Systems, Inc. www.greentreesystems.com

HR:Expert Suite Complete HRIS. Applicant tracking module is MatchMaker. See MatchMaker.

HRtrak Applicant tracking system. Maintains database of applicants. Has Web interface to enter jobs and applicant questionnaire on corporate Web site. Runs on AS/400, Unix, Windows NT systems. Vendor: Optimum Solutions, Inc. www.optimum-solutions.com

IRIS (Intelligent Résumé Input system) Reads and interprets the contents of résumés. Automates data entry, extracts important information and stores it into the R4W database. Requires R4W. Runs on Windows systems. Vendor: Knowledge Probe, Inc. www.recruiter.ca

MatchMaker Applicant tracking module. Part of HR:Expert Suite. Scans résumés, Generates letters, Matches job requirements to skills, integrates with Microsoft Office. Vendor: NuView Systems, Inc. www.nuviewinc.com

PC Recruiter Provides résumé entry, keyword searches on jobs, résumés, companies and names. Includes communications, bulk-mailing, contact scheduling. Can be purchased with either a Windows or a Web front-end. Vendor: Main Sequence Technologies. www.pcrecruiter.com

Personic WebBench Software that automates the functions of the hiring manager including creating requisitions, reviewing résumés, scheduling interviews, and generating offers. Allows the hiring manager to work from any browser. Interfaces with, and requires Personic Workflow. Runs on Windows NT systems. Vendor: Personic Software, Inc. www.personic.com

Personic Workflow Automates entire applicant tracking functions for corporations. Derived from EZaccess. Runs on Windows systems. Uses Oracle database. Vendor: Personic Software, Inc. www.personic.com

QSS96 Includes relational database, fax functions, contact log, letter writer (standard and customized), referral and interview tracking. Runs on Windows 95, 98 systems. Vendor: Quick Search Systems, Inc. www.qss96.com

R4W (Recruiter 4 Windows) Recruiting software that provides candidate, client, contact and job opening management. Includes an optional Internet Assistant modules provide secure two-way access via the Internet. Runs on Windows systems. Vendor: Knowledge Probe, Inc. www.recruiter.ca

RecruitMAX Applicant tracking system that includes résumé scanning, profile creation, and requisition management. Includes candidate, client and job order management functions. Available with a Windows or Web interface. Runs on Windows systems. HR edition for corporations, Professional edition for staffing industry. Vendor: Creative System Solutions, Inc. www.recruitmax.com

ResPro Résumé processing system. Works with scanned, faxed and e-mailed résumés. Sends printed or e-mail response to applicant, routes résumé to hiring managers and/or inputs to an applicant tracking system. Runs on Windows systems. Vendor: Chaparral Systems, Inc. www.chaparralsystems.com

RESUMate Résumé processing system for the staffing industry. Maintains records of people, companies, and job orders that are cross-referenced with each other. Is a relational database program. It maintains complete records of people (candidates and sales contacts), companies, and job orders. Runs on Windows systems. Vendor: RESUMate, Inc. www. resumate.com

Resume Assistant Decodes and analyzes résumés by skills. Cut and paste e-mailed, scanned or test résumé into Resume Assistant and it will analyze skills. Vendor: Knowledge Probe, Inc. www.recruiter.ca

Resumix Matches résumés to job postings. Manages and stores résumés. Provides access to a knowledgebase of skills for matching. Interfaces with major HRIS systems including PeopleSoft, Oracle HRMS, SAP and Lawson. Versions available 4,5,6 have different functions and options. Vendor: Resumix www.resumix.com

RezManager Complete applicant tracking system. Builds database with complete history for every candidate. Provides e-mail communication features such as sending an e-mail "thank you" note to all new applicants, and notifying recruiters through e-mail when a new job order arrives. In-house version of RezKeeper. Vendor: rezLogic, Inc. www.rezlogic.com

SmartSearch Complete applicant tracking system. Manages the recruiting process from job requisition, to posting jobs on the Internet, processing résumés, qualifying candidates, and making the offer. Runs on Windows systems. Web-hosted version available (SmartSearch Online). Vendor: APS (Advanced Personnel Systems). www.aps.com

Vista Complete HRIS system. Includes HR and Applicant tracking modules. Can be accessed through proprietary interface or Web browsers. Runs on Windows systems. Vendor: PDS (Personnel Data Systems) www. pdssoftware.com

Webhire Enterprise Applicant tracking system. Runs over corporate intranets. Former name: Restrak. Webhire Recruiter is Web-hosted version. Vendor: Webhire, Inc. www.webhire.com.

WebRecruiter Enterprise Allows hiring managers to fill out an online job requisition and software agents will then find candidates for that job. Uses Web-based interface. Integrates with Oracle Human Resources, PeopleSoft, SAP and other back-office systems. Runs on Solaris, Windows NT systems. Vendor: Com.Sortium http://com.sortium.com

IT SALARY SURVEYS

The following sites provide salary surveys. Most of the sites contain the actual surveys, but some require downloading. The amount of detail provided varies greatly.

www.abbott-langer.com/itsssumm.html	Salaries by skill sets. Purchase 351 page report.
www.bestjobsusa.com/annualsalarysurvey/ GetResults.cfm	Salaries by state. Download PDF files.
www.cnw.com/~sourcedp/survey.html	Source Services IT salary surveys.
www.datamasters.com	Provides tables by region and job title.
www.dataprorecruiters.com/salarysurvey.html	Salaries by region and job title.
www.dice.com/ratesurvey/ratesurvey_perm.html	Salaries for specific skills.
www.informationweek.com/731/salsurvey.htm	Provides salary ranges for general job titles.
www.itcareers.com	New location for ComputerWorld survey. PDF file.
www.jdapsi.com/client/CLIAPP99.HTM	Salaries for job titles. Both annual and hourly.
www.jdresources.com/salaryf.html	Salaries for job titles for past three years.
www.jobsmart.org	Lists surveys for specific skills.
www.planetit.com/techcenters/docs/ year_2000/news/PIT19990429S0011	Overview of salaries for general skill sets.
www.psrinc.com/salary.htm	Salaries by city, Canada. Purchase.
www.realrates.com/survey.htm	Survey of consulting rates.
www.rhii.com/resources/guide.html	Salaries for job titles. Request survey.
www.systemspersonnelinc.com/salary.htm	Geographic breakdown. Request survey
www.wageweb.com/im1.htm	Salaries by skill sets.
www.zdnet.com/enterprise/salaryzone/index.html	Provides salaries and other information by job title.

SUBJECT	LEGAL QUESTION	ILLEGAL QUESTIONS
Address	Where do you live?	How long have you been a resident of this state or city? How long have you resided at this address?
Age	None	How old are you? When did you graduate from college? What is your date of birth? How old are your children?
Arrests	Have you ever been convicted of a crime?	Have you ever been arrested?
Citizenship	Are you a U.S. citizen?	Of what country are you a citizen? What is the date of your naturalization? Are your parents or spouse naturalized or native-born?
Disabilities	None	May not ask about any physical or mental disability which has no direct bearing on the duties of the applicable job.
Driver's License	Do you have a valid driver's license?	May not ask to see it.
Education	What schools did you attend?	When did you graduate/finish?
Finances	Do you know of any reason why you might be refused bonding (if job requires bonding)?	May not ask about credit ratings, charge accounts, bank accounts, bankruptcy, property ownership (car, house), past garnishment of wages.
Language	What languages do you speak and/or write fluently?	What is your native language? How did you acquire your foreign language abilities?
Military	Did you serve in the US armed forces? Which branch?	May not ask about military service in other than the US armed forces or state militia. May not inquire about draft status or eligibility for military service. May not ask about applicants' whereabouts during time of war. May not inquire about date, type, or conditions of discharge.
Name	What is your full name? What name(s) are necessary to use in order to check your educational and/or work record?	What was your original name? What is your maiden name?
Organizations	What organizations do you belong to, excluding those whose name or character indicates the race, color, religion, national origin, or ancestry of its members? May ask about membership in a union, professional society, or other job-related organizations.	Please list the organizations to which you belong.
References	Names of people willing to provide personal or character references.	What is the name of your pastor, rabbi or other religious leader.
Relatives	What are the names of relatives already employed by our company?	May not ask any questions about relatives except those employed by the company.

In addition to these specific questions, the following general rules about questioning and requests for documentation must be followed:

MAY NOT ASK ANY QUESTIONS ABOUT:

Age	Disabilities	Race or color
Birth control	Height	Religion
Birth date	Marital status	Sex
Birthplace	Number of dependents	Weight

AFTER HIRING, MAY REQUEST:

Affirmative action statistics
Alien registration card
Baptismal record
Birth certificate
Driver's license
Marital status
Naturalization papers (proof of citizenship)
Photograph
Physical exam and drug testing
Social security card

Salary

Salary
Bonuses
Commissions
Stock options
Profit-sharing plans
Deferred profit-sharing
Deferred compensation
Tuition reimbursement
Royalties

Bonuses

Sign-on bonus
Completion bonus
Early salary review
Expense account
Credit cards
Provide computer
Club memberships
Company automobile
Transportation provided
Paid parking
Day-care facilities

Non-Financial

Work at home
Job sharing
Flex hours
On-site facilities (gym, dry cleaning, etc.)
Travel agency

Benefits

Moving expenses
Pension plan
Health insurance extras, dental insurance
Sick pay
Accident insurance
Group life insurance
Death allowance
Vacation pay
Leave of absence
Down payment on home
Purchase home for relocation

Status

Attractive office
Secretary
Business cards
Parking space
Exective dining room
Company name/reputation
Civic involvement, volunteerism
Title

Technical

Current technology
Training
Magazine subscriptions
Book allowance

QUESTIONS CANDIDATES MIGHT ASK

1. Why is this position open?
2. May I talk with someone who is currently doing this job?
3. How often has this job been filled in the past five years? What were the main reasons?
4. What happened to the person who was doing this job?
5. What would you like done differently by the next person who has this job?
6. What would be the next career step after this job?
7. What are some of the more difficult problems one would have to face in this position?
8. How visible is this position?
9. When could I expect a raise? How frequent are salary increases?
10. How is one evaluated and who conducts performance evaluations?
11. What significant changes do you foresee in the near future?
12. What technical training is provided?
13. What accounts for success within this company?
14. What freedom would I have in determining my own work objectives and schedule?
15. Will you provide a laptop? Will you let me connect my system to yours?
16. How many women/minorities are in management positions in this company?
17. Will I have access to, and free use of, the Internet?
18. Will I be paid royalties if the company sells software that I write?
19. Are performance bonuses standard?
20. Will I be given stock options?

ABILITY TO ACCEPT RESPONSIBILITY

1. Tell me about a time when you had to step in and cover for a co-worker? Who did you discuss this with?
2. Describe a time when you had to assume a responsibility beyond your standard job description.

ABILITY TO WORK UNDER PRESSURE

1. Describe a time where you were faced with problems or stresses that tested your coping skills.
2. Describe a situation when you had to make a quick decision.
3. Describe circumstances where you had to work under pressure and deal with unrealistic deadlines.
4. Describe a situation when the team fell apart. What was your role in the outcome?

DECISION-MAKING

1. Tell me of a difficult decision you had to make.
2. Tell me of an instance where you had to defend a decision you made.
3. Tell me of an instance where you had to reverse a decision you made.
4. Describe an instance where your supervision disagreed with a decision you made. How did you handle it?

DEPENDABILITY

1. Describe a situation where you had a personal commitment that conflicted with an emergency business meeting? What did you do, and why?
2. Describe a time when a scheduled vacation coincided with a critical due date. What did you do?

GETTING ALONG WITH SUPERVISORS

1. Describe a situation where your supervisor enabled you be more effective.
2. Describe a situation where your supervisor had to correct you. How did you react?
3. Describe a situation where you disagreed with your supervisor. How did you handle this?

GETTING ALONG WITH CO-WORKERS

1. What was your most challenging personal encounter with someone? How did you deal with that individual?
2. Describe a situation where you mediated a conflict within the team.
3. Describe a situation where one of your co-workers was angry with you. How did you handle that?
4. When working on a team project, have you ever had an experience where there was strong disagreement among team members? What did you do?

INITIATIVE

1. Tell me of a time when you pushed yourself to do more than the minimum.
2. What projects have you initiated? What prompted you to do so?
3. Describe a major goal you have recently set for yourself. What are you doing to attain that goal?
4. Describe a success that could not have happened without you being there.
5. In a past position, what problems did you identify that had previously been overlooked?
6. Tell me of a time when you did more than required in your job.

INTERPERSONAL SKILLS

1. Give an example of when you successfully predicted the behavior of a new employee?
2. Tell me about a time when you had to present complex information. How did you ensure that the other person understood?
3. Tell me about a time when you had to be assertive.
4. Describe a situation where a group of peers "ganged up" on another employee? What part did you take?
5. Describe a situation in which you were able to overcome a "personality conflict" in order to get results.
6. Tell me about a situation when you had to use written communication in order to get a point across.

LEARNING ABILITY

1. What is the most recent skill you learned? How did you learn it?
2. What was the newest thing you learned how to do? How did you learn it?
3. Tell me of a situation where you felt you needed additional learning even though it was not provided. How did you handle this?

LIMITATIONS

1. Describe an instance where you had to ask for assistance in completing a task.
2. Describe a situation where you failed to reach a goal.
3. What was your biggest mistake?
4. Describe a situation where you tried to get an assignment transferred to another worker.

MANAGERIAL/LEADERSHIP APTITUDE

1. Describe a time when you had to motivate or build team spirit with co-workers. How did you accomplish this?
2. Describe how you handled having to make an unpopular decision/announcement.

3. Tell me about a difficult situation when you pulled the team together.
4. Tell me about a time you had to lead people who didn't want to be led.

ORGANIZATIONAL SKILLS

1. Give me an example of how you set priorities in scheduling your time.
2. Describe a situation when you had many projects due at the same time. What did you do to get them done?
3. Describe a situation where you missed an important meeting. Why?

POTENTIAL FOR ADVANCEMENT

1. Have you ever changed the nature of your job? How?
2. Tell me of an instance where you had to be critical of someone. How did you handle it?
3. Tell me of an instance where you suggested something that saved the company time and/or money.
4. Describe an instance where you provided a solution that was out of the box.
5. What is the most creative thing you have ever done?

STRENGTHS

1. Tell me about an assignment that you really enjoyed?
2. Tell me about an assignment that you finished ahead of schedule.
3. Tell me about your greatest accomplishment.

SAMPLE QUESTIONS
TRADITIONAL

ABILITY TO ACCEPT RESPONSIBILITY

1. How do you plan and organize for a major long-range project?
2. What were/are your most important decisions on your last/current job?
3. In what ways has your current/last job prepared you to take on greater responsibility?
4. Tell me about a responsibility in your current/last job that you really enjoyed.

ABILITY TO WORK UNDER PRESSURE

1. How many projects can you handle at one time?
2. How do you remain effective when you are faced with difficult tasks or with things you do not like to do?
3. What would you do if a project's requirements suddenly changed and you were working under a non-negotiable deadline?
4. How do you handle it when two meetings are scheduled for the same time?

AMOUNT OF SUPERVISION NEEDED

1. How much time on your current/last job is/was spent working alone?
2. How often did you meet with your supervisor? For what purpose?
3. How often do you work at home, or evenings or weekends, with no supervision?

DECISION-MAKING

1. How would you rate your decision-making ability?
2. Is making decisions a major part of your present job?
3. What kind of decisions do you have to make in your present job?
4. What is the most important decision you ever had to make in a work situation?

DEPENDABILITY

1. What is the reason you left/are leaving your last/current job?
2. Have you thought about leaving your current/past position? If so, what held you there?
3. How do you feel about leaving information so you can be contacted while on vacation?

GETTING ALONG WITH CO-WORKERS

1. What kind of people do you like to work with?
2. What do you feel is the easiest type of person to deal with? The most difficult?
3. Let me describe the group you would be working with. How would you fit in?
4. What would be your ideal work group?
5. How do/did you get along with your current/last work group?
6. How do you handle social relationships with co-workers?

GETTING ALONG WITH SUPERVISORS

1. Describe the best job/supervisor you ever had.
2. Describe the worst supervisor you ever had.
3. What would you do if you disagreed with your supervisor?

INITIATIVE

1. How did you get your last job?
2. How did you hear about this position?
3. In your current/past position, what problems did you identify that had previously been overlooked?
4. What would you do if you had to make a decision without a procedure or precedent to guide you?

SemCo Enterprises, Inc.

INTERPERSONAL SKILLS

1. What form of communication do you prefer? Which do you feel is most effective?
2. In your current/past position, how important is/was communicating and dealing with others?
3. In your current/past position, what role does/did communication play?
4. When you begin to work with new people, how do you get to understand them?

LEARNING ABILITY

1. How do you learn?
2. What is your learning style (hands-on, research, by example)?
3. What are your educational ambitions?

LIMITATIONS

1. What are your weak points?
2. If I spoke with your current boss, what would he/she say was your greatest weakness?
3. What are some things that you find difficult to do? Why?

MANAGERIAL/LEADERSHIP APTITIDE

1. Do you prefer delegation or "hands-on" control?
2. Do you feel you have top management potential? Why?
3. What is your management style? Provide examples from work that demonstrate this style.
4. How do you determine where you stand with your subordinates.

ORGANIZATIONAL SKILLS

1. What tools do you use for planning and scheduling personal time?
2. What tools do you use for planning and scheduling work time?
3. Do you often find yourself repeating tasks? If so, how often, what kind of tasks?

POTENTIAL FOR ADVANCEMENT

1. What are you doing now to attain a goal you have set for yourself?
2. What are your long-term goals?
3. How do you keep informed professionally?
4. Where do you hope to be professionally in five years?

STRENGTHS

1. What are your strong points?
2. If I spoke with your current boss, what would he/she say was your greatest strength?

SOFTWARE FOR THE STAFFING INDUSTRY

This software was written for consulting firms and placement agencies who perform third party recruiting on a permanent and/or contract basis. The software listed here is written primarily for the staffing industry. Software that can be used by both corporate and staffing companies is listed under General Recruiting Software.

Adapt Software for the staffing industry. Logs daily activity into permanent records associated with clients, candidates, job orders and contacts. Runs on Unix, Windows NT. Vendor: Bond International Software. www.bondadapt.com

AgencySmartware Software for the staffing industry. Matches candidates against job openings, generates invoices. Runs on Windows systems. Vendor: S. Reynolds & Associates, Inc. www.applicantsmartware.com

AIMS Recruit Software for the staffing industry. Recruiter tool-set that uses agents to find résumés on the Web and match with corporate job requirements. The agents run 24 hours a day and can retrieve newly posted résumés. Web-based interface. Runs on AS/400, Macintosh, S390, Solaris, Unix, Windows systems. Vendor: JennerNet Software Company (Division of NotesETC, Inc.). www.jennernet.com

BRN (Bridgepath Recruiters Network) Web-hosted service for third party recruiters and staffing companies. Provides customer-relationship management including sending contacts newsletters, birthday cards, and other personalized communications. Vendor: Bridgepath.com. www.bridgepath.com

COATS (Complete Office automation for Temporary & Staffing Services) Complete HRIS for staffing industry. Includes résumé scanning, searching of employees for orders, client records and job order processing for recruiting functions. Runs on Windows systems. Vendor: Sarach Technologies, Llc. www.coats95.com

C-PAS Software for the staffing industry. Includes candidate, client, contact management and job order databases. Modules include C-PAS Agents (which includes a résumé robot) and C-PAS WebRecruiter (which posts job orders to corporate Web site and Dice, CareerMagazine, JobOptions and Net-Temps. Runs on OS/2, Unix, Windows systems. Stands for: Complete Placement Automation System. Vendor: VCG, Inc. www.c-pas.com

EmpACT Software for the staffing industry. Processes applications and résumés, conducts skill searches, manages customer orders. Used for permanent and temporary staffing. Includes back-office functions (payroll/billing, benefits, etc.). Runs on Windows systems. Vendor: Prairie Development, Inc. www.prairiedev.com

Encore Recruitment Environment Software for the staffing industry. Provides people management for candidates, contacts, sources, and clients. Also includes job order management, company management and timeline management. Runs on Windows systems. Vendor: The Cluen Corporation. www.cluen.com

EZaccess Software for the staffing industry. Works with the entire process including receiving résumés and job orders, matching and placing candidates, and generating customized management reports to track the entire process. Includes résumé agent which does Web résumé mining. Runs on Windows systems, uses Oracle database. Vendor: Personic Software, Inc. www.personic.com

iCIMS Web-hosted system for the staffing industry. Includes client, job, and candidate management functions. Vendor: iCIMS.com www.icims.com

Identity Software for the staffing industry. Tracks information about candidates, companies, and job orders. Recruiters can fax, e-mail, and scan directly into and out of the program, and automatically connects to the Internet. Can search on concepts or key words. Tracks activity for individual recruiters. Runs on Windows and Windows NT systems. Vendor: Identity Software Company. www.identitysoftware.com

MAESTRO Complete management system for the staffing industry. Includes financial functions, résumé management, contact management and report functions. Runs on Unix, Windows NT systems. Vendor: Allegro Software, Inc. www.allegrosoftware.com

PeopleMover Staffing industry application that works with permanent staff, temporary workers, consulting firms, and free agent contractors. .Interfaces with back-office packages like PeopleSoft. Web-based interface. Can run on a hosted platform or on internal Unix, Windows systems. Vendor: PeopleMover, Inc. www.peoplemover.com

PowerPlace, PowerPlace Internet Connect Management software for the staffing industry. Includes candidate, client, contact, project and job order tracking. Works with faxed, e-mailed, and scanned résumés. Internet Connect is Web-Hosted version. Runs on Windows systems. Vendor: Eclipse Technologies, Inc. www.ppnet.com/powerplace

Pro-Hunt Complete applicant tracking system for staffing industry. Automatically extracts information from résumés, matches candidates to job orders and clients, and handles scheduling. Runs on Windows systems. Vendor: Microtrends Computing Services Inc. www.microtrends.on.ca

Pursuant Software for the staffing industry. Includes client and candidate profiling, requisition and skill set management, contact management, and billing and timesheet management functions. Runs on Unix, Windows systems. Installation charge with monthly subscription fees based on number of sites and number of users. Vendor: More-O Corp. www.more-o.com

Safari HeadHunting System Software for the staffing industry. Manages applicants, clients, job orders, searches, placements, and invoicing. Handles both permanent and temporary staffing. Runs on Windows systems. Vendor: Safari Software Products. www.safarisoftproducts.com

Simply Visual Recruiting Software for the staffing industry. Runs on Windows systems. Maintains databases for candidates, clients, and job orders. Works with scanned, faxed, and e-mailed résumés. Records résumés, skills, appointments, interviews and correspondence. Vendor: Simple Solutions Software, Inc. www.simplesolutionsinc.com

SkilMatch Software for staffing industry. Manages all functions including billing and accounting. Works with scanned and faxed résumés. Runs on AS/400, Windows systems. Vendor: SkilMatch Staffing Systems, Inc. www.skilmatch.com

Sourcer and Apprentice Software for the staffing industry. Provides candidate tracking, résumé scanning, client management, skill matching, invoicing, and reporting features. Runs on Windows systems. Vendor: Sourcer Products. www.sourcer.com

TurboTrax (TTrax) Applicant tracking system for the staffing industry. Works with scanned and faxed résumés, tracks requisitions, manages contacts, and reporting functions. Runs on Windows systems. Vendor: Advanced Computer Technologies, Inc. (ACT) www.ttrax.com

WebPAS Web-hosted system for the staffing industry. Presents a personalized screen to each user showing where they were the last time they accessed the system. Provides client, job order, candidate and résumé management functions. Stands for: Web Placement Automated System. Vendor: VCG, Inc. www.c-pas.com

WinSearch Applicant tracking system for the staffing industry. Manages workflow, job orders, résumés and contacts. Runs on Windows systems. Runs on Windows systems. Vendor Relational Systems, Inc. www.winsearch.com

TECHNICAL TESTING PRODUCTS

www.knowitallinc.com	Test over Internet or set up on Intranet
www.proveit.com	Same as knowitall
www.quiz.com	QuizTek is name of IT tests. Run onsite or over Internet
www.reviewnet.net	Test over Internet
www.showmetests.com	Test over Internet
www.skillcheck.com	Purchase, run onsite
www.swcaliber.com	Test over Internet
www.teckchek	Tests installed onsite, transmitted to teckchek for scoring
www.teckmetrics.com	Service that provides certification through Internet tests

TRAINING FOR TECHNICAL RECRUITERS

These are instructor-led seminars that are presented on a regular basis for public enrollments and sessions are held in various cities. Check the vendor's Web site for specific schedule. Most vendors will arrange to bring seminars in-house for dedicated presentations; call for details.

Technology Seminars

SEMINAR/*VENDOR*	COURSE LENGTH (days)	VENDOR URL	FREQUENCY PER MONTH
Computers: Systems, Terms and Acronyms/ *SemCo Enterprises*	2	www.semcoenterprises.com	8–10
Technical Update/*SemCo Enterprises*	1	www.semcoenterprises.com	2–4
A Guided Tour Through I.T., & Adv. Tech./ *Dallas Training*	2	www.dallastraining.com	1
A Guided Tour Through I.T./*Dallas Training*	1	www.dallastraining.com	2
Computer Concepts/*The Breckenridge Group*	1	www.breckenridgegroup.com	1–3

Recruiting Process Seminars

SEMINAR/*VENDOR*	COURSE LENGTH (days)	VENDOR URL	FREQUENCY PER MONTH
Technical Recruiting/*SemCo Enterprises*	2	www.semcoenterprises.com	3–6
Sales and Recruiting Training/*Oz Enterprises*	2	www.ozenterprises.com	2
Professional Recruiter/*The Breckenridge Group*	1	www.breckenridgegroup.com	1–3
Life Cycle of Recruiting/*NV Training*	2	www.nvtraining.com	2
Sales and Recruiting Working Together/ *NV Training*	1	www.nvtraining.com	1

Internet Recruiting Seminars

SEMINAR/*VENDOR*	COURSE LENGTH (days)	VENDOR URL	FREQUENCY PER MONTH
AIRS I, II/*AIRS*	1	www.airsdirectory.com	10–13 each
AIRS III/*AIRS*	1	www.airsdirectory.com	4–6
Staffing & Recruiting (Hands-on)/*CareerX Roads*	1	www.careerxroads.com	1–2
Recruitment Sourcing Techniques/*Claybrooke and Associates*	1	www.claybrookeassoc.com	1–3
Strategic Internet Recruiting/*Claybrooke and Associates*	1	www.claybrookeassoc.com	1–3
Internet Recruiter/*The Breckenridge Group*	1	www.breckenridgegroup.com	1–3
Internet Recruiting Edge/*RISE (Barbara Ling)*	1	www.riseway.com	4–6
Techniques, Tools/ *NETRECRUITER*	1	www.netreceuiter.net	1 each

Part Six

Sample Letters and E-Mails

Sample letters and e-mails used throughout the entire recruiting process are provided. These letters may be used as is, or modified for individual use and/or e-mail communication. Of course any sample can be modified for either a written letter or e-mail.

CANDIDATE FROM INTERNAL DATABASE

Sample e-mail to candidate from internal database

To: candidate@aol.com
From: recruiter@abccompany.com

Subject: Job opportunity.

Dear Candidate:

I read your resume last (Month) and kept it on file because of your excellent credentials. We didn't have an appropriate job at that time, but now have new openings and a related opportunity has developed.

I am enclosing a complete job description and can be reached at 800-555-1212 to answer any questions you might have. If I am not available, Suzy Smith will be happy to help you. Please also fax (999.999.9999) or e-mail (recruiter@abccompany.com) a current resume.

We have not yet advertised this opening and, if you are interested, would like to hear from you as soon as possible.

Cordially,

Bill Brown

▰▰▰▰▰. CONGRATULATIONS ▰▰▰▰▰

January 1, 1999

John Doe
1 Main Street
Anytown, ST 99999

Dear John:

Congratulations on your job offer with the XYZ Corporation. You deserve it! I'm sure you were relieved, after weeks of telephone conversations and interviews, to hear that you were selected as the top candidate for the position. Your interview style was reported by all as professional. I wish you only the best in your endeavors at the XYZ Corporation.

I have contacted Jack Jones, one of your peers to assist you with any questions you may have regarding company logistics. His office is located in Section A of your department. If I am correct, your office is planned to be next to Jack's. Upon arrival at their offices, ask the receptionist to page Jane Smith, your manager. Her extension is 238.

I will be calling you sometime during your first week of work. Meanwhile, if you have any questions, my number is 999.9999.

Thank you for doing an exemplary job during the entire interview process. I am so proud of you, John. Best of luck.

Sincerely,

Bill Brown
Corporate Recruiter

January 1, 1999

John Doe
1 Main Street
Anytown, ST 99999

Dear John:

Your decision not to pursue career opportunities with ABC Company at this time is regretted. Your credentials are impressive, and your ability to speak clearly on the technical industry is above par.

I respect your decision and want to wish you the best of luck. If, however, in the future you have an interest in making another career move, I would appreciate your keeping our company in mind. I have enclosed a corporate overview and my business card for your information.

Again, thank you, John, for your time and best of luck in your future endeavors.

Sincerely,

Bill Brown
Corporate Recruiter

E-mail to Interesting Candidate

To: candidate@aol.com
From: recruiter@abccompany.com

Subject: Job opportunity.

Dear Candidate:

My name is Bill Brown and I am a recruiter at ABC company. I found your resume on the Internet and was very impressed. You seem to have the qualifications and background that would fit in with our staff. Although we have no job openings at present, I wanted to let you know that as long as you're agreeable we will keep your resume on file to contact you when we have an appropriate opening.

Please let me know if you have any objections.

Cordially,

Bill Brown

January 1, 1999

John Doe
1 Main Street
Anytown, ST 99999

Dear John:

As a follow-up to you joining the XYZ Company, I am writing to get an update on your progress. I realized I hadn't spoken with you since last quarter, when you accepted the position. How are you doing? How is your family? Give me a call when you get the opportunity. My telephone number is 999.9999. I am anxious to hear of your progress.

As for me, the open requisitions seem to multiply almost daily. In fact, I am now focused on multiple positions that have responsibilities very similar to what you are doing. You know the old saying "the work never ends." I must add to that cliché, however, "I enjoy every minute of it."

I'm looking forward to our telephone conversation.

Sincerely,

Bill Brown
Corporate Recruiter

January 1, 1999

John Doe
1 Main Street
Anytown, ST 99999

Dear John:

We are pleased to offer you a position as Senior Systems Programmer in our head-quarters complex at 1 State Street, Anytown, ST, starting on January 15, 1999. The salary will be $78,000 per year, payable semi-monthly. Our benefits package is defined in the enclosed pamphlet.

This offer is contingent on your passing the company physical and drug screens.

We look forward to having you join our organization and are confident that this will result in a mutually advantageous relationship.

Sincerely,

Bill Brown
Corporate Recruiter

E-mail to Prospective Candidate

To: candidate@aol.com
From: recruiter@abccompany.com

Subject: Job opportunity.

Dear Candidate:

My name is Bill Brown and I am a recruiter at ABC company. I found your resume on the Internet and it seems to fit one of our openings. We are looking for someone with xxxxx and yyyyy skills, and your resume looks very interesting. I am enclosing a complete job description of the opening, and invite you to visit our Web site at www.abc-company.com.

If you are interested in this position, I would like to discuss this opportunity with you and would like to see a current resume. I can be reached by phone at 800-555-1212. If I am not available, Suzy Smith will be happy to speak with you. Your resume can be faxed (999.999.9999) or e-mailed (recruiter@abccompany.com).

I look forward to hearing from you.

Cordially,

Bill Brown

January 1, 1999

John Doe
1 Main Street
Anytown, ST 99999

Dear John:

Thank you for your interest in ABC Company and the time you spent interviewing with us. It was not an easy decision, but after careful deliberation we felt other candidates were closer to our job specifications.

We regret that we cannot offer you a position at this time and wish you the best of luck in your career. With your strengths, you are sure to be an asset to many companies. We sincerely regret it couldn't be with ours.

Because our business is growing and requirements change over time, we would like to keep your application on file for future reference.

Thank you again for your time, and best of luck.

Sincerely,

Bill Brown
Corporate Recruiter

January 1, 1999

John Doe
1 Main Street
Anytown, ST 99999

Dear John:

Our conversations regarding opportunities with the XYZ Company/our company have been exciting and informative for me over the past week. I hope the experience has been mutual. The hiring team here is providing positive feedback on a daily basis regarding your interview last week. Once the remaining interviews and evaluations have been completed, I will be calling you immediately to inform you of the decision. Meanwhile, if you are entertaining other opportunities, John, I would certainly consider it an honor if you would allow us the opportunity to "win" your employment status.

I will notify you immediately with any "up to the minute" feedback concerning your opportunities with the XYZ Company/us.

Thanks again, and it was a pleasure meeting with you last week.

Sincerely,

Bill Brown
Corporate Recruiter

cc: Hiring Managers

SemCo Enterprises, Inc.

January 1, 1999

John Doe
1 Main Street
Anytown, ST 99999

Dear John:

It was a pleasure speaking with you on Monday. Your interview style is very professional, and we are very interested in continuing conversations with you. Our next phase involves management reviewing your résumé and interview data. Once I have received information, I will be in contact with you via telephone to provide feedback and discuss additional interview dates and times. I realize you are entertaining offers from other companies, therefore I ask that you please allow our organization to have the opportunity to entice you to one of the best working environments available—ABC Systems and Services.

If you have any questions, issues, or concerns, please call me at 999.999.9999 or page me at 1.999.999.9999.

Again, thank you, John, for taking time to come and discuss your background.

I expect to call you within the next week.

Sincerely,

Bill Brown
Corporate Recruiter

January 1, 1999

John Doe
1 Main Street
Anytown, ST 99999

Dear John:

It was a pleasure speaking with you on Monday, April 13. It is exciting to hear of your new project assignments and your continued success at ABC Corporation. In addition, I want to express my appreciation to you for providing me with a few names of associates you have in the industry, namely, Chris, Robin, John and Rosalyn. I have made an initial contact with each of them and look forward to phone conversations with them by next Thursday. I will keep you posted of the outcome.

As a token of my appreciation, please accept our company logo pen enclosed.

My conversations with you are always upbeat, and your humor continues to be refreshing.

Best of luck in your new assignment.

Sincerely,

Bill Brown
Corporate Recruiter

THANK YOU FOR PHONE INTERVIEW

January 1, 1999

John Doe
1 Main Street
Anytown, ST 99999

Dear John:

It was a pleasure speaking with you regarding your credentials on Monday. I have forwarded your résumé, as well as additional pertinent information that I believe will "sell" your abilities to complete tasks, for two open positions we have on file. As soon as I have received feedback concerning your career opportunities, I will call you to discuss the next step.

Meanwhile, please call me at 1.999.999.9999, if you have any questions or any additional information that we may have forgotten to discuss concerning your career opportunities. You have made a good impression thus far, and thanks for taking time to discuss your background with me on the telephone last Monday.

I will call you within the next week with follow-up data.

Sincerely,

Bill Brown
Corporate Recruiter

January 1, 1999

John Doe
1 Main Street
Anytown, ST 99999

Dear John:

Thank you for taking the time to speak with me regarding the reference review on Betty Brown. The information you provided was very helpful and I appreciate your taking the time to respond to my inquiries.

You mentioned in our discussion that you weren't aware of our company's services. I have included an annual report for your review, as well as a business card for your rolodex. Also please find a corporate gift enclosed in this packet. It is a small token of appreciation for your time.

If I can be of assistance to you, please feel free to call me at 999.999.9999.

Again, thank you, John.

Sincerely,

Bill Brown
Corporate Recruiter

Recruiting Glossary

Account manager	An employee in a consulting firm who receives job orders from client companies. Account managers are the contact point between the client company and the consulting firm. Also called account executive.
Active candidate	Someone who is searching for a new job.
Agency	Usually refers to employment agency. A company that conducts third party placement. A company that finds employees for other companies for a fee.
Applicant	See candidate.
Assignment	A task, or contract job.
Billing rate	Salary for consultants and contract-workers is usually expressed as an hourly rate which is also called billing rate, or daily rate (a multiple of hourly rate).
Candidate	A person applying for a job. The term is used interchangeably with applicant, although candidate often implies a level of pre-qualification.
Cold call	A phone call to a potential candidate who has no idea that a recruiter even has his or her name. Usually the persons contacted are passive candidates. Often when finding passive candidates on the Internet, all the recruiter has is an e-mail address, so the cold "call" is actually an e-mail.
Consultant	Someone who is brought into a company for a specific task, usually identified by a defined period of time. The consultant is paid by a consulting firm and he or she may be a permanent employee of the consulting firm or a free lancer.
Contract	Hiring someone for a specific task, usually identified by a defined period of time. The contract worker is not an employee of the contracting company and does not receive corporate benefits.
Corporate recruiter	One who works for a single company and recruits to fill openings in that company. Corporate recruiters hire all types of employees including full-, part-time, temporary, interns, and any other job type the company needs.
Counteroffer	An offer made by a candidate's present employer when the candidate presents a new offer. Counteroffers can be very effective because the present employer knows exactly what the new offer is. Recruiters must negotiate counteroffers, but must realize that often the counteroffer is too good to be turned down.
Daily rate	See billing rate.
Free lancer	A free lance worker is a self-employed person who works for various companies on a contract basis. Free lancers rarely receive benefits. Free lancers can be hired directly by a corporation to perform a specific task, but more often are hired by consulting firms who then get the assignments from corporations. Free lancers are also called independents, and contract workers.

Headhunter	Term usually used for a recruiter in an employment agency. It is a derogatory term and indicates someone who has no personal interest in the candidate. The term can be used for any recruiter, and, in fact, is often used to refer to anyone who cold calls into a company.
Hiring manager	The manager who has the job opening. The hiring manager is the one who provides the job description and is one who decided who to hire.
Hourly rate	See billing rate.
Ice breaker	See rapport building.
Independents	See free lancer.
Job order	See job requisition.
Job requestor	The person who gives a job order to a recruiter. In consulting firms this person is usually an account manager. In employment agencies the job requestor works for a client company and could be the hiring manager but more often is a member of the HR department. With corporate recruiting the job requestor is usually the hiring manager.
Job Requirement	Although used simultaneously with job requisition, a job requirement is actually something the candidate must have—something that cannot be negotiated. Typical requirements could be a college degree, or passing a drug test.
Job Requisition	The specific definition of an open position. Also called job order and job requirement. The job requisition can be for a permanent employee, or for a consulting assignment, although job order is often used to refer to a consulting assignment.
Negotiation	Negotiation is presenting the job opportunities to candidates, and handling any objections that come up in order to ensure that the candidate accepts an offer. The most commonly negotiated aspect of any job offer is salary.
Networking	A sourcing technique. Using contacts such as prior employees, other recruiters, and present candidates to find new candidates. Networking is really asking "Do you know anyone?" Networking is often considered to be the most effective sourcing technique.
Passive candidate	A passive candidate is one who is not looking for a job. Recruiters get names of passive candidates from many sources, and will try to come up with an attractive offer if the candidates has the right skills.
Permanent hire	Hiring someone to be a company employee who will receive whatever benefits the company offers, and will stay employed until either the employee or the company decided to terminate the employment. Permanent placement can be full-time or part-time.

Permanent placement	Recruiting for corporate employment. Usually used to refer to refer to the work employment agencies do.
Pipeline	Pipelines are built for open jobs and for candidates. The job pipeline shows how many candidates are applying for each job and where in the pipeline they are, eg. how many résumés have been received, how many candidates have been interviewed, etc. The candidate pipeline shows how many candidates the recruiter is working with at any given time regardless of job, and shows eg. how many interviews a recruiter has scheduled.
Process control	Process control is the methodology used to manage the entire recruiting process. Process control includes established standards, such as "all job openings will first be made available to internal candidates." It also includes standard forms such as Pipeline Reports that help control recruiting activity.
Queue	A queue is simply a line. Used in recruiting it usually refers to the "line" of candidates for a job, or the "line" of jobs that need to be filled. Used interchangeable with "pipeline."
Rapport building	Also called "ice breaking." Rapport building refers to the time taken by recruiters to build a relationship with a candidate. The term is usually used to refer to the opening of an interview and can reflect actions, such as getting coffee, or questions, such as "Did you have trouble finding us?"
Screening	Screening is often also called qualifying, and is the process of evaluating applicants based on reading a résumé and/or application and conduction a screening (usually brief) interview.
Soft skills	Soft skills are interpersonal skills, such as leadership ability, communications skills, and growth potential. These skills are hard to measure objectively and behavioral questions are often used to identify them.
Sourcing	Developing a list of applicants for a job; gathering résumés of applicants for a job.
Staffing industry	Companies that conduct third party recruiting and placement. Includes employment agencies and consulting firms.

SemCo Enterprises, Inc.